Work-Life Effectiveness

Bottom-Line Strategies for Today's Workplace

Karol Rose

Alliance for Work-Life Progress™

An Affiliate of WorldatWork®

About WorldatWork®

WorldatWork.
The Professional Association for
Compensation, Benefits and Total Rewards

WorldatWork is the world's leading not-for-profit professional association dedicated to knowledge leadership in total rewards, compensation, benefits and work-life. Founded in 1955, WorldatWork focuses on human resources disciplines associated with attracting, retaining and motivating employees. Besides serving as the membership association of the professions, the WorldatWork family of organizations provides education, certification (Certified Compensation Professional — CCP®, Certified Benefits Professional® — CBP, Global Remuneration Professional — GRP® and Work-Life Certified Professional — WLCP™), publications, knowledge resources, surveys, conferences, research and networking. WorldatWork Society of Certified Professionals™; Alliance for Work-Life Progress (AWLP)™ and ITAC, The Telework Advisory Group, are part of the WorldatWork family.

About AWLP

Alliance for Work-Life Progress™
An Affiliate of WorldatWork®

Alliance for Work-Life Progress (AWLP) is a membership organization committed to the development and advancement of the field of work-life effectiveness. Founded in 1996, AWLP addresses work-life issues through publications, forums and professional development strategies. AWLP strives to influence better integration of work and family life. An affiliate organization of WorldatWork, AWLP is headquartered in Scottsdale, Arizona.

WorldatWork Staff Contributors
Publishing Manager: Dan Cafaro
Research Assistant: Cheryl Stuck
Production Manager: Rebecca Williams Ficker
Editorial Assistant: Wendy McMorine
Graphic Design: Erika Freber

WorldatWork Global Headquarters
14040 N. Northsight Blvd., Scottsdale, AZ 85260
480/951-9191 Fax 480/483-8352 www.worldatwork.org

Author Acknowledgments

I am fortunate to have been part of the work-life field virtually from its inception. It has been a phenomenal learning experience for me, and I've been privileged to meet and work with so many talented people along the way — as colleagues, clients and mentors. Each has taught me more than I can thank them for. I've also been fortunate to have positions in organizations that allowed — and, in some cases, encouraged and expected — me to think about issues related to work and personal life from a variety of perspectives.

I've been able to "play" with and develop new ways of thinking about work-life effectiveness. Through affiliation with leading organizations including Alliance for Work-Life Progress, I've been able to express ideas and explore new ways of addressing work-life issues with others who are also trying to "push the envelope." I've learned that in many cases, it's the person or situation that is most negative that actually encourages you to move forward and learn ways to break through the resistance that continues to persist in our field. I'm also excited to be starting a new venture with Sandy Burud to explore what we believe is the next evolution of work-life — fitting it into the larger context of a human capital framework.

Throughout my career I have been fortunate to have the support and inspiration of my wonderful family and friends, who have helped me understand and appreciate the challenges of managing work and personal life from many diverse perspectives. To my family — my mother, an amazing role model, and my ever challenging husband, Bob, and our children, Alex, Ashley, Ilana, Michael and Rich, and grandchildren, Hannalina, Shoshana, Zoe and Jackson — goes all my love and thanks. Thanks for being you and thanks for loving me. This one's for you.

Table of Contents

Preface

This book is the latest work by an amazing figure in the work-life field. Karol Rose is a woman with many talents, but two, in particular, are rarely found in one person. Karol has the savvy to identify trends, even as they emerge, and the ability to quickly convert them into practical information so practitioners can respond. She has written a litany of publications that organizations in the United States and other countries use as their primary reference source for planning work-life strategies.

One reason these materials have worked so well for their readers is Karol's prolific history in the work-life field and the discipline that comes from 25 years of working directly with organizations. Karol has advised some of the largest and/or most successful organizations in their respective industries. That experience has given her a clear sense of how managers and HR leaders think and what they need.

This new book is the ultimate field guide for smart organizations that want to respond to the dynamics of today's workforce. It is the practical information that all types and sizes of organizations need to plan and implement critical work-life activities. Once again, Karol has taken the complexities of work-life strategies and made them manageable and clear.

As a work-life thought leader since before the term "work-life" existed, Karol recognizes that timely, practical information must fit in a larger context as the relevance of work-life effectiveness evolves. And, Karol has now expanded the context of work-life effectiveness — which she explains is the synergistic notion that "when work is effective, life benefits, and when life works, work benefits" — with another leap forward. She recognizes that work-life responses are integral to managing people as human capital and that it is impossible to manage people as human capital without recognizing all that they are and all that they can bring to their work.

Always on the threshold of change in the field, Karol has embraced this new direction. I am thrilled that Karol and I joined efforts, forming a new consulting practice, Rose&Burud, to combine this emphasis on practical application with the new human-capital conceptual framework that incorporates and expands the importance of work-life effectiveness.

This human-capital perspective not only reinforces the wisdom, but also broadens the definition, of work-life effectiveness to encompass the aspects of organizational life that create demand for work-life responses — workload, pace, pressure, job quality, how good work is defined and many others that can have as much effect on people's lives as the more tangible work-life strategies. This new perspective also shifts the rationale, making a human-capital management approach (to which work-life is key) more than simply desirable — but essential for organizations that rely on human talents for their competitive advantage. In this knowledge era, as Peter Drucker wrote, human talents are the commodity in shortest supply. They are the "constraining resource," because what only people can do — the ability to develop and share knowledge, to sustain durable relationships and to innovate — creates advantage. That is what it means to be in a human-capital environment and why only organizations that invest in people and manage them as assets, rather than costs, will thrive.

There is no question that organizations like those using this great resource book will outpace those who do not yet understand this powerful shift in what drives performance. They will pay attention to the short- and long-term well-being of people, because it is in their best interest to do so. In this context, work-life morphs from something done "for employees," to something done to protect the value of the organization's key asset — its people. What is good for people is what is good for the organization.

Creating a "Best Practice" organization requires a conceptual understanding of what has changed and practical knowledge about how to respond. Karol's book provides that necessary, on-the-ground information. This book's readers will find it invaluable, and will find they refer to it many times in their work. By adopting these very smart practices, their organizations will become the great places to work they try so hard to create and, therefore, their organizations will be more effective in the marketplace.

— Sandy Burud, Ph.D.
Author of *Leveraging the New Human Capital: Adaptive Strategies, Results Achieved and Stories of Transformation* (Davies-Black, 2004)

Introduction

T his book simply could not have been published at a more fortuitous time. Consider the following factors:

- The work-life field is entering its third decade and Alliance for Work-Life Progress (AWLP), its professional membership organization, is celebrating its 10th anniversary.

- The empirical evidence has burgeoned for the positive impact on the bottom line of management strategies that treat employees (at least) as well as customers.

- Business enterprises of all sizes and industries show signs of waking up to the fact that the talent war isn't a skirmish you win just once.

- Change seems to be picking up speed in every domain at once: economic globalization, workforce demographics, business models, technology and even within the family, which is the core unit of society.

- Stress and overwork have become so ubiquitous in a "24/7 world" that few seem to be able to find an acceptable "off" switch, a chronic condition that is contributing to deleterious health, energy and motivation outcomes.

- Time has become the new currency, now that it is more scarce (and thus, more valuable) than money.

- The employment value proposition is in a state of flux as companies vigorously cut costs wherever possible (with the striking exception of executive compensation) so that employees are bearing more of the financial burden for their own safety net.

In response to the impact of these dynamics on the workplace, WorldatWork has chosen this moment to launch the most significant reframing of its Total Rewards Model since the turn of this century, when the organization broadened its focus and its name. (See Figure A: The New WorldatWork Total Rewards Model on page 4.)

This major redesign is not accidental. When AWLP decided to join forces with WorldatWork at the end of 2003, the affiliation was undertaken in deliberate response to a confluence of values and world views. The newest and most profound insight was the mutual realization that in the 21st century what is (totally) rewarding to everyone who works is neither homogenous nor simple — one size does not fit all.

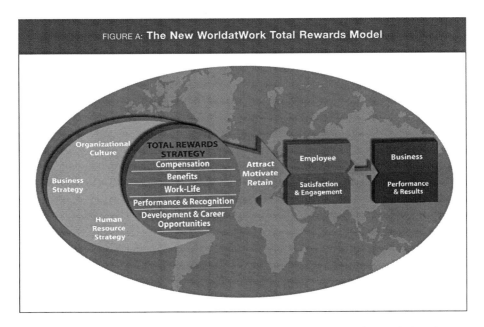

FIGURE A: **The New WorldatWork Total Rewards Model**

As affluence has grown, as ethnic and generational diversity in the workplace have become more pervasive, as the time bind has strengthened its vise-like grip, people work for very different reasons — or not at all. As a consequence, there is a widening disparity of expectations and values about the nature of work, the nature of workers and the increasingly turbulent intersection between work and personal life.

This is the stuff that turning points are made of. At issue here is nothing less than the integration of work-life effectiveness into the total rewards mix, until now a misunderstood, frequently overlooked and underappreciated management tool that is coming into its own.

Work-Life Effectiveness as a Business Imperative for Attracting, Motivating and Retaining Talent

Since this book makes it clear how broad the work-life charter can become, it is obviously not a stand-alone function. In most organizations, the portfolio expands in well-defined stages over time as the employer responds to first one need, then another workforce constituency's need, to integrate personal and professional demands more effectively. It overlaps and augments other people strategies inside and sometimes outside of the human resources function. It fits most appropriately at the heart of total rewards strategy, since work-life options are primarily non-monetary in nature and yet widely valued by employees. When used in conjunction with compensation and traditional benefits offerings, the potential variety of motivators that can be customized to meet individual and team needs are bounded only by the creativity of managers and their employees.

The integration of work-life into the total rewards mix encourages new thinking about how to define and reward success. It also lends a fresh source of empirical evidence about which people practices have the most impact on the attraction, retention or motivation of talent. Although some practices can improve more than one business outcome, what follows is a first attempt to align all of the components of the Total Rewards Model with the drivers to which they primarily relate. This is done through a work-life lens, and is intended to illustrate the power and utility of looking at the workplace in an integrated fashion.

Figure B on page 6 organizes these practices based on research findings from the pages of this book, as well as the following sources:

- Towers Perrin's Talent Report (2003)
- Gallup Organization's *Engaged Workers Index* (2003) and Q-12 research
- WFD Consulting's *The Drivers of Employee Commitment: Tools for Creating a Competitive Workplace*, Charles S. Rodgers (1998)
- *National Study of the Changing Workforce*, Families and Work Institute, 2002
- Watson Wyatt's *Strategic Rewards* report
- Watson Wyatt's Human Capital Index research, presented in most detail in the book, *The Human Capital Edge: 21 People Management Practices Your Company Must Implement (or Avoid) to Maximize Shareholder Value*, Bruce N. Pfau and Ira T. Kay (2002)
- 550 studies' findings that were summarized in *Leveraging The New Human Capital: Adaptive Strategies, Results Achieved, and Stories of Transformation*, Sandra Burud and Marie Tumolo (2004)
- The Great Place to Work Institute, San Francisco
- Catalyst, New York City.

The same core people strategies not only result in stronger attraction, higher retention and greater levels of engagement, but this entire "virtuous circle" of behavior has been demonstrated to increase shareholder value — the ultimate outcome measure of corporate success.

Work-Life Effectiveness: Why 'Balance' Does Not Suffice

To fully comprehend the value that work-life brings to the implementation of 21st-century total rewards strategy, you must first understand the nature and scope of the work-life body of knowledge. Karol Rose deftly begins this book by defining *work-life effectiveness*, explaining why the notion of "balance" as a goal is not applicable to the individual, and certainly does not suffice as a description within the organizational setting. No individual or company has ever achieved the static state of work-life balance, although today most companies strive to find ways to help employees become more *effective* at navigating the white water of work-life conflict throughout their employees' career and personal life cycles.

FIGURE B: Differential Impact of HR Practices on Business Outcomes		
Attraction Practices	Retention Practices	Desired Outcome: Employee Motivation[1]
Market-based, competitive base pay	Appropriate, timely incentive compensation	Genuine pay for performance
Company image, reputation	(Opportunity for) community involvement	Numerous and continuous community awards for good corporate citizenship
Placement on "Best Company" list(s)	(Perception that) company genuinely earns its way onto the list(s)	Overall work-life effectiveness; respect for the whole person; supportive supervisors and co-workers
Prospect of challenging, rewarding work	Respect; recognition as a valued contributor	Rewards tied to contribution; frequent, objective, results-oriented performance feedback
Potential career and development opportunities	Satisfactory career movement; personal growth	Career advancement and responsibility based on fair, objective performance standards
Benefits and policies that include "non-traditional" offerings such as workplace flexibility	Equitable access to workplace flexibility; adequate control over working conditions	Continual team-driven work redesign to eliminate low-value work and inefficient processes
Perception of values alignment (individual and organization share common values)	Tangible input into management decision-making	Empowering leadership; high levels of two-way trust and communication
Evidence of concern for employee well-being	Proactive health and wellness strategy	Reasonable workload, pace and pressure; well-established stress reduction and burnout-prevention techniques
Safe working conditions; appropriate tools to do the work	Skill acquisition and development	Continuous learning; belonging to a "learning organization"

[1] Employee motivation has different levels of outcome including satisfaction, commitment and/or engagement, depending on the impact of the practice and the stage of the employee's life cycle.

The Notion of a Work-Life Portfolio

During the past decade, organizational support for work-life effectiveness has clustered into seven major categories, each defined by a robust suite of responses that weave together a number of related policies, programs and practices. Each category of responses has been shown by empirical evidence to provide differential returns on investment over different timeframes. (See *Categories of Work-Life Effectiveness: Successfully Evolving Your Organization's Work-Life Portfolio* in the Appendix.) Research also demonstrates that the power of the whole is greater than the sum of the parts. That is, as employees use more and more work-life options across multiple categories in response to the numerous and predictable work-life conflicts encountered in the course of a typical career, the greater the benefits that can be documented for the business, workforce and other stakeholders, such as clients and shareholders. (*The Human Capital Edge*, McGraw Hill, 2002).

The work-life professional's unique contribution is to build the architecture, to expand and manage this dynamic and ever-changing work-life portfolio to the measurable benefit of both the organization and the individual, thus illuminating an actionable path to the end of the 20th-century zero-sum game. Within the work-life framework, neither personal nor professional priorities win at the permanent expense of the other; they coexist in response to a changing workforce that becomes increasingly adept at fluidly time-swapping between the two domains, as need dictates. In this book, Karol performs the invaluable service of explaining how to chart an overarching strategy, and then how to go about building most of the pillars of the work-life portfolio.

Caring for Dependents (Child Care and Elder Care)

The first work-life conundrum employers encountered centered on child-care options, since work-life's origins are rooted in the huge influx of women into the workforce following World War II, a workforce trend that challenged employers to problem-solve with employees to create workable solutions for taking care of children while their mothers worked. Although not a new development, since on-site childcare, hot meals and laundry service had been provided to mothers temporarily pressed into service during the Civil War and every national conflict thereafter, the magnitude and permanence of the need was unprecedented.

Karol devotes two chapters to this one category of work-life support, because of its dual nature. Given the aging of America toward the latter half of the 20th century, it wasn't long before the emergence of the "sandwich generation," the growing contingent of working parents who must also cope with primary responsibility for the care of their own aging parents.

Although not considered a traditional benefit, or a clearly defined type of compensation, the fact is that organizational support for dependent care does effectively put money in the pockets of employees, and has come to be considered so important to working parents' effectiveness that companies are now given tax relief for providing it. It is also a source of competitive advantage, since parents and the many employees who become parents during their careers are more likely to choose to join such family-friendly employers, and to stay with them longer once hired.

The other categories of organizational responses to all the other work-life conflicts that arise include the following:

- **Proactive Approaches to Health and Well-Being**

  Stress reduction is the central premise of work-life effectiveness. Because the negative impact of stress-related illness has been shown to eclipse the combined annual profits of the *Fortune* 500 companies, focusing on this category of work-life support holds the most promise of contributing to the reduction of escalating health-care costs.

- **Creative Uses of Paid and Unpaid Time Off**

  Time to spend with loved ones is the most fundamental pillar of work-life support. Some cutting-edge innovations in this category include sabbaticals, paid family leave for new fathers as well as mothers and paid or release time off for community service.

- **Workplace Flexibility**

  This category encompasses the critical management strategy of optimizing employee control over when, where and how work gets done — a factor so central to retention, engagement and productivity that it has come to define "employers of choice."

- **Community Involvement**

  This is one domain in which employer and employee interests are naturally in close alignment, because both the workforce and customers come from the community in which the organization operates, and every enterprise wants to be visible and perceived as a responsible and ethical contributor, whether community is defined as a neighborhood, city or the world.

- **Financial Support**

  Providing financially for oneself and loved ones from career entry through retirement is why people work in the first place, and thus core to the work-life effectiveness of everyone who works. As companies undo traditional financial supports such as defined pension plans and place more of the financial support burden squarely on employees' shoulders, it is more important than ever that compensation, benefits and work-life professionals collaborate to research and redefine what new combinations of monetary and nonmonetary incentives will attract, engage and retain 21st-century workers.

- **Managing Cultural Challenges**

  Creating meaningful support for work-life effectiveness across all of these categories for everyone at all organizational levels requires strong leadership in the areas of culture-change management, new types of management training to create an optimally collegial, flexible work environment, and continual experimentation with and streamlining of work processes. Additionally, in order to eliminate any residual barriers to the full engagement and productivity of every contributor, it is sometimes necessary to launch specific interventions to eliminate gender (and/or other) inequities. Thus, there is a strengthening link between work-life effectiveness, diversity initiatives, women's advancement, mentoring, networking, organizational effectiveness, health promotion and other efforts that share the goal of making the organization a better, healthier place to work.

Challenging the Status Quo
Many profound issues about work, workers and workplaces are discussed herein. It is the nature of the work-life professional to challenge the status quo because responding nimbly and appropriately to change has become the organizational norm, and no employer has successfully met new challenges by coasting uphill. Our goal is to team up with the professionals at the helm of all other people strategies to keep raising the bar and make every workplace a continually better and healthier place to work. This book is guaranteed to make you think and debate and discuss what kind of workplace you want to be known for, and then get on with creating the strategy and action steps to get there.

— Kathie Lingle
Director, Alliance for Work-Life Progress

Chapter 1
Why Work-Life Effectiveness?

1

It has been said that the only thing we can be certain of is change. That's certainly true in today's business environment. In addition to constant change in the way companies do business, employees' personal lives continue to change and have become far more complex than ever before. Dramatic change in the world of work and in people's lives has accompanied us into the 21st century. The focus on a competitive, fast-paced global economy; the ever-changing challenges of personal and family life; and the dramatic impact of technology have forced profound changes in how we define the workplace, the workforce, work and our personal lives.

Companies have long said employees are their most valuable assets, and today they face a human capital crisis. More than ever before, organizations are realizing that, if they want to remain competitive, they must find innovative ways of engaging employees that encourage and support their commitment and improve their performance. Companies today actually compete to become the employer of choice, the best place to work, the best work environment and so forth in order to attract and retain employees and to improve productivity.

In response to these dramatic changes, companies now view implementing effective work-life initiatives as a business imperative. Companies need to distinguish themselves from their competition by "connecting the dots" between issues such as overwork, stress and increased health-care costs, and realize the advantage they can gain by implementing preventative approaches, such as work-life effectiveness. In a knowledge economy, more than ever before, employers are realizing they must understand and address the diverse needs of their workforce in order to survive and thrive. Effective work-life practices — which include programs, policies, benefits and practices — are a critical way to "walk the talk" when it comes to corporate values and to create a culture that "puts its money where its mouth is" when it comes to human-capital assets.

Changing Demographics

In most countries, companies and their workforce do not look very much like their counterparts of just 10 years ago, and the impact of these changes has given birth °to the phenomenon we generally refer to today as "work-life." The dramatic increase of women in the workforce, resulting in the rise of the dual-focus worker — workers focused on work and family, rather than on work or family — and the aging of the workforce are among the most critical factors shaping today's workplace and affecting the way people live and work.

Let's take a look at demographics, the workforce and the family. As Sandy Burud and Marie Tumolo describe in their book, *Leveraging the New Human Capital* (2004), the change in the old male "breadwinner" profile of worker — 56 percent of employees in 1950, and as of 2000, only 21 percent of employees — is driven by the fact that, today, primarily for economic need and personal satisfaction, large numbers of women are working outside the home.

Consider these facts, according to Burud:

- In 55 percent of families, women earn more than half the household income.
- In one in five families, since no male is present, women are the sole support.
- Most married women are now employed, an increase from 37 percent in 1967 to 61 percent in 2000.

And, according to the Bureau of Labor Statistics, consider these facts:

- As of 2002, the workforce was almost even — 53 percent men to 47 percent women — and almost half of all graduates from professional programs today are women.
- As of 2003, the majority of mothers of young children worked outside the home — 51 percent of mothers of infants under one year, and 56 percent of mothers of children under six.
- In 2001, more women with children under 18 were employed (73 percent, the same as the percentage of all men employed) than were women without children (55 percent).

In addition to child care, with the aging of the population and the aging workforce, employees also have to deal with elder-care issues. As a result, the majority of today's employees (53 percent) have either children or elders whom they care for. These demographic changes have resulted in changing employee needs. In a 2001 Radcliffe Public Policy Center survey, 82 percent of men surveyed and 85 percent of women ages 20 to 39 placed family time at the top of their work-life priorities. In a Rutgers University and University of Connecticut study of that same year, 90 percent of working adults said they were concerned that they do not spend enough time with their families. Caregiving responsibilities are impacting the way employees feel about their work.

Work-life has also become a recruitment issue, because new entrants into the workforce are asking how they are going to manage both their work and their personal lives. Headhunters often report that candidates now ask, "How flexible is the work environment?" and "What kind of work-life programs does the company offer?" These questions are even being asked globally, according to a 1997 PricewaterhouseCoopers survey of 1,200 business school graduates worldwide, which found work-family support at the top of the list of important factors in selecting a job.

Managing a workforce with diverse needs has grown to a position of paramount importance as knowledge workers have taken their place in the majority of organizations as their companies' most precious asset. These organizations must find new ways to accept, incorporate, empower and engage the vast array of human talent available. Companies must do whatever is necessary to help each and every employee work up to his or her full potential, no matter what their personal or family responsibilities. In other words, companies simply must create work-life effectiveness for individuals and organizations or lose their competitive advantage.

The Evolution of Work-Life Initiatives

The work-life field has evolved along with the workforce itself. The work-life field first emerged on a wide scale in the United States in the early 1980s in order to address the child-care needs of working mothers who entered the paid workforce in record numbers. In the mid-1980s elder care was recognized as another area that impacted women's ability to participate fully in the workforce, and dependent-care information and resources and child-care centers were seen as the "solution" to what was then called "work-family" issues. Most of the responses to these needs were designed primarily to make it possible for the employee to be able to work, not to change the workplace, or necessarily to change the way work was done or to accommodate personal needs.

In the early 1990s, with the advance of technology and increased work demands, the issue of "time" became a major focus as women and men realized that multitasking could only stretch the day so far. At that point, organizations began to implement flexible work arrangements to address the need for more options for where and when to work. In the late 1990s and today, these issues continue to exist, along with an effort to "connect the dots" and change the organization's culture by redesigning work; address escalating health-care costs due to stress and overwork; and redefine benefits and total rewards — all to attract, energize and engage employees. While the focus in many organizations is still on responding to real or perceived employee needs, progressive companies see real advantages in taking a preventive, proactive approach to work-life issues and linking the effort directly to business goals.

Figure 1 on pages 16 and 17 outlines some of the major milestones in the evolution of the work-life field in the United States along with business and societal trends that accompanied them (*Fortune* magazine work-life special feature, 2003).

Work-Life Effectiveness: A Definition

Today, companies are thinking more strategically about the words they use to describe their work-life initiatives. This is more than semantics; it's a critical, as well as a philosophical and organizational, issue. Vocabulary is very important, as are labels, especially in an evolving field. The words we use shape our thoughts, and

FIGURE 1: The Evolution of Work-Life Initiatives		
1980	1985	1990

Dependent-Care Focus

Flexibility in Work Arrangements

Demographic Drivers

Women in workforce	Dual-income households	Working fathers
Women in professions	Working mothers	Sandwich generation
Women in management		Generation X

Business Drivers

Mergers and acquisitions		Downsizing/delayering/reengineering
	Total Quality Management	Cross-functional teams
	(TQM), continuous improvement	Customer focus
	Global markets	Managing change
	Cost controls	

Source: Families and Work Institute and WFD Consulting

there are many opportunities for misunderstanding when we're talking about "work-life" — I prefer the term "work-life effectiveness," meaning, "When work is effective, life benefits; and when life is working, work benefits." This message seems to resonate with both managers and employees.

Still, work-life means different things to different people depending on where they are in their lives and career cycles. For many employees, work-life effectiveness means being able to take care of child- or elder-care needs while working; for some, it's having the time to take care of their own or a family member's medical needs; for others, it's the ability to go to the gym when they want to, or to learn a new skill; and for still others, it's being able to avoid commuting during peak traffic periods. Whatever the need, what is clear is that many of the policies, programs, benefits and practices in organizations today were designed for the needs of the "traditional family" (i.e., stay-at-home mom, working dad) — which, according to the Bureau of Labor Statistics, represents less than 20 percent of the workforce, and not the rest of us, the 80 percent. Clearly, change should be on the way.

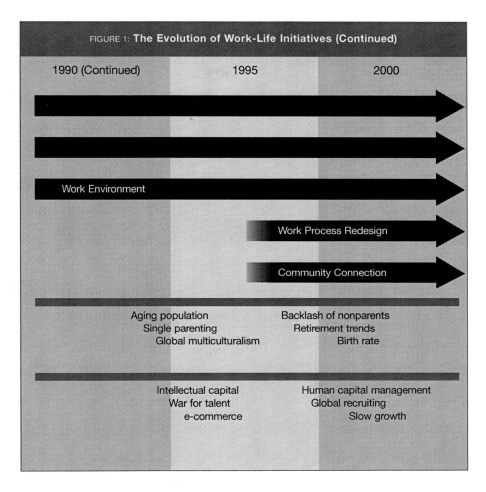

FIGURE 1: **The Evolution of Work-Life Initiatives (Continued)**

| 1990 (Continued) | 1995 | 2000 |

Work Environment

Work Process Redesign

Community Connection

Aging population
Single parenting
Global multiculturalism

Backlash of nonparents
Retirement trends
Birth rate

Intellectual capital
War for talent
e-commerce

Human capital management
Global recruiting
Slow growth

Work-life has become part of the culture-change process that is taking place in the most progressive companies as they work to engage employees, create a more results-oriented organization, foster productivity and compete more effectively for talent. Organizations are beginning to move from the notion of "work-life balance" — which no employee seems to have and most employers don't want, since it implies a win/lose situation — to work-life effectiveness, where the goal is for both the organization and the employee to work together for effective management of personal life and work. While that may be common sense, it hasn't always led to common practice. Today, employers of choice and the best places to work are trying hard to make common sense be the common practice. In these companies, work-life has become a package of total rewards — a combination of programs, policies, benefits and practices designed to address both changing business and employee needs.

Work-life effectiveness is often organized in companies as: programs, policies and practices. While there are many other ways to define and organize work-life initiatives, the following description highlights the relationship between the plans and the outcomes.

Figure 2 uses "8 Ps" to describe the organization of work-life effectiveness and the outcome of this effort — the return on investment (ROI). It highlights how work-life programs, policies/benefits and practices, designed and implemented effectively and aligned with the company's culture and mission, can help prevent absenteeism, turnover and stress; improve productivity; and increase employee passion as well as "presenteeism." Presenteeism in this case is not the opposite of absenteeism, but rather the discretionary effort or engagement that organizations need from their employees to remain competitive in the future. When these results are achieved from work-life effectiveness, the bottom-line impact is increased revenues or ROI.

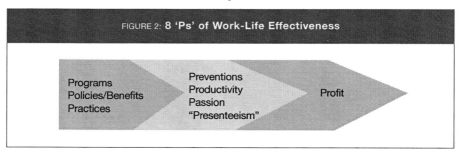

FIGURE 2: **8 'Ps' of Work-Life Effectiveness**

Programs
Policies/Benefits
Practices

Preventions
Productivity
Passion
"Presenteeism"

Profit

Some other labels that are still being applied to this field include: work-life balance, integration and harmony. Of course, each organization must select the best terms for its purpose. However, it is important to think about the message behind the label. In the case of "balance," balance has been shown to imply a zero-sum game, where if one side wins (the employee), then the other side loses (the company). This makes it more difficult to "sell" or overcome management's resistance to work-life. The terms "harmony" and "integration" both seem to imply that employees and the organization can just mix everything together and it will come out all right. However, increases in stress-related illness and depression, as well as reduced engagement, loyalty and commitment, show that this is not the case.

How an organization defines work-life depends on its culture, leadership and in some cases, the length of time the company has had a work-life initiative in place. For some organizations, work-life is simply a collection of programs, policies and benefits. In the most progressive companies, work-life has come to represent culture-change efforts or practices that include changing work, the way employees are managed and how productivity is measured. Some of these companies are beginning to "connect the dots" between traditional benefits and "non-traditional" work-life efforts. In some cases, this means including a broad definition of health and wellness as part of the work-life effort with the goal of reducing stress and health-care costs. It can also involve an ongoing examination of the way work is actually done with the goal of reducing "low value" work and inefficiencies. Work-life effectiveness, because of the uniqueness of each person's personal work and personal life cycle, also relates to diversity. And, it often involves assessing how well the process and methods of communication and the messages and branding for work-life meet the goal of ensuring a focus on a broad range of life-cycle and career-cycle issues.

According to the Alliance for Work-Life Progress (AWLP), work-life effectiveness is a specific set of organizational practices, policies and programs along with a philosophy that recommends aggressive support for the efforts of everyone who works to achieve success both at work and at home. The organization also includes those efforts initiated by employers to create a supportive work environment that acknowledges the personal and family commitments of their employees, supports them in fulfilling those commitments, and improves work and personal effectiveness in the process. Clearly, work-life is not an easy concept to get one's arms around, and that may be why responsibility for work-life can be found in almost any area of a company that deals with people strategy, including benefits, personnel, human resources, employee relations, training, diversity, and health and wellness.

Why Companies Address Work-Life Issues

There are at least eight very important interrelated business-related reasons why a company must have a comprehensive work-life initiative:

No. 1: To Attract and Retain Valued Employees

For many companies, the main reason for work-life initiatives is to attract and hold on to talented people. Even in a difficult economy, good people are hard to find and keep. Recent studies indicate that as the job market improves, many employees who have been frustrated and dissatisfied in their current situations will begin to look for other opportunities. In surveys and focus groups, employees frequently report they have considered looking for other jobs because their companies are not supportive of their work and personal needs. According to the 2005 Society for Human Resource Management (SHRM)/Career Journal *U.S. Job Recovery and Retention Survey*, more than one-half of the currently employed respondents indicated that with continued improvement of the economy they were very likely to begin to search for another job.

Work-life initiatives have given corporations a human face that can help prospective employees tell one corporate face from another. When companies set out to recruit today's stars, they're not only offering a job and benefits, they're also selling an identity. "There are plenty of very good places to work," says Ray Baumruk, a consultant with Hewitt Associates. "But the best organizations are taking a different tack, much as a product brand would do in a consumer market. The message has to be: 'We stand for something that others don't. We're special. We're relevant.'" This message is especially significant in an era of corporate scandal and mistrust.

Companies are also using their work-life initiatives to bring people who wouldn't otherwise be available to do the job into the workforce. These new workers may include new mothers who want to spend time with their babies; other parents or caregivers who will work as long as their schedule allows them to care for family members; young people who want to continue their education while working; older workers looking for more flexibility; the disabled who can work from home or from an office with accommodation; and workers, otherwise unavailable, who can participate remotely across the globe with vital skills.

IBM's 2004 global work-life survey demonstrated that, for IBM employees overall, flexibility is an important aspect of employees' decision to stay at the company. The survey incorporated both a work-life balance index and a flexibility index with nearly parallel results (i.e., employees with higher work-life balance scores also had higher scores on the flexibility index). Based on responses from almost 42,000 IBM employees in 79 countries, the survey found that work-life balance — of which flexibility is a significant component — is the second leading reason for potentially leaving IBM, behind compensation and benefits. Conversely, employees with higher work-life balance scores (and, therefore, also higher flexibility scores) reported significantly greater job satisfaction and were much more likely to agree with the statement "I would not leave IBM."

Forward-thinking companies are doing their best to let prospective employees know they respect the importance of their lives, their involvement in the community, their families and their ability to simultaneously manage multiple demands. They want employees to know how valued they are as "whole people." Post-9-11, these issues have become even more salient. A 2001 study by Aon Consulting, *United States Back @ Work*, found that 82 percent of workers surveyed felt that in light of the September 11th attacks, employees wanted to spend more time on personal, family or community activities, and less time on their jobs.

Many research studies show that when companies offer staff ways to help them manage work-life priorities, including flexible schedules, there is a lower rate of job turnover, and higher job and customer satisfaction. Lower turnover saves money. According to a 2005 survey by Managing Work/Life Balance, 29 percent of "best practices organizations" say they have data that shows their work-life strategies have contributed to a reduction in staff turnover, and 35 percent say that the strategies have helped increase employee motivation and satisfaction.

Merck and The Saratoga Institute, among others, have documented the cost of turnover. Typically they find that it costs 150 percent to 200 percent of an exempt person's yearly salary to lose that employee, and 75 percent of a nonexempt person's salary. Deloitte has quantified the cost savings that can be attributed to flexibility by calculating the cost of turnover for those professionals who say they would have left the firm had they not had a flexible arrangement. Based on this calculation, the firm has determined that it saved an estimated $41.5 million in turnover-related costs in 2003 alone.

A professional services firm recently documented its losses at two times salary. When the people leaving are not ones the organization wants to lose — undesirable losses — this is clearly not good for the bottom line. These are numbers senior management should be paying attention to.

Figure 8 on page 66 provides an example of a way to quantify the potential cost to a company from turnover related to work-life issues based on a survey conducted for the author's client.

Employee satisfaction or lack thereof is directly linked to turnover. While many companies have not calculated the cost of turnover, they ignore this expense at the risk of losing competitive advantage. Companies can maximize the investment in their human capital by being more responsive to employees' needs.

Companies Want to Retain Women

Many companies are becoming more sensitive to the proportion of women they recruit and retain, especially now that women graduates represent more than half of all professional programs (e.g., accounting, law, MBAs, etc.). Often, work-life issues are the underlying cause for women leaving an organization. In fact, recent company studies have shown that frequently it is the women the organization has a significant investment in — those with five to seven years of experience — who are leaving in large numbers. Typically, these highly competent women, who are in demand elsewhere, are looking for more supportive work environments and, specifically, more flexibility to manage their work and personal lives. Now that half the workforce is female, and more women are taking critical roles in their organizations, it has become even more important to find ways to retain and develop them.

The 2001 Women in Cable & Telecommunications Foundation Best Practices Benchmark & Survey indicates that the more a company strives to attain balance between work and home for employees, the higher the retention rates and morale and the more committed the employees.

While 61 percent of AstraZeneca men say that flexibility is "very important" in their intention to stay at the pharmaceutical company, 80 percent of women say so, according to survey findings from AstraZeneca.

No. 2: To Raise Morale and Job Satisfaction

The second reason to actively support work-life effectiveness is to raise morale and job satisfaction. Wilson Learning Corporation studied 25,000 workers and concluded that the single most important thing a company could do to improve its performance and bottom line is to increase employee morale. Sears, MCI and Northern Telecom all conducted studies that found when employees are satisfied, both customer retention and financial returns go up. Work & Family Connection Inc. surveyed 153 companies for *Working Mother* magazine, querying them about their work-life programs, how they had evaluated them and what they had found. Out of 40 different work-life initiatives, all but five had been found to increase employee satisfaction and morale.

The Family and Work Institute's *National Study of the Changing Workforce* also found job satisfaction improved when the work environment was supportive.

In the 2004 *Overwork in America Study*, findings show that employees are less likely to feel overworked if they have the following:

- Jobs that provide more opportunities to continue to learn
- Supervisors who support them in succeeding on the job
- The flexibility they need to manage their job and their personal and family life
- Input into management decision-making.

This holds true even when these employees work long hours and have very demanding jobs.

Survey findings from AstraZeneca, the pharmaceutical company, show that commitment scores are 28 percent higher for employees who say they have the flexibility they need compared to employees who do not have the flexibility they need. And, according to *Business Impacts of Flexibility: An Imperative for Expansion* by Corporate Voices for Working Families (November 2005), at Bristol-Myers Squibb, commitment scores of users of flexible work arrangements were higher than that of nonusers, especially in relation to the effective elements of commitment associated with loyalty, job satisfaction and recommending the company as a good place to work.

No. 3: To Increase Productivity

The third reason to implement a work-life initiative is to make the people you have more productive. Companies that have studied the results of their work-life programs have found they reduced absenteeism and increased productivity, which makes sense. People who feel they have more control over how they manage their work and personal lives can focus more intensely on their work. More than half the companies surveyed by Work & Family Connection found work-life programs increased productivity. Many other companies have reported increases in productivity after initiating a work-life effort. Scott Paper Co., for instance, said its work-life programs increased production by 35 percent. In the case of telecommuting, many studies have found productivity eventually rises when employees can work from home or a more convenient location, even for only a few days a month.

According to the *Way Ahead Report on the Year 2005 Survey* (Managing Work Life Balance International, Australia), 24 percent in best practices organizations, compared with 2 percent in lower-ranked groups, say they have reliable data that shows their work-life strategies have contributed to a positive impact on productivity.

Reducing absenteeism means increasing productivity. The *2004 Unscheduled Absence Survey* by CCH Inc., a provider of human resources and employment-law information, revealed the hidden costs of unscheduled absences due to work-life issues ranged from an average of $60,000 for small firms to more than $1 million for large companies.

No. 4: To Increase Commitment and Engagement

Increased productivity doesn't tell the whole story. Employee commitment and engagement are becoming more important with the increase in knowledge and service workers who can take their knowledge and expertise with them if they leave the job, and whose emotions — how they feel — impact how they do their jobs on a daily basis. A 1995 study by S.L. Grover and K.J. Crooker of a cross section of U.S. workers found higher levels of commitment in organizations that offered family-friendly policies, regardless of whether the employees anticipated directly benefiting from the policies. When employees notice when little mistakes are made, try to make sure they're putting out quality work, spend some time thinking about how to do a better job, use time more wisely, don't listen when others put down management or co-workers and give their discretionary effort to the job at hand, that's called engagement. Among employees in effective workplaces, more than twice as many (82 percent) express high levels of job engagement and commitment as employees in ineffective workplaces (36 percent), according to *When Work Works*, a summary of findings from the national *Study of the Changing Workforce* (Families and Work Institute, 2002).

In 1997, Hoechst Celanese found employees who were more aware of the company's work-life efforts were 20 percent more committed and more likely to say they'd "go the extra mile" for the organization.

No. 5: To Reduce Health-Care Costs

The fifth reason to implement a work-life initiative is to cut the rise in health-care costs. Duke University Medical Center reported in a 1997 study that workplace stress, especially in tandem with a lack of job autonomy, heightens the incidence of depression, anxiety, anger and a whole range of physical health problems. According to the Stress Institute of America's latest figures, stress is costing U.S. employers about $300 billion per year in lost productivity, health-care and replacement costs. In a 1990 study by Northwestern Medical School, depressive disorders within the workplace were much higher than anticipated and were associated with the highest medical plan costs of all behavioral-health disorders. The National Institute for Occupational Safety and Health (NIOSH) reported in 1999 that because the nature of work is changing at whirlwind speed, job stress poses a threat to the health of workers and, in turn, to the health of the organization. In 2000, the World Health Organization reported that by 2020, clinical depression was expected to outrank cancer and follow only heart disease to become the second greatest cause of death and disability worldwide.

It is widely believed that lack of control over one's job can lead to major health problems. *The New York Times* (June 1, 1999) reported on a large-scale study of civil servants in which employees were asked to rate the amount of control they felt over their jobs. Managers also rated the amount of control employees actually had. Job control, the researchers found, varied inversely with employment grade: the higher the grade, the more control. The less control employees had, as defined either by their own or their managers' ratings, the higher the employees' risk of developing coronary disease. Job control, in fact, accounted for about half the gradient in deaths from pay grade to pay grade.

Another study in 2000 by the Health Enhancement Research Organization found the health-care bills of employees who suffer from (clinical) depression are 70 percent higher than those of other workers. The study tracked the medical bills of 46,000 employees from several major U.S. companies for up to three years. When several risk factors associated with heart disease were combined — smoking, high blood-glucose levels, high cholesterol, high blood pressure, high body weight and poor exercise habits — medical costs were more than three times those of low-risk workers, and combining stress and depression led to costs nearly two and one-half times higher. The findings come at a time when downsized workforces are being pressured to be productive. The cost of such pressure could be more significant than has been previously acknowledged.

Employers are realizing that to get to the root of the health-care cost problem, they must take a more active role in managing the health of their employees. Programs that focus on managing specific diseases and help workers make lifestyle behavior changes aimed at weight management, exercise and smoking cessation can go a long way toward slowing rising costs over the long term. Nearly seven of 10 respondents (69 percent) are using disease-management programs through a health plan this year, a 50-percent increase over last year, according to the *2005 Watson Wyatt Health Survey of Large Employers*. Similarly, the number of employers adopting lifestyle behavior change through a health plan doubled to 40 percent this year. Additionally, 32 percent offer obesity-reduction programs, compared with just 14 percent in 2004.

No. 6: To Combat Burnout

"Burnout" may be hard to define, but both employees and their employers feel its effects. Employees who feel burned out tend to leave the organization, have less commitment and focus, be depressed and have a host of stress-related illnesses that include heart disease and cancer as well as headaches and other minor but debilitating ailments. One study found burnout and stress were very closely related, and four out of every 10 workers told researchers they thought about quitting because of it. While most companies think stress is too "soft" an issue to demand their attention, 50 percent of workers surveyed said job stress and burnout had reduced their productivity. Of those who reported having "severe" stress, 59 percent wanted to quit, and 55 percent said they became ill more frequently.

Sixty-one percent of workers say their workloads increased over the last six months of 2005, contributing to increased stress levels and dissatisfaction with work-life balance, according to the results of the CareerBuilder.com annual survey that projects recruitment and job-search activities for the coming year. Thirty-one percent of those same workers say they are struggling to balance both professional and personal commitments.

A 2001 study by the Families and Work Institute (FWI) found that one in three U.S. employees experienced feeling overworked as a chronic condition. In a follow-up 2004 study, FWI found that 26 percent of employees were overworked often or very often in the last month; 27 percent were overwhelmed by how much work they had to do often or very often in the last month; and 29 percent often or very often didn't have time to step back and process or reflect on the work they were doing during the last month. This study also found that 44 percent of U.S. employees were overworked often or very often according to these measures. The more overworked employees are, the more likely they are to make mistakes at work and to feel angry with their employers for expecting them to do so much.

AON Consulting's 1999 *America@Work* study found more than half of the 1,800 workers surveyed said they were burned out by job stress. A 2005 study showed that employees at Bristol-Myers Squibb who use flexible work arrangements are significantly less likely to report feeling stressed and burned out. Those on flexible arrangements scored, on average, 30 percent lower in stress and burnout (Corporate Voices for Working Families, 2005). A New England-based financial services company found that employees who say they have the control they need over their work schedules have burnout index scores less than half that of employees who do not have control over their work schedules. And WFD Consulting found that employees who have control over their work schedules are more committed to their employers and are less likely to suffer from burnout.

No. 7: To Attract Investors

The seventh reason is that shareholders increasingly value companies that are good citizens, are good to their employees and are active in their communities. There are a number of new studies that show such supportive companies are more profitable, including one from Cornell University. That study concluded that the way a firm treats its employees may be a window on both its stock price and survival rate. When companies treated their workers well — offering stock options and profit sharing, providing training, emphasizing employee relations — they would be more likely than other new companies to still be doing business five years down the road.

The Cornell study tracked the 136 nonfinance companies that went public in 1988 and found personnel policies were an important factor for the 60 percent that survived five years later. Theresa Welbourne, study author and professor, concluded, "In the long run, employee rewards get you the performance you need in an organization." And according to Harvard Business School Professor Rosabeth Moss Kanter, a comparison of the 20-year performance of progressive companies (those with a variety of human resources programs) and nonprogressive companies found that the former had significantly higher long-term profitability and financial growth.

Watson Wyatt's Human Capital Index found that firms with high employee satisfaction have decidedly higher market value — and that a flexible workplace is associated with a 9-percent change in market value.

First Tennessee Bank also used flexibility as a centerpiece in putting the service-profit chain theory into practice. In several branches, the bank trained managers on flexibility practices and focused on creating a work environment in those branches that was supportive of flexibility and people's personal lives. The result was that employee retention in these branches proved to be 50 percent higher than in other branches, and this contributed to a greater retention rate of customers at these branches. The bank demonstrated that as employee satisfaction increased, customer retention increased by 7 percent, which translated into a $106-million profit increment in two years' time.

In an analysis of its employee survey results, Ernst and Young found that individuals' perceptions of their own flexibility are highly predictive of level of commitment, which in turn was found to be highly predictive of revenue per person as well as retention. The firm found that business units in the top quartile of people commitment scores had revenue per person that was seven percentage points better than business units in the middle half, and 20 percentage points better than business units in the lowest quartile of people commitment scores. This led the firm to conclude that having flexibility is an important driver of performance and, ultimately, of financial results.

No. 8: To Be a Good Corporate Citizen

The eighth reason is simply that it's the right thing to do and it can demonstrate support for the community from which both clients and the workforce are drawn. Companies are becoming more aware of the connection between their employees, their customers and the larger community. Some companies, such as Prudential, are beginning to examine ways to link their volunteer initiatives with employees' career development, benefiting employees, the company and the community. Today, the most progressive companies focus not only on their employees' needs, but also on the larger community in which they live and work. In some cases, companies leverage their corporate contributions and community relations resources to support this win-win effort.

Ways to Address Work-Life Issues

One way to describe work-life efforts is to separate them into categories according to programs, policies and benefits, and practices, as described earlier. While the following is not an exhaustive list, it does provide some examples of each category.

Programs

Often the intent is to offer "something for everyone" in terms of work-life programs. While every employee won't use every program, during their careers, most employees will make use of some of the following offerings:

- Adoption assistance
- Car maintenance or repair services
- Career planning
- Child-care assistance to find and manage care
- Company cafeteria or store
- Corporate discounts, reserved spaces and preferred customer status at child-care centers
- Child-care centers, on site or nearby
- Educational scholarships or tuition reimbursement for employees and/or their children
- Dependent-care reimbursement accounts
- Educational seminars for employees to help them handle personal responsibilities
- Elder-care case management and other elder-care support services
- Emergency or back-up care subsidy or on-site emergency-care centers
- Fitness centers, on or near site, and/or local centers (subsidized)
- Housing assistance (either financial aid or help in locating housing)
- Information and support for both elder-care and child-care needs
- Literacy and remedial education mentoring
- Nursing room and lactation assistance
- Overnight travel child-care expense subsidies
- Pagers for expectant fathers
- Peer-support groups
- Recreation site for family use
- Relocating assistance for families
- Reserved parking for pregnant employees
- Summer camp or other summer care; summers off
- Warm line for after-school phone calls
- Wellness and prevention programs.

Policies and Benefits

The trend among leading companies is to re-examine and redesign policies and benefits to ensure that they reflect the company's commitment to mutual trust and respect, treat employees like responsible adults and reduce health-care costs while focusing on outcomes and results. In some cases, companies are examining their time-off practices and are allowing employees to take all their paid leave days — personal or emergency days, vacation and sick days — for whatever purpose they want without having to present their need, make the case and secure permission. This type of "paid leave bank" has grown in use and is being found not only to raise morale and save money, but to give employees more control over their time. This helps make employees feel as if they're being treated like adults instead of children who have to ask permission for every day off and present the reasons to someone for approval. Companies are also realizing that employees need true time off, time away from work, to regenerate, which can help reduce health-care costs while improving productivity.

Many companies are examining their benefits to determine if a life-cycle approach is more appropriate to meet increasingly diverse employee needs. Some companies have instituted flexible (cafeteria) benefits that allow employees to select from a menu of options and make choices based on individual career and life stage. While most cafeteria plans primarily focus on traditional benefits, in some cases companies are experimenting with including work-life related benefits as well. For example, Xerox implemented a life-cycle benefit that allowed employees to use a $10,000 lifetime account to help pay for child care, buy a home and finance other work-life related needs.

Other work-life related polices and benefits might include the following:

- Gradual return to work after parental, family or disability leave
- Flexible work arrangements
- Phased retirement
- Time off to volunteer or for community service
- Sabbaticals
- Family sick days
- Subsidies to pay for child- or elder-care services
- Convenience services
- Financial assistance to equip a home office
- Group insurance policies for life, home, car
- Subsidies for health/fitness classes, gyms and so forth.

Innovative companies are taking a strategic approach by analyzing their existing policies and benefits, examining employee needs and identifying gaps in services. It is important that such an analysis include a review of those policies and benefits based on usage, value and cost.

Practices
Workplace practices and culture are inextricably tied together; it is impossible to view one without the other. Enlightened companies are changing the way work is done in order to become more efficient and to alter their company cultures. Flexibility is the

work-life practice most frequently requested by employees, and most major companies claim to offer it. But for most companies that means a policy that says, "If it's OK with your manager, it's OK to be flexible." *Fortune* magazine's annual "Best Companies To Work For" issue includes criteria such as whether a company surveys its employees. Great Places To Work Institute conducted the research for *Fortune* and found that employee answers and company executives' answers about company flexibility were often different.

The goal for leading-edge companies now is to treat employees as trusted, responsible adults with unique personal and career needs. Rather than focusing on obeying rules, their focus is on outcomes and results. The flexible scheduling tools that facilitate this change include job sharing, telecommuting, compressed workweeks, part-time work, temporary part-time work and informal flexibility (which allows employees to leave work when necessary and make up the time and/or work later).

Supportive Work Environment

The impact of a supportive work environment cannot be overestimated. A study by Stewart Friedman, of the University of Pennsylvania's Wharton School of Management, and Jeff Greenhause, Drexel University, sheds new light on ways that a supportive work environment impacts the workplace, its workers and their home lives. The researchers reported in March of 1999 that they had tracked 861 graduates of Wharton and Drexel, questioning them several years after they graduated about their work, their families and the impact each had on the other. In every case where the organization was perceived as supportive (family-friendly), flexibility and self-control were present. Those in a supportive work environment felt better about their performance at home, took more time for personal relaxation, worried less about work when they did and reported no difference in work performance. Their families interfered less with work, and they experienced fewer work-life conflicts. They were more satisfied with their jobs and their careers. They were more likely to align their future career plans with the future direction of the firm. They were more committed to the long-term interests of the organization. Working parents rated themselves more highly as parents.

The study drew a clear picture that, in truth, summarizes 10 years of learning about work-life. It indicates that work and life are irrevocably connected. Work and personal life have a circular impact; one cannot be experienced without a reaction from the other. Friedman has since extended that work by creating a process for improving leadership skills that involves aligning personal goals for family and community along with business objectives. Implemented at Ford Motor Company, these tools are beginning to be used by other companies and organizations.

Company Culture

Each corporation has a unique company culture, its own way of doing business. Factors that influence a company's culture include:

- Company's leaders and values
- Type of industry
- Age and size of the company
- Geographic location
- Union or nonunion
- Centralized or decentralized
- Private or public institution
- Structure of the company (pyramid organizational structure or flatter organizational structure)
- Workforce demographics.

All of these factors combined create a unique workplace — one that has different cultural norms, different resources and restrictions and unique ways of addressing workplace issues. Each corporate culture dictates the way business is conducted. If the corporate environment is extremely conservative, a strong "code of conduct" may exist that discourages alterations to the traditional office-based, 40-hour, 9-to-5 and five day-a-week schedules.

But studies increasingly point to the need to change the way work is done. The Ford Foundation sponsored a three-year study (1993-1996) at Xerox, Tandem Computers and Corning to see if taking steps to integrate work and personal life would improve business performance, work-life effectiveness and gender equity. The study found that traditional assumptions should be re-examined and work tasks reengineered. It showed that business concerns are inextricably tied to work-life issues and the same innovative, systemic changes that ease work-life dilemmas will also help achieve business goals.

Academics from Radcliffe Public Policy Institute, working with New England-based Fleet Financial Group (now part of Bank of America), quantitatively measured the impact of work redesign on both home life and work. The study posed three questions to workers: How is work organized and what are the business measures for success? How does the way work is organized affect employees' personal lives? How can changes in the way work is done positively affect both business outcomes and employees' lives?

Researchers heard from staff about sleepless nights, neglected families, too much work and a sense of frenzy about getting everything done. Employees began to brainstorm in order to come up with suggestions for how their work might be redesigned. The changes they chose seem simple at first glance: a shifting of administrative tasks, a new way to assign credit applications, a new form designed to yield more complete information and, of course, new flexibility — flex time at one site and telecommuting at both sites.

With strong leadership, a company culture can change rapidly. For work-life efforts to succeed, champions must make every effort to obtain resolute support from top management; to set clear, measurable goals; and to assess progress and reward managers who demonstrate supportive behavior. As companies move from implementing work-life programs toward work redesign and culture change, many new challenges and rewards will surface.

Work-Life Strategy

Just as with other business undertakings, in order to successfully develop, implement and manage a work-life initiative, there must be a strategy that is aligned with the overall business strategy. The Boston College Work & Family Roundtable for Employers recommends the following guiding principles to help shape a work-life strategy. These principles can be used by organizations of any size as a guide for a self-assessment process.

The guiding principles are as follows:

- The employer recognizes the strategic value of addressing work and personal life issues.
  - Business is practiced with sensitivity to employees' personal life needs.
  - Work and personal life solutions are aligned with business goals.
  - The employer's commitment to addressing work and personal life issues is viewed as a long-term investment.
  - Work and personal life strategies are flexible enough to meet changing transitional and employee needs.
- The work environment supports individual work and personal life effectiveness.
  - The employer's informal culture supports healthy work and personal life management.
  - The employer provides meaningful work and personal life programs and policies.
  - The employer is committed to ongoing education of key stakeholders: employees, management and the community.
  - The employer strives for continuous improvement through ongoing evaluation and assessment.
- The management of work and personal life effectiveness is a responsibility shared by employer and employee.
  - Managers and employees are empowered to develop solutions that address both business and personal objectives.

- Managers and employees are held accountable for their behavior in support of these objectives.
- The employer develops relationships to enhance external work and personal life resources.
  - Partnerships are formed to maximize the value of employer and community resources available to employees and community members.
  - The employer serves as an active role model.
- The employer is open to working with the public sector to strengthen policies that benefit both employers and individuals.

Developing a Work-Life Vision

A work-life vision can help shape your strategic plan. In many cases, organizations have developed mission or vision statements that, while they may not state it explicitly, may have elements related to work-life issues. For example, if the organization's mission statement includes concepts related to people, the community, respect, excellence, customer service and so forth, these can all be linked to work-life.

To develop a work-life vision statement, it is helpful to start with a "straw man" or sample statement and ask key people in the organization to react to it. The process of developing a work-life vision encourages the company to recognize the connection between the work-life initiatives and the organization's purpose. It provides a roadmap for current and future decision-making regarding programs, policies, benefits and practices.

Marketing Work-Life Initiatives

As work-life programs, policies, benefits and practices are developed, marketing becomes critical. The process of internally marketing work-life programs requires creativity and perseverance on the part of all those involved. It also requires considerable knowledge about the organization, its culture and the relevance of work-life issues to the company's goals and concerns. In terms of marketing the work-life agenda, it is important to know whom to target and the likely obstacles or resistances that will be encountered.

Effective marketing is necessary if any new concept or product is to survive. Marketing new products and/or services and dealing with new ideas is very difficult and challenging. In many ways, marketing work-life programs and policies is similar to marketing any other human resources program. The key to getting a company to adopt work-life programs and to making them successful is to take a basic marketing approach and sell the ideas as part of an overall business strategy that meets corporate objectives. Promoting work-life is an ongoing process that must include constant feedback and communication. Packaging the work-life message, customizing communication for different target audiences and involving employees all contribute to the long-term success of a work-life agenda.

Marketing can be defined as the performance of business activities that direct the flow of goods and services from producer to consumer or user. Some basic principles that apply to marketing work-life are as follows:

- **Know your customer(s) and assess needs.**
  Conduct an informal or formal work-life needs assessment. Identify the key audience(s) and separate those groups in terms of their different needs. For example, identify the employee segments that a new program is most likely to benefit. Then estimate the size of the segment and project the benefits to the company that are expected from the program. Quantify the benefits as much as possible. Always include ongoing market research — ask customers what they like, dislike, want, don't want, etc.

- **Know your culture.**
  What works in one corporate culture may not work in another. Companies are like families; in some ways they are very similar, and in many ways they are very different. Consider what has been effective in your organization in the past and why. Develop a work-life marketing plan that takes into account the "personality" of your organization. Know current "hot" issues in the company, where the "pain" is (recruitment, retention, absenteeism, etc.). Involve someone in the process who really understands the corporate culture. Be aware of the image the company wants to project. Know if there is a new division, product or market niche that is being developed.

- **Attach a work-life agenda to business needs.**
  Establish a positioning strategy that defines the work-life program in terms of its benefits to the target audience(s) and to the organization's short-term and long- term goals. Find out if the company is concerned about quality, diversity, productivity, morale, cost savings, downsizing and so forth, and use this to promote the work-life agenda.

- **Check out the competition.**
  Benchmark the activities of your competition. This competition can be from different companies or within the company or division. Sibling rivalry, which is in keeping with the work-life tradition, can be useful in getting senior management's attention. Consider ways work-life programs and policies can help define your organization as different/better than the competition. Find ways to keep people informed about what the competition is doing on work-life issues. Also assess competing issues or products that may draw needed resources and attention away from the work-life agenda.

- **Identify key decision makers and their preferred influence style.**
  Know who has to be convinced and find out how she or he prefers to be influenced. Consider visual, verbal, written, face-to-face and phone, as well as formal, presentations. Anticipate objections that will be raised and develop tactics to overcome those objections.

- **Position work-life in its broadest context.**
  Develop a sequential or staged approach for focusing on different audiences and/or objectives. Try not to compartmentalize each work-life initiative as a separate item; package the whole "product" instead. Work-life is not one thing (for example, child care), but a combination of many policies, benefits and programs. Consider the life cycle of employees and include the needs of singles, retirees and so forth in your plans.

- **Use internal and external resources.**
  Explore a wide range of methods and approaches to communicate about work-life programs and policies. Internal resources might include newsletters, posters, e-mail messages and so on. External resources might be the local press, community organizations, and so forth. Also involve a wide range of resources in your information-gathering and evaluation process, including consultants, professional organizations, and publications and conferences.

How to Begin

Marketing involves understanding and addressing your customer's needs and wants and getting feedback. It is important not to assume that the customer's needs/wants are known. Programs have failed when they were implemented for the wrong audience and/or the wrong reason. In many companies, the decision maker for work-life issues is senior management. The person who is often responsible for selling programs to senior management may be the head of human resources or benefits. Each person has his or her own agenda. The work-life strategy must take into account the interim decision makers as well as the final decision maker.

Getting to know your customer is critical to planning a successful work-life program. As it was said about Alice in Wonderland, "If you don't know where you're going, how will you know when you get there?" A work-life strategy must be carefully thought out and developed. The word "strategy" is taken from the Latin word meaning "battle plan," and that is what is required. Too often, work-life initiatives are undertaken because someone thinks they are "nice to do." Work-life programs can be implemented for many reasons — to keep up with the competition, to recruit and retain the desired workforce, to improve morale and/or productivity and so forth — but how work-life programs and policies will serve the needs of the intended audience must always be clear.

In developing a marketing plan, it is important to determine where support will come from and where there might be a restraining factor. In some cases, the support or restraint will be a person, and in other cases it might be an organizational issue or resource. Whatever the case, successful marketing requires that you make the best use of supportive forces while you cope with or minimize the restraining forces.

In the best of all possible worlds, the organization's values dictate its mission.

Strategies evolve from the mission and indicate tasks that need to be accomplished. When this kind of organizational structure is in place, the marketing strategies for work-life initiatives can be clearly determined. However, in most organizations, there is not such a clear definition of purpose or direction. This makes it somewhat more difficult to determine the appropriate strategy for creating and marketing work-life programs. Deciding the appropriate course for marketing work-life programs and policies involves research, advertisement, public relations and communication.

Source of Commitment

It's clear that the more senior management support there is for work-life issues, the better. The reasons why a company begins to address the work-life needs of employees vary greatly. The reasons might be organizational, personal or those that result from some external influence. In some companies, unions are influential in getting work-life on the agenda. In other organizations, there is an informal network, often of mothers, that may work for years trying to determine the needs and then presenting ideas to management. In some cases, the work-life agenda surfaces when the company realizes it is having recruitment and/or retention difficulties with a particular segment of the workforce.

Some companies respond to their competition's activities and initiate programs and/or policies in an attempt to "keep up with the Joneses," especially when another company's initiative receives positive press. In some companies, work-life programs are implemented because they are consistent with the organization's philosophy or culture. In other organizations, if the CEO or other senior leader experiences a work-life problem personally, that is when the organization develops a response. Whatever the originating cause for implementing work-life programs, once started, they tend to continue and expand.

It is important to note that there is no guarantee for successful marketing of work-life programs. One might assume that with top management's involvement, support from all levels within the organization will be forthcoming. However, that is not necessarily the case. Senior management may have indicated support for work-life initiatives, but to sustain work-life programs, this support needs to be continuously nurtured and expanded to middle managers.

Anticipating Problems

Be prepared to respond appropriately to obstacles. There will always be resistance to implementing work-life initiatives. One thing to check is the vocabulary that is used to describe the initiatives and how they are communicated and marketed to the various stakeholders. There are many "messages" that are heard within organizations that may or may not be accurate but are often given as the reason why a particular work-life initiative cannot be undertaken. In many cases, these obstacles can be counteracted with timely, accurate information. What is important is to identify the obstacle, to understand what it means, especially taking into consideration its source, and then to prepare to counteract it.

Developing an Appropriate Marketing Strategy

The appropriate marketing strategy depends on where the company is in the process of developing a work-life initiative. The strategy will be somewhat different for a company that is at the beginning stages of developing a work-life agenda versus a company that wants to expand an existing program or a company that is involved in changing its corporate culture.

A needs assessment can be conducted to find out what kind of work-life initiatives are appropriate and what the priorities might be. The involvement of an experienced work-life consultant can be invaluable when conducting a needs assessment. The assessment might be formal or informal. A formal needs assessment could involve focus groups, questionnaires and/or an attitude survey. It might be done to investigate the company's goals, employee needs and/or community resources. A task force, steering committee or other interested group can conduct an informal assessment.

For a company at the beginning of the process of developing a work-life agenda, one of the first steps might be just to get official permission to study the issue or to gather information. A work-life task force can be an effective method of collecting information and making recommendations. If a task force is formed, it is important to include members representing diverse groups or positions within the company. If possible, a high-level champion should function as the group's leader or spokesperson. The task force's goal is to define a direction for the company regarding work-life issues. Individual issues must be handled in such a way that they can be easily explained and related to the overall business strategy of the organization.

In some companies, the first job of a work-life task force is not to solve a particular problem but to position work-life as part of a larger effort to improve productivity. In this way, the value of work-life to the organization is clear, and the mission of the work-life task force is seen as relevant to the organization's success. The task force should go about obtaining the necessary information on work-life issues just as it would for any other business issue it might be investigating. If necessary, contact other companies to find out how they have handled particular situations. It is not necessary to reinvent the wheel!

Calculating the Return on Investment

For the success of work-life initiatives, it is important to strategically determine the most appropriate programs, policies, benefits and practices for each organization. In order to accomplish that goal, an analysis of current and future programs, policies and practices is critical. The process includes documenting all work-life related initiatives and determining their real and perceived value to employees.

These findings can then be used to determine the most highly valued and cost-effective programs, policies and practices, as shown in Figure 3.

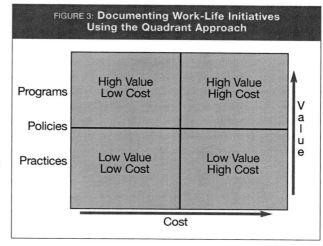

FIGURE 3: **Documenting Work-Life Initiatives Using the Quadrant Approach**

Cost and Value

By analyzing existing polices and benefits according to business or employee value (real and perceived) as well as cost, it is possible to see where the greatest return on investment (ROI) exists. Clearly, those initiatives that are low in cost and highly valued, as well as possibly those that are high in cost yet have high value, are the ones the organization most likely should retain and support. Those with high cost and low value, or low cost and low value, might be modified or eliminated.

Developing the most appropriate combination of work-life effectiveness programs, policies and practices will lead to improved prevention, increased productivity and "presenteeism" as well as employee passion. These are all necessary for bottom-line success, that is, improved profitability.

The Future of Work-Life Effectiveness

The Society for Human Resource Management (SHRM) asked a panel of HR experts to make predictions for the future of HR. The top 10 predictions for work and society point to the importance of work-life initiatives for the future. Their predictions, presented in the order of importance, were as follows:

1. Family and life interests will play a more prominent role in people's lives and will be a greater factor in people's choices about work — there will be more of a "work to live" than a "live to work" mentality.

2. Employees will demand increases in workplace flexibility in order to pursue life interests.

3. Dual-career couples will refuse to make the sacrifices required today in their family lives, and more people (not just women) will opt out of traditional careers.

4. Families will return to the center of society; work will serve as a source of cultural connections and peripheral friendships.

Putting It All Together — Checklist

You may find that employees may rate individual work-life programs as marginally important or unimportant when they are considered separately. However, when presented and described as a group under one umbrella, employees will most likely rate them as very or extremely important. It all depends on how these initiatives are developed, implemented and communicated.

Consider the following when planning your overall work-life strategy:

☐ **Know your customers.** This may include management, employees, those within the organization, representatives from the community and so forth.

☐ **Package the product.** Create a look, a logo that communicates the message you want to convey about work-life initiatives.

☐ **Deliver a consistent product over time.** This helps build awareness and manage employee expectations.

☐ **Develop linkages/connections** to other work-life related programs, policies and practices.

☐ **Think long term,** but propose in stages/phases/segments. Be aware of what you want to accomplish over the long term, but if it helps sell the program or policy, present it in smaller segments. Once that part is proven successful, then you can return and ask for approval for another part of the program.

☐ **Pilot, pilot, pilot.** It may be easier to sell a program or policy to senior management if they know it is a test. This is also helpful because it allows you to experiment and modify as you go along. Letting employees know that the program is a pilot is also useful because they can understand if something has to be changed to make the service more effective.

☐ **Live by "just enough" or "just manageable difficulty" motto.** It helps to give senior management the information that they need to know to make a decision, but no more. Too much information can be overwhelming, especially when you are not familiar with the subject. There have been situations where a work-life task force or committee has worked for long periods of time to research the topic and when it finally presents to senior management, it tries to review everything it has learned and recommend everything it wants to accomplish for the next five years. This is too much. Determine what the goal is for senior management. Is it to get buy-in, make a commitment to begin, to adopt a work-life strategy or to implement a particular program or policy? Chunk down — overkill usually does not work.

☐ **Evaluate and report progress.** Emphasize the process, not just the product. Track the number of employees who use a particular program or policy. Count those who sign up for a program, as well as those who show up. That way, you can choose to report both numbers (usually sign-ups exceed show-ups). Be creative with cost/benefit analysis information. It may be difficult to obtain hard data to document the cost/benefit of all work-life programs.

5. Workers will continue to struggle with their need for work-life effectiveness, and it will get worse.

6. Integration of work with quality-of-life initiatives will create solutions to problems formerly seen as the responsibility of government.

7. Community involvement and social responsibility will become part of an organization's business vision.

❑ **Watch for "smoke screens" of resistance.** Some companies have conducted extensive research on work-life options, and when they were finally presented to the president, they were not approved. In some cases, the reasons given had to do with liability and insurance. In reality, these were not real problems, but management could not be convinced at that time. The same kind of argument is sometimes given for not implementing flexible scheduling — that everyone will want to work part-time, or that there will be no way to know that people are really working if they work from home. In these cases, providing examples of other companies' experience can often alleviate these fears. In other cases, proposing a pilot project over a specific period of time can be a way to get started.

❑ **Consider the message and the medium.** Effective marketing requires that you think about both the content and the media that can be used. There are many ways to "cross market" work-life programs.

❑ **Use a variety of vehicles/tools for marketing work-life programs.** A good marketing strategy does not depend on one kind of media to convey its message. Try to use a variety, including e-mail, newsletters, activities like an expo, videos, speeches or talks, brochures and so forth. Even meetings that promote the work-life agenda can be considered marketing. Sometimes just including an influential person on the distribution list of relevant material can be part of a marketing strategy. A good marketing strategy might tie a program or activity to a "theme" to help employees remember to use it.

❑ **Consider internal and external marketing activities.** Some of the most effective marketing efforts within companies have begun with an article in the local press. The article might even be talking about your competition.

❑ **Promote your success stories.** You must be your own best advocate. Be sure the internal newsletter covers work-life activities and programs. If there is an example of job sharing, perhaps the partners can be interviewed. If an employee writes a letter praising a particular service, find a way to share that praise, if only with senior management. Keep track of employee contacts about programs and requests for additional services. Document any contacts from the press or media. When there are articles about your work-life programs and policies, be sure that they are copied to all those involved. Keep your communication network very active.

❑ **Collect other companies' materials.** Share your materials (brochures, flyers, booklets, Web sites, etc.) with others and ask them to do the same. A great deal of information and many good ideas can be gathered from examining these materials. Even if you are not ready to implement a marketing idea today, keep a file of these materials so that when you are ready for the next step, the material will be at your fingertips.

8. "Cocooning" will become more popular as workers look to their homes for refuge from the pressures of a more competitive workplace and depersonalized society.

9. Companies will take on increasing responsibility for elder care, long-term care and other social needs through cafeteria-style benefits programs.

10. Those people who refuse or are unable to adapt to new technologies will find they're working harder and accomplishing less.

Only time will tell if these predictions will come true, but one thing we do know: The issue of work-life effectiveness will continue to grow in importance as long as work depends on people to get the job done.

Chapter 2
Assessing and Evaluating Work-Life Strategies

2

E mployers can implement a wide range of work-life programs, policies, benefits and practices to address employee and business needs. Determining what to do, why and when to do it is critical to the success of any endeavor. A variety of measurement approaches can be applied to work-life initiatives, including benchmarking against other companies and conducting internal surveys, focus groups and interviews. Such an assessment can be valuable regardless of the organization's stage of work-life involvement. In some cases, an assessment may be conducted to decide whether to implement a new initiative. In other cases, the assessment process is used to evaluate or justify existing programs. No matter what the purpose, conducting an assessment process will help determine the perceived and actual benefits to the corporation and its employees that could result, or that have resulted, from providing specific work-life options. Such an assessment process is applicable to all types and sizes of companies. A comprehensive work-life needs assessment often includes determining the company's goals and business needs, employees' needs and community resources.

In order for a work-life assessment to be carefully thought out and clearly articulated, it is helpful to begin by answering questions such as the following:

- Why should the organization conduct this assessment? What's the purpose?

- How should the assessment be conducted? What methodology should be used?

- Who should participate in the assessment? Who should be involved in the process and what audience should be surveyed?

- When is the best time to conduct the assessment? What other factors need to be considered?

- What are the plans for sharing the results from the assessment? Who needs to know what, and how will they be told?

It is important to determine if the assessment will be local — in only one or a few locations — or global, across the whole enterprise. If the company participates in other assessment processes — perhaps an employee climate, opinion, satisfaction, engagement or benefits survey — these processes may be coordinated and possibly even consolidated into one assessment process. When implementing an assessment process, think about whether this is a one-time event or something that the organization intends to repeat over time. The same assessment tools — focus groups, interviews and surveys — can also be used to conduct evaluations of existing programs, policies, benefits and practices. Use of these methodologies to evaluate initiatives will be discussed at the end of this chapter.

The success of any assessment, including a work-life assessment, relies on several critical factors:

- Supervision or sponsorship of the process by a senior manager who has decision-making authority
- Leadership, commitment and ongoing support from the CEO and/or senior management
- Allocation of sufficient resources and staff to conduct the assessment
- Representation of key management and employee groups in the process
- Clear goals and plans to communicate and act on the findings.

There are many approaches to identifying and analyzing work-life needs. In some cases, there may be an initial assessment followed by some program implementation. Some companies plan an ongoing assessment of work-life needs as part of their HR strategy. Some hire a work-life consultant to do all or part of the process, including conducting the initial research, designing employee and community needs assessments, recommending a company response, overseeing implementation actions, and evaluation of appropriate programs and policies. Other companies look at what the competition is doing, benchmark and respond accordingly. Still others implement programs and policies, perhaps on a pilot basis, and then evaluate their effectiveness.

Many organizations actually start an assessment process informally, using information from work-life workshops or focus groups. Others do it more formally by conducting a survey. Whatever the approach, there is frequently some concern about raising employee expectations when there is no guarantee that the company can provide solutions to meet all the identified needs. When the approach to assessing employees' work-life needs is carefully planned, organizations find they are able to respond appropriately to employee concerns.

Needs-Assessment Task Force

Every work-life assessment begins with gathering information. Usually an individual or a group of employees is asked to investigate work-life issues. For many companies, the exploration into work-life programs and policies begins with the formulation of a task force.

Ideally, the task force should be made up of a cross section of employees representing various areas of the company, such as human resources, benefits, technology, marketing, legal, community relations, corporate contributions,

Work-Life Needs Assessment

A work-life needs assessment must take into account company goals, business needs and resources, as well as employee needs and community services.

Company Goals, Business Needs and Resources

One of the factors in developing an appropriate work-life agenda is analyzing how work-life fits with the business in terms of short-term and long-term goals. Understanding corporate attitudes will help determine which options will be most appropriate for each company. Existing work-life-related programs, policies, benefits and practices must also be considered. Some of these initiatives may be "owned" by various departments in the organization, but it is best to "cast a broad net" when assessing work-life. A broad perspective will also help define modifications that must be made for a program or policy to be successful. The following are some of the issues and related questions that should be considered.

- **Corporate culture and management style**
  The following questions can help determine the corporate culture and management style. Answers will affect how work-life policies and programs are developed and which ones will best fit with the company's current management style.
  - Is employee participation a corporate priority?
  - How supportive are managers of employees' work-life needs?
  - Are there work teams focused on quality of life, great place to work or other workplace change processes?
  - What messages has senior management conveyed related to work-life issues?
  - Does the company recognize the value of its human capital?
  - What work-life related policies, programs, benefits and practices are currently available?

- **Company characteristics**
  Basic characteristics will be important in determining the design and delivery of work-life programs and benefits.
  - What type of business(es) is the company in?
  - How large is the company?
  - Does the company have more than one location or operate for more than one shift?
  - Are human resources issues responded to locally or is decision-making centralized?

- **Fiscal concerns**
  The company's overall financial condition must be considered before making decisions about implementing new programs and policies.
  - Is it feasible to consider investing resources in work-life programs at this time? If so, how many resources and in what amounts?
  - How do the company's costs for recruiting, retraining, absenteeism and turnover compare with those of other companies in the industry?
  - What is the cost and benefit of implementing work-life programs at this time?

- **Labor market**
  This is a key ingredient in work-life decision-making.
  What are the current and projected workforce needs of the company?
  What is the competitive situation with regard to key employee groups?
  How are recruitment efforts impacted by work-life needs?

government affairs, employee relations and so forth. Each member should bring some needed expertise. For example, a human resources specialist can provide information about trends in hiring and recruitment issues, an employee relations expert can offer insight into employees' points of view, a financial expert can help analyze costs and a technology expert can anticipate technology issues and possibly help organize and summarize data from a survey. The importance of such a diverse group is to strengthen political support, capture the key perspectives and issues, share ideas and expertise, and divide up the work.

In addition, most businesses try to make sure that the task force is representative of race, sex, seniority and job assignments within the company. Whoever takes responsibility for the issue will need to be knowledgeable about the way in which the company makes decisions, for example, the kind of information that's needed and how it should be presented.

Reasons for including a number of people in the general thinking and planning from the start include the following:

- To assess how work-life fits with the company's goals and business needs
- To determine positive and negative aspects of creating a work-life initiative
- To educate key personnel and bring people from all levels of the organization into the process
- To help key personnel feel involved in the process
- To develop a shared understanding of how work-life programs and policies might fit with the current company philosophy and its future plans.

The work of a task force can take a long time. There may be many starts and stops along the way, because the issues are often complex. The task force should be large enough to handle the work that needs to be done, but not so large that communication becomes unwieldy. In general, a task force usually contains six to 20 members and often, smaller groups are more effective.

Collecting General Demographic Data
Without professional assistance, the time required and the real cost of an assessment process can actually be much higher than anticipated, because employees who are paid to do other jobs must spend many hours gathering information that is not readily available to someone not familiar with the field. To limit the expense, a consultant can be brought into the project at key points to provide guidance and direction to the task force or other designated employees, to develop assessment tools/processes, to conduct the assessment, and to analyze data and make recommendations.

The task force, or whoever is responsible for determining the company's work-life agenda, should be familiar with the range of work-life options that other companies

Employee Needs

An important component of the needs assessment is a review of the workforce itself. It is essential to identify characteristics related to work-life in order to understand employee needs and to develop an appropriate strategy for the company. Some of the issues that should be considered include the following:

- **Workforce composition**
  - What percent of the workforce has family responsibilities?
  - What is the ratio in the workforce of female and male employees?
  - What is the age distribution of the population?
  - What is the average tenure?
  - Are there certain key job categories, and if so, what are they?

- **Evidence that employee stress is related to work-life issues**
  - Is there evidence of employee morale problems?
  - Do employees report difficulties in finding or managing suitable child care or elder care?
  - Do employees express concern, in general, about the care of family members (child, spouse, elderly relative)?
  - When do employees return after the birth or adoption of a child?
  - What percent do not return from parental leave? Do they indicate they will return, but change their minds?
  - Are there other indications of family-related stress, such as lateness, absenteeism, requests for part-time work or leaves, high turnover and so forth?
  - Is there evidence of overwork or reported health-care issues in certain groups or areas of the company?
  - Do co-workers complain about colleagues who have dependent-care responsibilities?

- **Employee preferences**
  - What types of benefits or policies do employees indicate they want most (child care or elder care, information and support, financial assistance in paying for care, services at the workplace, flexible work arrangements, etc.)?
  - How much are employees willing to pay for specific work-life services?

(Continued on page 48)

support and should obtain benchmark information, if possible (especially for those companies in the same industry or geography that are competing for employees in the same local and national labor market). It is also important to obtain information on the types of relevant programs that exist in the immediate community, nearby communities and areas where employees live to determine where gaps in services might exist.

A great deal of information can be obtained without asking employees directly about their specific work and personal needs. National demographic data can often provide information on two-earner families, single parents, working mothers, working fathers, children whose mothers work, adoption, the elderly and the disabled. Although these general statistics can be useful, they should be interpreted

(Continued from page 47)

Community Services

It is important to explore community services in order to be able to make appropriate decisions. Questions about community services can be approached in the same way that many companies routinely analyze health care, schools and transportation systems in the community. In some cases, information about community services can be obtained through informal discussions with employees. There may already be awareness on the part of human resources professionals in the company of certain limited community resources because of knowledge of situations when employees reported difficulties with inadequate services.

In most cases, companies will want to maximize their use of available community services rather than compete with these resources. Government or local agencies have typically documented work-life related community services that may be appropriate, but you may decide to conduct your own assessment, possibly in conjunction with other businesses or community groups, or with the help of a consultant.

Issues that should be considered when looking at community services include the following:

- Are there any local child-care or elder-care resources for information regarding child care and elder care?
- What local agencies are available to provide family-support programs?
- What is the child-care delivery system like in the community (how many programs exist, for what ages of children, what are their hours of operation, where are they located, what do they cost, how good are they, etc.)?
- What kind of support is available for elder-care needs (in-home companions, day care, caregiver education, etc.)?
- What kind of convenience or time-saving services are available through community businesses?
- What is the level of corporate involvement in the community?

carefully, because the company's employee population may differ greatly from the general population.

Other sources of information about employee needs include company programs where employees may have expressed family concerns, that is, benefits forms, insurance claims, exit interviews and so forth. This information provides another way to determine employee needs without raising expectations. Some of this information may not be easily accessible, because few companies organize their personnel records according to employees' family structure, and much of this information may be confidential. However, in some companies, data can be tabulated in such a way as to indicate the scope of employee needs without sacrificing confidentiality.

The combination of internal data and government statistics can provide information that can help determine company-specific work-life needs. For example, internal data merged with census data can provide some general estimates about the number of female employees likely to bear children during their work careers as follows:

- If 60 percent of the workforce is female, and 80 percent of these women are between the ages of 21 and 40, a general estimate of childbearing can be determined.
- U.S. data indicate that approximately 75 percent of these women will get pregnant at some time during their employment.
- Therefore, for a workforce of 1,000 employees, approximately 360 would have children while employed at the company.
- That is, more than one-third of the entire workforce might need maternity leave and support for parenting/child care at some point.

Exit interviews can also be useful in providing information about work-life needs if the right questions are asked. There may be a record of the number of employees who left the company because of child-care or elder-care problems, or difficulty getting the support they needed, such as flexibility, to manage their work and personal lives. It is also possible that a trend may emerge, such as problems associated with a specific department or division of the company due to work hours, supervisory policies, overtime expectations and so forth.

Interviews and Focus Groups

A great deal of information can be obtained through conversation with individuals or groups of employees. Face-to-face interviews can capture the emotional impact and intensity of work-life situations. Individual interviews are most frequently used with senior managers and or others who may not be appropriate to include in a group discussion. Interviews are usually about 30 to 45 minutes in length, and often the questions are similar to those used for the focus groups, but from a management perspective.

Interviews allow the collection and analysis of management's responses, and they can also be used to effectively educate managers about work-life issues. Management representatives whose support may be most instrumental in the success of a work-life initiative are frequently the ones who are invited to participate in individual interviews. Analysis of management interviews is then included in the final assessment report.

In interviews and focus groups, participants use their own words to express their opinions, and the moderator can ask questions to clarify comments. In some cases, focus groups are the only source of data used to determine employee needs. However, focus groups are often used to shape the content of a survey or to help in more clearly understanding issues identified in a survey.

Focus groups are particularly useful for the exploration of a range of issues, employees' perceptions of issues and the intensity of their feelings. The major limitation with focus groups is that they provide subjective data rather than objective data. Even though they may not be considered "scientific" because they cannot provide a complete picture of the company and its employee population, focus groups can provide a rich source of information and capture employees' voices.

It is important to assure confidentiality when conducting focus groups. Focus groups should be set up so that participants feel they can reveal their true feelings. Many companies structure the groups so that an employee and his or her supervisor are not in the same group. This helps the individuals feel free to fully participate in the focus group. Focus groups also help management communicate its interest in work-life issues and clarify issues about which there may be misperceptions in the minds of employees. Employees who participate in focus groups gain a better understanding of management's attitudes toward work-life issues. They can also obtain a more realistic understanding of the possibilities and limitations of the work-life options that the company may elect to support. Employees' misunderstanding of company policy can be discussed in a focus group and shared with management so that appropriate changes can be explored.

Structure of Focus Groups

Focus groups often are most effective when led by an objective third party who has experience in conducting such group meetings. In many cases, an outside facilitator is hired to design, conduct and analyze focus-group sessions. The facilitator often works closely with the company representative responsible for making sure that results reflect the company's major concerns. Questions asked must be couched in language that is appropriate to both the personal life situations employees face and the needs of the workplace. The final report usually defines the major concerns raised by employees, provides sample anecdotes and quotes, and defines the mood and tone of each group.

The group must be facilitated in such a way as to bring out the opinions and attitudes of the entire group, not just a few individuals. Groups should contain eight to 10 people and last about two hours during the workday. If focus groups are to be the only source of information and the findings will be used to develop specific programs, it is wise to organize groups that include approximately 5 percent to 10 percent of the employee population. If focus groups are used in conjunction with a survey or to get an impression of issues and concerns, a smaller sample will suffice.

The groups are usually made up of employees who are more or less at the same job level. Separate groups may be conducted for women and men, hourly and salaried employees, parents and non-parents, supervisors and subordinates, and so forth, according to the varying needs of each group. Care must be taken to assure participants that the information provided will be kept confidential. Some people may be reluctant to talk about themselves in a group setting. If this is the case, they can be invited to meet with the expert privately. In most cases, representatives from the company with responsibility for HR or work-life issues are not present during focus group meetings. The decision to include such representatives must be given careful consideration. On the one hand, these people know the organization and can relate to the information provided from that perspective. Such exposure might also give them a more personal identification with employees' concerns. On the other hand, employees may be much less forthcoming if someone from HR or management is present.

If it's necessary to get a representative sample, employees from targeted groups may be randomly selected to participate. These individuals may be selected because they represent a specific work-life situation, such as single parents or employees caring for elderly relatives, or because they represent a specific employee group, such as exempt or nonexempt, union or nonunion, or senior female manager or male technician. Since participation is usually not mandatory, some companies offer food, a raffle prize or promotional gift to encourage attendance.

An alternative approach is to announce the groups and allow employees to volunteer. Again, such groups can be targeted by asking for employees with young children, school-age children, elderly relatives and/or those with specific work-life issues to volunteer. When holding voluntary focus groups, it is possible that some employees with problems will self-select themselves into the group.

It is important to note that information from focus groups may not accurately reflect the attitudes of the entire population. As a result, the complaints of a few employees might be overemphasized, or the concerns of a group of employees not included in the focus groups might be overlooked. Collecting reliable information from a diverse population may require many group sessions, which can be time-consuming and costly.

Content of Focus Groups

Topics covered in focus groups depend to a great extent on the purpose of the sessions and their role in the overall needs-assessment process. If focus groups precede a survey, they typically concentrate on current programs and benefits as well as areas of work-life conflict. If the focus groups are conducted after a survey, they often are used to expand on or explain the results. Specific topics might also provide feedback on the company's decisions for work-life support. To avoid having focus groups become general gripe sessions, it is important to control the communication, define the parameters and carefully plan the questions.

The following are types of questions that can be used to obtain relevant information from an employee focus group:

• **Family and child-care support**
  - What child-care or elder-care arrangements do you currently use? What do you like or dislike about these arrangements? What would you recommend to improve them?
  - Ideally, what kind of child-care or elder-care arrangements would you feel most comfortable with for your dependents?
  - What kind of support do you get from family members (your spouse/partner, older children, other relatives, etc.) to help you care for your dependents?

- How do you manage when an emergency arises, such as when the child or elder dependent gets sick or you face necessary (or unexpected) overtime or travel?
- **Community support**
  - What kind of community programs would help you better manage your work and personal responsibilities?
- **Workplace support**
  - How supportive is your supervisor of your personal needs?
  - Have you had situations when work was interrupted for personal reasons? Describe them.
  - What are the greatest sources of conflict between your work and your personal life?
  - What types of programs, policies and benefits and/or practices would make it easier for you to manage your work and personal life?

Workshops and Seminars as a Source of Data

Workshops that are held to provide employees with information about work-life issues can also serve as a means of identifying employees' needs. When these sessions are structured as facilitated discussion groups in which employees have a chance to talk about specific issues, a great deal of information about employees' concerns can be obtained. In sessions on topics such as "Finding and Managing Child Care" and "Resources for Elder Care," data about things such as cost of care, types of care used and where people live may be generated. Obviously, this information must be kept confidential. However, summaries of the data can be included in the assessment process and report.

To stimulate discussion, the leader should ask open-ended questions, such as, "What do you like about the care you are using now?" and "How did you find that nursing home?" Because of the spontaneous nature of employees' responses, information gathered in this way cannot be considered representative, but it can be used to highlight other findings. To make the information collected in workshops more standardized, it is possible to distribute a minisurvey. Such a document might consist of a few targeted questions related to the topic under discussion. Results can provide a snapshot view of a select group of employees' needs.

Designing and Disseminating an Employee Survey

A formal needs assessment uses an instrument for obtaining specific information about large numbers of employees, usually through a written survey, or possibly with telephone interviews. The survey should relate specifically to the information needed for decision-making. It is important that the instrument be easily understood, designed to yield usable data and distributed in such a way as to assure a significant response. When large numbers of employees are involved or the survey is complex, computerizing the survey can allow for more complete analysis.

A survey should not raise expectations that cannot be met. This is one of the most important characteristics of a survey. For example, if an on-site child-care center is not viable, there should not be any questions about such an option. Focus groups are sometimes conducted prior to a survey for the purpose of defining key issues that the survey will cover. Work-life surveys are sometimes repeated over a period of time in order to gather comparative data, though they can also be administered just once.

Process

When conducting a survey, it is important to sample a sufficient number of employees in order to be able to generalize the findings to the whole population. The following table, created by Kenneth Nowack ("Getting Them Out and Getting Them Back," *Training and Development Journal*, April 1990), indicates that the minimum sample size depends on the following statistical factors:

- The expected response rate of the survey (a 50-percent rate is generally considered good)
- The precision of the population estimate (e.g., within plus or minus 5 percent)
- The confidence level (e.g., a 95-percent level of confidence means that 95 out of 100 times a sample will provide the desired precision level).

Figure 4 summarizes the minimum sample sizes required for different target population sizes. The minimum sample sizes given will provide a 95-percent confidence level that the sample is within plus or minus 5 percent of the actual population estimate. If the return rate is at least 50 percent, one can feel confident that the sample is providing information that is truly reflective of the target population.

Nowack also suggests the following 10 ways to increase the survey response rate:

- Make sure that participation is voluntary and either anonymous or confidential. Employees who feel coerced may comply but may provide incomplete or biased answers.
- Provide a complete cover letter addressed personally to each employee and signed by the highest-level executive possible.
- Make it easy for employees to return the survey, typically using e-mail.

FIGURE 4: Minimum Sample Sizes Required for Different Target Population Sizes

Target Population	Minimum Sample Size
10	10
50	44
100	80
300	169
500	217
800	260
1,000	278
3,000	341
5,000	357
8,000	367
10,000	370
20,000	377
30,000	379
40,000	380
50,000	381
100,000	384

- Make sure the survey looks professional and be sure it is long enough to be reliable (or to have internal consistency or integrity), but not so long that it discourages employees from completing it. In general, as the length of any survey increases, its reliability increases and the compliance rate decreases.

- Include a separate demographics page with the survey, either at the beginning or at the end. Limit demographics to variables that are relevant to the project and that will be analyzed statistically. As demographic requests increase, the compliance rate will decrease slightly.

- Place controversial or potentially upsetting questions toward the end of the survey. Research has shown that compliance on controversial questions increases when they are placed in the middle or at the end of the survey.

- Alert managers and employees ahead of time that a survey is being developed and will be sent out.

- Provide incentives that reinforce employee compliance. Inexpensive incentives such as discount movie tickets, books, training programs, meals, discounts in the company store and organizational paraphernalia such as coffee mugs, briefcases and pen sets can be very effective.

- Send follow-up e-mail reminders to increase the response rate.

- Provide employees with feedback about the survey results. This is one of the most powerful ways of ensuring participation in a survey. Feedback can occur in a variety of forms and can even be targeted to special audiences. Management and employee briefings, written reports, executive summaries and newsletter articles are useful feedback tools.

Survey Structure and Format

It is possible to address all of the research questions in one survey, but several surveys may be planned over a period of time. In some cases, only a specific group of employees is surveyed, such as women over 35 who are caring for an aging relative, or employees who have children less than three years of age. In other cases, a company may be planning to implement a particular program and will survey only those employees who are potential users to test their reaction to it. If there is information that the employer feels will be difficult for employees to provide, or is especially sensitive, that section can be optional.

To test a survey, give it first to a small group of employees. This allows for evaluation of individual questions, clarity of instructions, estimated length of time it takes to complete the survey and willingness of employees to complete it. To be effective, it should be possible to complete the survey in about 15 to 20 minutes. The more time a survey requires, the less likely it is that employees will complete it.

Confidentiality must be stressed. Employees must be confident that their interests are protected. In most companies, management includes a cover letter with the survey to explain who is conducting/analyzing the survey data, that no individual employee's answers will be identified and that an honest response is best because it will help the company design its approach to work-life concerns.

Survey Sampling

Whether or not to survey all employees is a decision often based on the size of the company. In situations where there are fewer than 3,000 employees, companies often include all employees. In larger companies, a 10-percent sample is usually representative of the entire population. To include specific subgroups of the employee population, random samples are taken within individual employee groups, for example, exempt and nonexempt. If it is especially important to have information about a particular group of employees, for example, women in their childbearing years, they can be surveyed more extensively.

There are several advantages to including all employees in the survey process. First, it allows all employees to feel they are taking part in the project, even if their information is not analyzed in order to make recommendations. In addition, it gives a more complete picture of the entire company and might surface a particular employee group that could benefit from a special response. Surveying all employees provides information about those groups whose needs are likely to change.

Survey Construction Tips

The following are suggestions to guide you in survey construction:

- The words should be simple, direct and familiar to all respondents. For example, some people do not know their marital status, but they certainly know if they are married, single, divorced, separated or widowed.
- Wherever possible, lists of possible responses (multiple-choice answers) should be provided. First, this makes analysis easier. Second, some people feel that writing an answer might help to identify them, and others are uncomfortable with the idea of expressing themselves in writing.
- Instructions should be simple and clear, and only one subject should be covered in each question.
- If rating scales are used, the "best" answers should not always be in the same place (i.e., at the right margin).
- If any questions are not applicable to all respondents, the instructions for those questions should clearly state which groups they are intended for and should include appropriate directions for skipping to the next applicable question.
- Keep the question as short as possible without sacrificing information that may be needed. It is easier to discard a question than it is to go back to get more data.

Analysis of Results and Recommendations

The recommendations from any work-life needs-assessment process can only be as good as the process of information gathering and analysis. When designing the needs-assessment process, it is important to take into consideration expected or possible outcomes. Recommendations should be based on a synthesis of information about the company's perspective, employees' needs and the community's resources from surveys, focus groups and/or interviews. Wherever possible, include write-in comments from participants in the final report. Management is often moved by the "voices" of participants more than by the statistical analysis.

Analysis of all data should be compiled in a report with an executive summary. It is often helpful to create a Microsoft PowerPoint presentation of the overview of findings and recommendations. Recommendations should be organized according to the priority of findings and should be reviewed with the task force or company representative in charge of the project before finalizing the report. The results and recommendations may be tailored to a specific audience, which may include senior management, middle managers, line managers, human resources, employees, other companies and/or the media.

Based on the findings from the assessment process, the range of options can be reduced to those that the company is prepared to consider from a philosophical and financial perspective. Issues that need to be considered when making recommendations include the following:

- Will the initiative(s) be targeted to meet the needs of a particular employee group, such as middle managers or clerical workers?
- Are the programs designed to meet the needs of female employees, males and females, or employees in a specific age range?
- What are the expected benefits for target employees? For example, will they feel less stress as they manage work-life responsibilities?
- What expectations have these employees expressed in focus groups or surveys?
- What advantages to the company are assumed — greater employee productivity, retention, engagement, commitment and/or reduced absenteeism? What are the anticipated levels of employee participation in the program or service?
- Can employees afford to use the benefit or service, such as unpaid leave for child care, or can they pay the cost of on-site child care? Will employees be asked to share the cost of the program or service? If so, will there be a sliding scale based on income? Which of the organization's operations will be affected by the work-life program or policy?
- Will the proposed work-life program or policy have top management's support?
- To what extent does success of the proposed plan depend on outside factors over which the company may have little or no control, such as the response of the community, delivery service or local government?

Recommendations should also include a plan to communicate findings and next steps to employees.

Implementation Plans

Before a work-life initiative can be undertaken, detailed implementation plans should be developed for each possible program and policy. Based on the assessment, there should be a clear description of employees' work-life needs, the company's goals and community resources.

Some of the procedures that must be considered include the following:

- Develop a budget that specifies the start-up and operating costs of the proposed program or policy, including all direct costs such as consultants' fees. Use the experience of other companies to make accurate estimates of costs.
- Develop a realistic timetable that includes when each task should be completed.
- Plan how management and employees will be kept informed at each stage of development.
- Provide for management orientation and training on new policies and programs.
- Develop written descriptions of each new program and policy.

In addition, it is important during this planning period to consider what the benefits or return on investment (ROI) of implementing specific work-life options may be for the company and its employees. Outcomes that might be measured include the following:

- Recruitment
- Retention/turnover
- Absenteeism
- Tardiness
- Employee use of the work-life program or policy
- Employee productivity
- Productivity and quality of the service
- Employee morale, engagement, commitment
- Manager-employee relations
- Favorable publicity and community relations
- Improved labor relations.

How the Company Responds

While it is clearly helpful to obtain information about specific options employees feel will be beneficial, care must be taken not to raise expectations for solutions that are not possible. Survey questions should be carefully formulated and worded. Some companies have difficulty interpreting the results of questions that ask employees if they would like things such as a child-care center. In these cases, the questions may not be clear and employees' responses may require expert

Developing Survey Questions

A series of questions can be asked to determine if there are similarities or differences among divisions, regions, jobs or income levels. The objective is to obtain demographic data and a work history of the employee population. The following points provide guidelines in terms of the categories and topics to consider.

Demographic Information

Possible topics include the following:

- Exempt or nonexempt, length of service, age, sex, race, number of dependents, marital status of employee, including whether the employee is living with a partner
- Those expecting or planning to have children within the next two years – responses can be separated from those who already have children; those with or without elder-care needs
- Educational achievement
- Department and job title.

Work History and Responsibilities

Possible topics include the following:

- Determination of how employee needs break down among job categories, divisions or plant locations
- Number of days/hours worked, length of career, number of interruptions in service
- Commuting time and method of transportation, especially if a child-care center is being considered, also for flexible scheduling
- Job tenure (current position)
- Previous positions with company.

Nature of Employees' Family Needs

Asking employees about their current dependent-care arrangements is one way to assess their needs. Because dependent-care needs tend to vary from day to day and situation to situation, this complex process requires expertise to design questions and analyze responses correctly.

Subcategory: Characteristics of Employee's Household

Possible topics include the following:

- Employee's marital status.
- Employment status of household members and hours worked
- Ages of household members
- Number of children present, related children not present
- Household income
- Plans for (additional) children.

Current Dependent Care

Possible topics include the following:

- All forms of care for each dependent, both children and the elderly
- Terms must be clearly defined: babysitter or caregiver may mean different things to different people
- Type of care used

Developing Survey Questions — Continued

- How current arrangement was located
- Problems encountered in arranging child care or elder care
- Child-care or elder-care services not available or difficult to locate
- Time spent in locating child-care or elder-care arrangements
- Back-up child-care or elder-care arrangements
- Location of child-care or elder-care (proximity to work or home)
- Cost of child care or elder care
- Degree of satisfaction with child-care or elder-care arrangements.

Family Issues and Productivity

Asking employees how family issues affect their work behavior can shed light on things such as absenteeism, morale, turnover and stress. This type of information can be very useful in planning the company's response to these problems.

Employee Views on Company Involvement

Asking managers for their opinions about the company's involvement in work-life issues is one way to determine their level of support for future programs and policies. It is also possible to assess employees' general attitudes toward the company if such support is currently offered.

Effects of Personal Issues on Employee Productivity

Possible topics include the following:

- Frequency of absences, tardiness, unproductive time on job due to specified child-care or work-life problems
- Perceptions concerning amount of overwork and of work-life related stress
- Impact of family and personal considerations on availability for work and career advancement
- Impact of work schedules on work-life issues
- Interest in part-time work or flexible schedule
- Degree of support from supervisor in accommodating worker's personal needs.

Employee Views Concerning the Employer's Role

Possible topics include the following:

- Providing work-life support
- Developing policies that assist employees, including working families, in managing work and personal responsibilities
- Expecting supervisors to be supportive of employees' work-life needs.

Employee Preferences Concerning Employer Responses

Possible topics include the following:

- Checklist of range of options related to work-life programs, policies, benefits and practices, and degree of personal interest in them if provided by the company
- Awareness or utilization of policies, benefits and services related to work-life issues that company currently provides.

interpretation and analysis. For example, usually only a small percentage of employees who say they will use a child-care center on a survey actually register when the center opens.

One of the most common times for companies to conduct a work-life survey is when they are considering developing a child-care center. While the survey must be carefully tailored to the company's needs, keep in mind the information that is required. When assessing child-care needs, it is helpful to organize the data into subcategories based on employee family types. Four groups that should be examined are as follows:

- Employees who have dependent children
- Employees who do not have children yet, but are planning to have them within the next several years
- Employees who have children and intend to have more within the next several years
- Employees who do not have and do not intend to have children in the near future.

Surveys can also determine employees' awareness of, use of and satisfaction with existing work-life programs, policies, benefits and practices. Figure 5 on page 61 provides a small sample of survey questions to help measure awareness, use and satisfaction.

Benchmarking

Benchmarking can be used to evaluate the quality of different aspects of a company's work-life programs, policies, benefits and practices by comparison to "best in class" companies or competitors. The questions in Figure 6 on page 61 can be used to profile the scope of a company's work-life initiative.

It is also possible to compare initiatives according to the effectiveness (utilization, satisfaction, outcomes for employees and the company), efficiency (simplicity of administration, timeliness, etc.) and cost (implementation cost, vendor cost, etc.). The questions in Figure 7 on page 61 could be used to benchmark these aspects.

When selecting work-life practices to benchmark, consider which areas are most important to the company, its employees, managers and so forth. Also take into account where competitive pressures are being felt, how work-life fits with the organization's mission and strategy, and ways work-life initiatives address business needs and so forth.

Benchmarking studies can involve collecting qualitative and quantitative data. They can be used to determine the critical elements of a specific work-life initiative, to determine the difference between the offerings of different companies and/or to develop targets to measure planned improvements in work-life programs or policies. In some cases, a benchmark study is conducted in conjunction with a larger work-life assessment. Findings of the benchmark study should be reported to contributing companies as a token of appreciation for their participation, while recommendations should be reserved for management of the sponsoring company.

Are you aware that the company offers the following work-life programs?

☐ Yes ☐ No

- Information and support for dependent care
- Financial assistance

Sample: Measure of Utilization and Satisfaction

	Yes	No	Not Satisfied	Very Satisfied
Have you ever used any of the following work-life programs, policies or practices?	☐	☐	☐	☐
• Information and support for dependent care				
• Financial Assistance				
Would you use any of these in the coming year?	☐	☐	☐	☐

Work-Life Issue	Extent of Availability		
	Available to All	Some	Case by Case
What policies, programs or practices help employees manage work and personal life?	☐	☐	☐
What policies, programs or practices provide managers with help for work-life issues?	☐	☐	☐

	To a Minimal Extent	To a Moderate Extent	To a Great Extent
What policies, programs or practices help employees manage work and personal life?	☐	☐	☐
What policies, programs or practices provide managers with help for work-life issues?	☐	☐	☐

Evaluating Work-Life Initiatives

As implementation plans are being made, it's a good idea to also consider how the initiative will be evaluated. A plan for evaluation should be an integral part of the recommendations for any work-life program or service. A system for tracking and measuring the outcomes and costs of the work-life programs and policies should be developed with the company's goals and objectives in mind. The tools for evaluation might include checklists, written or oral reports, observations, interviews and comparison of data before and after the service was initiated. A follow-up survey and/or focus groups might also be included.

Ongoing monitoring allows the company to refine and improve its work-life program to best meet business objectives and employees' needs. If possible, records should be modified to include factors such as recruitment, absenteeism, turnover, etc. and their relationship to work-life initiatives. Additionally, accounting systems can be modified to include relevant cost and benefits data.

In determining the effectiveness of work-life initiatives, it is important to match performance with the original objectives for the program. Assessment by users of the program or service is essential. During the early months of a program, it may be valuable to solicit feedback more frequently. Feedback should be designed to be constructive, not merely positive or negative. For example, employees can be asked for suggestions rather than complaints. Questions could include the following:

- How did you hear about the program?
- Why did you choose to use it?
- What did you like most about the program? What did you like least?
- What suggestions, if any, do you have for improving the program?

Another way to assess the effectiveness of work-life initiatives is to start with a restatement of what the company hopes to achieve and then set up a "before and after" comparison. If the company hopes to demonstrate improved recruitment, lower turnover rates or decreased absenteeism as a result of program use, there must be prior documentation for comparison. Even if statistics show change for the better, it will be necessary to interview employees to confirm that the program is responsible, at least in part, for the changes. For example, if one objective is improved recruitment, new hires could be asked if they knew about the program, and if so, how it influenced their decision to take the position. It is also possible to compare certain variables such as absenteeism and tardiness among employees using the service and those not using the service.

"Last things first" should be your motto when it comes to evaluating the impact of work-life initiatives. In other words, evaluation plans should be determined before the program even gets off the ground. Knowing what you want to accomplish and how you will know if you get there are integral parts of the initial planning. In other words, if the work-life program were a success, what would success look like?

Evaluation should address the following:

- Were the work-life program goals and objectives met? These should be the goals and objectives that are most crucial to management and employees.
- What specific measures or outcomes will be used to track the accomplishment of these goals and objectives?
- How will you evaluate the work-life initiative? What methodology will be used?
- Why do you need to evaluate the work-life program? What will happen with this information? Who is it for?

For instance, if one objective is improved community relations, a telephone survey of a random sample of merchants and community residents, both before and after the program is instituted, might help measure whether their attitudes toward the company have changed. Although these may be rough comparisons, they will provide a general impression of the program's effectiveness.

You will need to decide whether the evaluation will be pragmatic and accomplished by your internal staff, perhaps with some consulting support, or whether you wish to participate in an experimental longitudinal study with control groups. Most employers don't have the time or resources to conduct long-term research. They simply want to know what programs they should implement, and if the programs are helping employees and having a positive impact in management's eyes. If you want to conduct formal work-life research, you have the option of working with researchers at universities or other consulting organizations. Another approach might be for employers to band together to fund a study, which can keep costs down for individual companies and can produce comparative data.

The following suggestions for program evaluation are for employers who want to conduct their own pragmatic evaluation. Whatever method you use, it is important to understand the limitations of evaluation. Other initiatives or organizational changes may also be affecting employees. Therefore, while it is important to measure the effectiveness of work-life efforts, be careful about making definitive claims.

What Should Be Measured

There are two major types of data that can be used to evaluate work-life programs. These include process data and outcome data. Process data include program costs, number of sessions and so forth. In other words, process data are used to describe what happened. Outcome data are used to describe the results or impact of a program on participants, customers or business drivers. Examples of outcome data are savings or return on investment, reductions in absenteeism, increased employee satisfaction and enhanced image. Outcome data can address both subjective (e.g., attitude) and objective (e.g., absenteeism) measures and can also measure the business impact and impact on employees' personal lives. In addition to looking at intended results, you may also wish to examine unintended consequences, both positive and negative. Again, what you measure is a function of what is important to know about the work-life program within the limitations of time and resources.

How to Measure

A number of practical tools to evaluate work-life programs, similar to those used for a needs-assessment process, include the following:

- Employee surveys
- Management surveys and interviews
- Return-on-investment analysis
- Focus groups
- Organizational profile.

It is possible to simply describe work-life program activities in terms of cost, number of events and participation by employees. Additionally, current program status can be compared with the goals articulated in the original program proposal or plan:

- Accomplishment of overall goals and objectives
- Specific program, budget and utilization goals
- Inventory of current programs and gap analysis
- Comparison with original plan
- Problems encountered
- What worked.

It is possible to apply accounting measures to the evaluation of work-life initiatives. These measures can include: return on investment (ROI), cost/benefits analysis, breakeven analysis and productivity measures, among others. Regardless of the approach, it is important to specify the goals and expected outcomes, select financial (or some equivalent) measures for the outcomes, collect the data and make calculations, and then make recommendations to maximize the financial benefits.

Work-life initiatives can be viewed as an investment in helping the company's most valuable asset (its employees) better manage their work and personal lives. The ROI compares the relative profitability of a program with the investment required to implement and maintain it. A cost/benefits analysis compares all costs (direct and indirect) associated with the development and implementation of a program with the cost savings (direct and indirect) or increased profits associated with the use of the program.

Questions that might be asked regarding these approaches include the following:

- What are the goals for the work-life initiative?
- What financial measures can be used to document the extent to which work-life policies and programs meet financial objectives?

- Which nonfinancial outcomes for work-life initiatives can be translated into monetary equivalents?
- What level of investment has the company made in work-life initiatives?
- What are the costs associated with the company's work-life initiatives?
- What are the savings/expenses associated with the company's work-life initiatives?
- What are the financial gains/losses associated with the company's work-life initiatives?
- What should the company do to maximize the financial contributions that work-life initiatives can make to the bottom line?

It is important to note that there are many areas that are likely to be impacted by work-life initiatives, such as reductions in health-care cost if employees are less stressed. These areas are often very difficult to measure quantitatively, but they may have very high value.

Calculating the Return on Investment

ROI is frequently used as a measure of the value of work-life programs and policies. A number of studies highlight ROI-related findings. These include:

- Watson Wyatt: *Linking Human Capital and Shareholder Value* (2000) — This study found that specific HR practices, including well-established work-life and total rewards approaches, increase a company's value.
- Vanderbilt University and Hewitt Associates' study of *Fortune* magazine's "100 Best Companies To Work For" (2000) — This study found that companies on the list outperformed similar companies that were not on the list and showed a "substantial financial performance advantage."
- Cap Gemini Ernst & Young Center for Business Innovation (2001) — This study found that 35 percent to 40 percent of portfolio decisions by money managers are based on nonfinancial information such as employee morale and corporate culture. It also found that the only statistically significant difference between successful and nonsuccessful IPOs from 1986 to 1997 was nonfinancial factors such as "giving people a place where they are happy to come to work, where they are respected."

ROI information can be collected in a variety of areas, including turnover, absenteeism, productivity, stress-related health care, morale, commitment, engagement and job satisfaction. Some of the sources of the data used for ROI include HR information systems, business-unit revenue, health insurance enrollment and claims, salary, survey results, performance and promotion data.

There are a number of formulas that can be used to calculate ROI, including the following:

- ROI = Change in Operating Revenue/Investment in Program. This compares the relative profitability of a program with the investment required to implement and maintain it.

Example: $500,000 return on $200,000 investment = return of 2.5.

- Cost Benefits Analysis = Cost (direct and indirect)/Savings or Profits (direct and indirect).

This does not actually measure return on investment, but rather overall profitability.

- Breakeven Point = Fixed Costs/Cost Savings per Unit. The usage rate needed to recoup costs.

Example: $800,000/$25,000 = 32 people need to use the service.

- Payback = Net Initial Investment/Expected Net Annual Related Profits and/or Savings. This measures how long it will take to recoup an investment.

Example: $1,000,000/$250,000 per year = 4 years.

Figure 8 is an example of ROI calculations based on survey results.

FIGURE 8: ROI Calculations Based on Survey Results

Annual Cost: Turnover Related to Work-Life

Of 2,727 survey respondents, 42.4% report actively looking or considering looking for a job at a different company to better manage their work and personal life.

Assuming only 1/3 of those looking or considering looking actually leave, the estimated annual replacement cost of turnover related to work-life at Company X is $22,440,000.

Calculation

Assumption: Average salary (exempt) = $50,000
- Assumption: Average salary (nonexempt) = $28,000
- Assumption: 70% of the population is exempt, 30% nonexempt
- 42.4% of 2,727 employees = 1,156 employees
- Assuming 33% of the 1,156 employees looking to leave actually leave = 382 employees leave.
- Replacement cost* per exempt employee = ($50,000 X 1.5) = $75,000
- Replacement cost* per nonexempt employee ($50,000 X .75) = $21,000
- 267 separated exempt employees X $75,000 = $20,025,000
- 115 separated nonexempt employees X $21,000 = $2,415,000

*Source: Using research from Merck and others indicating that employee turnover costs a company roughly 150% of an exempt employee's annual salary (finding a replacement, getting that person up to speed, etc.) and 75% of a non-exempt salary as a guideline.

Chapter 3
Flexible Work Arrangements

3

N eeds, values and priorities of employees and employers have changed dramatically over the last decade. At all levels of the organization, men and women are struggling to find new ways to manage the time they spend working so they can spend more time living. In boardrooms, executives want to find ways to attract — and keep — the best employees so they can continue to survive and thrive in the highly competitive global economy.

Interestingly enough, solutions to the changing needs and priorities of employees and employers are being found in one idea — workplace flexibility. This idea is proving to be a win-win strategy for today's leading-edge organizations. In many organizations, informal flexibility — employees working flexibly periodically, such as working at home occasionally or coming to work after a doctor's appointment — has become the norm. This is an important aspect of flexibility that reinforces the importance of mutual respect and an adult-adult relationship in the workplace. In addition, flexibility can be seen in the move toward more flexible benefits and a move toward more diversity and a "life-event management" approach to policies and practices. At the same time, more formal flexible work arrangements have become recognized as an important business tool that offers a real return on investment.

All forms of flexibility, but particularly flexible work arrangements that include customized schedules such as telecommuting, flex-time and part-time work, can help employers expand their recruitment pool to include people who are unable to work traditional office hours due to family or personal commitments. The provision of flexible work arrangements is also a good tool for motivating and engaging employees. Allowing responsible workers the flexibility to plan their own schedules boosts morale, improves productivity and engagement, and cultivates loyalty. The benefits of working flexibly are not confined to a booming economy. Flexible work arrangements, like hiring temporary staff and part-timers, allow organizations to respond rapidly and efficiently to changes in workload demands. In particular, workplace flexibility can help management during difficult periods that might otherwise require downsizing.

During the 1990s, the attitude of organizations toward flexible work arrangements (FWA) changed dramatically. Inspired by the Clean Air Act and the women's movement, which focused on new ways to commute and to work and parent, these arrangements have been evolving since the early 1970s. The Clean Air Act promoted staggered working hours and telecommuting as a means of cutting air pollution from automobiles. Once used as an ad hoc response to individual employees' needs, companies are now realizing that they can use flexibility as a cost-effective strategy to accomplish business goals. Where once an FWA was used as an accommodation to the request of a highly valued individual employee (typically a woman), employers today are realizing the business value of encouraging flexibility and often institutionalizing FWAs.

According to the Monthly Labor Review from the U.S. Department of Labor, from 1991 to 1997 the percentage of full-time wage and salary workers with flexible work schedules on their principal job increased from 15.1 percent to 27.6 percent. There are many benefits to working flexibly. According to the 2005 Families and Work Institute's *When Work Works* project, in flexible organizations, the following applies:

- 66 percent of employees report high levels of job engagement and commitment, and the number drops to 56 percent in organizations with low levels of flexibility.
- 72 percent of employees plan to remain with their employers for the next year, as opposed to only 49 percent in organizations with low levels of flexibility.
- 67 percent of employees report high levels of job satisfaction, whereas only 23 percent do in organizations with low levels of flexibility.

Workers 50 years old or older are more likely to stay on the job when they control hours and have workplace flexibility, job autonomy and learning opportunities, according to the 2005 report, *Context Matters: Insights about Older Workers* from the *National Study of the Changing Workforce* (The Center on Aging and Work/Workplace Flexibility at Boston College).

The study also found that 26 percent of wage and salaried employees, particularly younger employees (43 percent of workers under 30 years old), plan to "be their own boss," strongly suggesting that employers need to devote serious attention to creating work environments that embody some important positive characteristics of self-employment and business ownership, such as control over hours, workplace flexibility, learning opportunities and job autonomy.

As more companies recognize the value of workplace flexibility, they are using it as a way to help define, or redefine, the culture of the organization. In this chapter we focus on formal flexible work arrangements that follow company guidelines, are consistent over some period of time, meet business and employee needs, and are based on an agreement between employees and managers. We do not include informal flexibility, which allows employees to occasionally be away from work to attend to personal needs.

Clearly, both informal and formal flexibility are important, but informal flexibility doesn't usually require policy or guidelines. Managers are just encouraged to use their good judgment. However, with formal flexible work arrangements, companies are moving away from the old model of primarily accommodating the personal needs of a few highly valued employees. The new paradigm is one that encourages formal FWAs as a way to meet employee and business needs. It's important to make sure that the terms used to describe flexible work arrangements are consistent. While there are variations, flexible work arrangements typically include flex time, telecommuting or flex-place, part-time work (including job-sharing) and compressed schedules. Each of these will be discussed in more detail in this chapter.

Experimenting with Flexibility

Many organizations have experimented with flexible work arrangements with positive results. Research and experience can now document that flexibility can be used to accomplish the following:

- **Improve productivity.** Employees are less distracted; make better use of quieter times when fewer people are in the office or when working away from the office; and work with better morale from the confidence of being respected and valued. Work may be better organized and managed.

- **Retain valued employees.** When allowed to manage their own time, employees respond with a greater commitment to the organization, thus protecting the company's investment in them.

- **Motivate employees to achieve their full potential.** In an environment where trust and mutual respect prevail, employees are more likely to contribute their discretionary energy to their jobs, which also translates into improved customer satisfaction.

- **Retain quality employees.** Employees are willing to work harder in return for the flexibility that helps them work smarter. Research indicates one of the main reasons people join — and leave — organizations is to gain control over time.

Specific types of FWAs produce their own particular bottom-line benefits. For example, consider the following:

- **Flex time** helps reduce tardiness and absenteeism and can be implemented at low cost.

- **Telecommuting or flex-place** maximizes the use of equipment and office space, and can be used to respond to the needs of many employees, including the disabled.

- **Compressed work schedules** enable businesses to expand coverage and service, especially across time zones, and to make better use of equipment.

- **Part-time schedules** can make it easier for businesses to adjust to variations in business cycles and to recruit from a new population of employees.

Persistence of Resistance

Despite the documented successes of flexibility, resistance in many organizations is still widespread. This is true on both the senior- and middle-manager level. One problem seems to be caused by the ad hoc flexible arrangements themselves. In many organizations, these arrangements were established without clear guidelines or expectations. When they do not work, which under these circumstances is often the case, management may decide that flexible work arrangements can't work in their organizations at all. This is similar to "throwing out the baby with the bath water." In most cases it's not the FWA that does not work; it is the way it is implemented that's the problem.

On the senior-management level, "stonewalling" often occurs because many top decision makers do not themselves experience the struggle to manage work and "have a life." They don't "get it" because they don't experience "it." This barrier grows out of viewing flexibility as an accommodation to individual employees rather than as a business tool to use to accomplish business goals. When viewed strategically, that is, as a coordinated organizational effort to solve business problems – such as containing costs, improving customer service, attracting and retaining good employees, meeting the demands of expanding market — the value of flexibility stands on its own. The strategic view does not regard flexibility as a reward for "star performers." It sees flexibility as a means of helping all employees function more effectively, both at work and at home. This is still a relatively new way of thinking about achieving business goals, however, and has yet to be embraced by all areas of the business community.

On the middle-management or supervisor level, resistance is understandable. One of the greatest barriers to a flexible workplace is the continued prevalence of work overload. Managers, after all, are responsible for getting the work done, and their concerns — for example, loss of control, how to supervise someone who isn't there and so forth — must be addressed. Some of these concerns are misperceptions that can be addressed through education, communication and training. Others are very real obstacles that must be addressed through avenues such as policy change and work redesign.

In some cases, it's not clear how a particular employee group, for example, exempt workers, can make use of flexible work arrangements such as compressed or flex-time. This is because they don't have a set number of hours to work. It's hard to see how they can compress their jobs into fewer, longer days, or start later, and so forth. In reality, this concern is related to the connection between face time and productivity. If a reasonable output is expected, it shouldn't matter when or where the work gets done.

Change is always difficult, and workplace flexibility touches every facet of the employee-manager relationship. Many managers have been unwilling or unable to make the transition to managing for results. Relying on "face time" as a means of supervising employees continues to be the more familiar and more comfortable mode. Managing flexibly requires adult-adult relationships between managers and employees. It requires that managers learn new ways of managing — coaching, mentoring, empowering and allowing their employees to work more flexibly, as well as harder and smarter.

Making It Work

Implementing FWAs is an evolutionary process that requires long-term and more immediate plans. Components of a successful strategy include the following:

- Involve all levels of management, starting at the top of the organization, and making sure the FWA initiative is endorsed by senior management as a business imperative, with appropriate alignment with the business strategy.

- Establish an FWA committee, cross-functional team or task force with a visible senior-management champion to lead the FWA change process and address important issues such as technology support, changes in benefits, record-keeping, performance management, recruiting and so forth.

- Design a communications plan that includes appropriate messages, messengers and communication vehicles for both short-term and longer-term promotion.

- Plan and implement an educational process that helps managers and employees approach FWAs as a business issue in order to identify key concerns, devise solutions and take ownership of results. This process should be integrated with existing or planned manager and employee training, and it should include orientation and supervisor training.

- Provide training in skills necessary for successful FWAs: negotiating techniques, managing by objectives, proven approaches to communication and problem-solving techniques.

- Develop and disseminate guidelines for managers that define roles and responsibilities and that help them implement, manage and conclude flexible work arrangements.

- Involve HR representatives or others in providing guidance and coaching for managers and employees so they can successfully develop, manage, modify and end FWAs.

- Provide guidelines for employees that clarify that they, too, have responsibilities, and include tools to help them assess their own situations in terms of business needs, make reasonable proposals, negotiate terms and manage themselves.

- Frequently re-evaluate policies that affect FWAs such as head count, performance evaluations, rewards and recognition, eligibility for advancement, benefits, pensions and so forth.

Changing the Way Work Is Done

When flexibility is integrated with strategic business goals and corporate culture, it is more likely to produce a win-win situation. At the most progressive companies, flexibility is an ongoing initiative that is part of a culture-change effort. Bringing about culture change requires a change in the way work gets done — how it's organized and its impact on productivity and on employees' lives — all of which requires that management look more closely at traditional assumptions and weed out work processes that are counterproductive to business and personal goals.

The process of challenging old assumptions and cultural beliefs frees managers and employees to think more creatively about work in general and provides companies with a strategic opportunity to achieve a more equitable, productive, cooperative and innovative workplace. Some experts believe that well-designed workplace flexibility initiatives can open the door to innovation and creativity that translate into the competitive edge needed for the 21st century.

Creating a Flexible Workplace

Organizations achieve successful flexible work environments in stages or phases — it's typically evolutionary rather than revolutionary. It is also an ongoing initiative. Workplace flexibility should be part of an overall long-term strategy, because much of what is involved may run counter to traditional management views about matters such as scheduling, employee on-site visibility, methods of supervision and performance evaluation. The goal should be to maintain productivity when implementing FWAs, not necessarily improve it.

The following are some recommendations for an implementation process when introducing workplace flexibility:

1. **Gain support for the initiative.**

   - Make the business case for the use of flexible work arrangements using external data (benchmarking competitors) and internal data (surveys, focus groups, interviews) that involve quantitative and qualitative analysis.

   - Describe ways in which workplace flexibility will enhance support for internal and external customers.

   - Determine a time frame, as well as roles/responsibilities to introduce, implement, manage and evaluate workplace flexibility initiative.

2. **Identify a top-level planning group or task force to be responsible for the following:**

   - Investigate what similar organizations have done with regard to these options.

   - Inventory existing FWA experience in the organization.

   - Define objectives and desired results.

- Develop a draft policy statement for review.
- Develop an action plan and timetable for evaluating the new initiative.
- Set up a system for gathering input to the planning and implementation process and for generating feedback during the initial phases of the initiative.
- Revise the policy and action plan as appropriate.
- Determine the initial scope of the initiative. Will it start out as a pilot? Will it be companywide or apply to selected units only? Will it be introduced incrementally?
- Set up a process to provide ongoing support for those charged with implementing the change and reiterate top management's commitment to increasing flexibility.

3. **Set up the initiative's administration.**
   - Implement specifics of the initiative devised by the task force.
   - Coordinate and develop technical assistance for supervisors and employees.

4. **Design the initiative.**
   - Developing the initiative may be the responsibility of the task force or a subgroup that it designates, and/or a consultant.
   - Review current policy for compatibility with new objectives and form new policy where necessary (e.g., tools for employee success measurement that will be equitable across function and department).
   - Consider issues such as eligibility, application process, effect on employee status and reversibility.

5. **Develop resource materials.**
   - Have materials for both employees and managers.
   - Include description, educational and technical-assistance materials, as well as training, to explain new options and policies and provide support and guidance.
   - Use the intranet, if available, to disseminate resource information.

6. **Announce the initiative.**
   - Determine if the initiative is launched companywide or as a pilot.
   - Take an assertive posture rather than waiting for employees to request a flexible schedule.
   - If appropriate, make information available to all employees, managers and HR staff.

7. **Promote the initiative.**
   - If an organization and its employees are to take full advantage of any of the new work arrangements, the program must be promoted on an ongoing basis. From management's perspective, the benefits associated with most of the options come from a multiplier effect. That is, when many employees use the program on a voluntary basis, the organization enjoys greater benefits.

- Educate managers/supervisors to recognize opportunities, such as a major life event or a change in how a job is performed, to suggest flexible work arrangements.
- Promote/communicate on a regular basis and in a variety of ways, including in recruitment efforts.
- Reassure employees that working flexibly will not have an adverse effect on how they are perceived or on their career or earning potential.
- Actively encourage managers to model flexibility.
- Reward managers who effectively use flexibility.
- Consider external promotion in local and/or national publications, media events and so forth.

8. Evaluate the initiative.

- Build evaluation processes into the design of the program.
- Consider whether the initiative has had the desired effect. If not, why not? What are the problem areas? Any unexpected benefits? How have customers, clients, employees and managers reacted?

9. Fine-tune the initiative.

- Use information from the evaluation process to address specific areas of concern.
- Involve the task force in recommending next steps.
- Develop a processes for obtaining feedback from managers and employees as an ongoing component of the flexibility project.
- Communicate results and next steps to all involved.

Types of Flexible Work Arrangements

In the most general sense, flexibility is a way of structuring work that involves a change from the traditional or standard arrangement of how, where or when work is done. There are always two different perspectives on flexibility: that of the organization and that of the employee.

To an organization, flexibility means being able to adjust quickly to changing economic conditions: expanding, contracting or reallocating the labor supply as needed. Also included in the ability to adjust to new conditions is becoming more competitive by increasing productivity and decreasing costs. To employees, flexibility means being able to adjust the time or place of work when personal needs are in conflict with the current schedule. This includes being able to alter starting and quitting times; reducing paid work time in order to return to school, start a family or recover from burnout; and attending nonwork functions without being penalized. Both perceptions reflect a work world in which people and organizations are under increasing pressure to do more with less and must be able to react quickly to external demands and ongoing change.

It is important to note that substituting one kind of rigid schedule for another is not being true to the real meaning of flexibility. Some organizations introduce a single FWA option, such as a compressed schedule, and require everyone to work four 10-hour days a week. The company may even be known for its "family-friendly" policy. However, employees frequently report difficulty in adjusting their lives to the new "flexible" schedule. True flexibility takes into account both business and personal needs.

Flexible work arrangements can take many forms. The most common are flex time, telecommuting, compressed work schedule and part-time work (which includes job sharing and work sharing). Each arrangement has advantages and disadvantages for both the employer and the employee. Critical to the success of any flexible work arrangement is the commitment of both management and employees.

Flexible work arrangements can be divided into two types: (1) Restructured full-time work (e.g., flex time, telecommuting, compressed work schedule) that generally does not affect salary, benefits or career-advancement time frames, and (2) Reduced-time work (e.g., part time, job sharing) that does impact salary, may impact benefits and is likely to alter career-advancement time frames (depending on the arrangement, the length of its duration and company policy). When looking at types of FWAs to offer employees, employers must consider how well the arrangements align to applicable federal and state laws regarding issues such as overtime.

The most common flexible work arrangement options are:

Restructured full-time work

- *Flex time.* A schedule that permits employees to choose their starting and quitting times within limits set by management. Requires a standard number of hours during a five-day week within a given time period. Usually features core hours when all employees must be present.

- *Compressed work schedule.* A full-time schedule that enables employees to work fewer than five days a week. Among the schedules used are four 10-hour days, three 12-hour days and nine workdays totalling 80 hours, with an extra day off every other week.

- *Telecommuting.* An option that allows regular employees to work at home or from another location all or part of the time, often linked to the office electronically by computers, fax machines and telephones.

Reduced-time work

- Regular part time. Voluntary, less than full-time work that includes the same degree of job security available to regular full-time workers. Other privileges may also be included on a prorated basis. In some cases, benefits may be provided as well.

- *Job sharing.* A form of regular, part-time employment where two part-time employees voluntarily share one full-time position, with salary and benefits prorated.

- *Phased retirement.* A program that allows older employees to retire gradually by reducing their full-time commitment over a set period of years without negatively impacting their retirement benefits.
- *Leaves and sabbaticals.* Authorized periods of time away from work without loss of employment rights. Paid or unpaid leaves are usually extended for family, health care, education or leisure time. Sabbaticals are usually paid and occur on a regular basis, in addition to vacation time.
- *Work sharing.* A management decision to share the work as an alternative to layoffs.

Although the most common options, these are by no means the only flexibility options available. New ideas and variations are constantly being developed in response to particular needs. "Hoteling," for example, which is a practice wherein employees who spend most of their time out of the office do not have a permanent desk, is a variation on telecommuting that is gaining momentum. Other types of flexibility include paid time-off programs that combine vacation and holidays with sick time and sabbaticals.

Advantages of Flexible Scheduling

In focus groups, interviews and surveys, employees consistently talk about the need for greater flexibility and control over their time. Research confirms that flexibility can significantly benefit a company's bottom line by doing the following:

- Improving retention, recruitment and productivity
- Responding to cost concerns related to turnover, absenteeism, overstaffing and office space
- Reallocating labor to cross-train employees, extend service and staff peak demand hours.
- Avoiding or minimizing layoffs
- Building employee morale and commitment
- Creating the image — and the reality — of an "Employer of Choice" or "Great Place to Work."

There are many ways that flexibility has demonstrated positive outcomes for employers. Some are as follows:

Flexibility protects the company's investment in good workers.

When a company loses good employees, it loses the investment it has made in those individuals and also incurs additional costs of downtime and recruitment, both of which have a real bottom-line impact. In addition, the company loses the "relational capital" that comes from knowing who does what and how to get things done. The changing values and priorities of the workforce have made quality of life an important issue to employees. There is strong evidence that companies can retain good workers by offering flexibility.

Flexibility helps gain a recruitment edge in a tight labor market.
Workers who have the skills and competencies many employers are seeking today place a high value on having personal time available and control over when they take it. To attract those workers, many organizations are being forced to change in many ways, particularly around issues of time. Advertising the availability of flexible work arrangements like job sharing, flex time or telecommuting increases the number and quality of candidates who respond.

Flexibility reduces office space and overhead expenses.
Working off site, in less expensive satellite centers, in shared office space, such as a "virtual office" or a "hoteling" facility, or from home can reduce the need for high-priced office space. Extending hours through compressed work scheduling, job sharing and part-time employees also means expanded use of expensive equipment and new ways to meet customer demands, providing a real return on investment.

Flexibility improves productivity, morale, commitment and engagement along with the quality of work.
Despite widespread fear that flexibility would hinder productivity, there is a great deal of evidence that the opposite is true. Most studies report no fall-off and even an increase in productivity when flexible work arrangements are used properly. In general, productivity improvements are credited to the higher energy that comes from reduced stress or better morale; improved quality of work; more focus on task rather than time; and extended service with the same number of employees. Flexibility also improves morale and commitment. When employees feel good about their jobs and are less stressed, they're more willing to "go the extra mile" for the employer.

Flexibility downsizes labor costs rather than staff.
During business downturns, work sharing or voluntary unpaid leave can help reduce payroll costs while retaining trained employees, which can result in higher morale and fewer employees job hunting.

Flexibility improves coverage.
Flexible schedules and new forms of part-time work let companies redesign schedules for positions or work units that need broader or more intensive coverage. By overlapping their schedules, job sharers can provide double coverage during peak periods of activity and don't lose productivity during vacations. A combination of full- and part-time employees will give employers more staffing options, particularly if the work flow or demand for service is uneven.

Flexibility helps upgrade and expand employee skills.
Allowing a full-time employee to reduce his/her work schedule can provide another employee with an opportunity to work in that job part time and learn new skills.

Sabbaticals help enrich a worker's skill level by providing opportunities for cross-training or ongoing education.

Flexibility retains older workers' skills and experience.

Many firms are, or will soon be, experiencing "brain drains" as a result of early-retirement programs. Polls indicate that a significant number of older workers would continue working if they could do so on a part-time basis and not lose retirement benefits.

Flexibility creates a more responsive organization.

Companies continually face challenges such as departmental "baby boomlet," recruitment for a particular job classification or external pressures like the introduction of new technologies, the onset of a recession or a disaster. Managers must be able to respond creatively and quickly with flexible policies that are already in place when or before a crisis hits.

Potential Obstacles to Flexibility

Despite all the documented success, resistance to flexibility continues in many different areas, including an unsupportive culture, skepticism on the part of management, concern about productivity and client satisfaction, subtle and not-so-subtle messages about employee commitment, the need to comply with state and federal laws, administrative difficulties and work overloads.

Corporate Culture

There are many ways in which the culture of a company may not be supportive of flexibility. The company may possess a value system that holds (explicitly or implicitly) that employees' personal issues do not — and should not — have anything to do with the company. Management may hold the belief that employees who cannot manage their work and personal lives effectively are at fault.

Sometimes the culture is dominated by control: achieving business goals means keeping a tight watch on how, where and when people work. Controlling behavior works against the team autonomy, self-directedness and empowerment that characterize successful flexible environments. Often company cultures reward the heroic behavior that causes stress rather than change the work processes so they won't be stressful.

Corporate culture can be a very intangible thing, but workplace values have a dramatic impact on the effectiveness of work-life initiatives. To understand the values that form a company's culture, it is important to observe what behavior is or is not rewarded or encouraged. Does senior management support flexibility? Do any executives model it or visibly encourage it? Do managers view employees who use flexible work arrangements as less serious and less committed to their jobs? Do employees perceive that to be the case, whether or not it's true? Other common assumptions intrinsic to many company

Management Skepticism or Lack of Support

An organization's unwillingness to offer flexibility to employees is often due to misconceptions about flexible work arrangements, as seen in the following examples:

Misconception:

Flexibility is inequitable. FWAs are designed to meet the needs of a few employees and have no impact on business goals.

Fact: In the increasingly diverse workforce, everyone doesn't have the same needs. Equity no longer means that every employee must have the same options; it means everyone should have access to the options they need. As FWAs become more commonplace, they are being used by employees at all levels and in all jobs to meet a wide variety of work responsibilities and personal needs. These include people with child- or elder-care responsibilities, those with educational or community commitments, employees who interact with people in other time zones and those who wish to reduce commuting time.

Misconception:

Flexibility has a domino effect. If we let a few employees have flexibility, everyone will want to do it.

Fact: Research and experience have shown that this has not been the case. The fact is that most people prefer a full-time job and a regular schedule. Most people cannot afford to significantly reduce their work time. However, even in situations where large numbers of employees opt for some form of flexibility, the needs are generally so varied that schedules can be worked out through collaboration and negotiation. In addition, FWA policy guidelines always give managers control over whether to allow flexible work arrangements, and it's the manager's role to make sure that business needs are addressed.

Misconception:

Flexibility only works in low-level or routine jobs, not in positions with a lot of responsibility.

Fact: Flexible arrangements work successfully in a variety of functions, including supervisors, employees who have clients and those who travel on a regular basis. Some work part time in top-level jobs, some work at home several days a week and others are on flexible schedules.

Misconception:

Flexibility is disruptive.

Fact: Most change is disruptive unless it is well managed. Losing good people because they need more flexible schedules is disruptive. Layoffs are disruptive. Using new forms of workplace flexibility can actually help reduce disruption.

Misconception:

Most supervisors dislike flexibility — it makes more work for them.

Fact: Supervising flexible work arrangements requires a new kind of management style, one that emphasizes results rather than oversight. Some managers are more comfortable with this change than others. Indeed, many supervisors report they have less work once they have some experience managing flexible scheduling arrangements. Working flexibly often enhances self-management. Managers of job sharers comment that partners tend to supervise each other and compensate for skill deficiencies.

(Continued on page 82)

(Continued from page 81)
Misconception:

Unions are against flexible scheduling and staffing arrangements.

Fact: Unions vary in their positions. Some oppose part-time and work-at-home across the board while others do not. Unions try to represent their members' interests. When members express a need for more flexibility, labor representatives try to include that issue in their negotiations. There is no doubt that unions will look very hard at the fairness of any flexible arrangement.

Misconception:

Flexibility works best if it is limited to a ring of contingent employees so that benefits and salary costs can be cut.

Fact: Higher energy and improved morale are the productivity gains most often cited in relation to flexible work practices. Supervisors' major criticism of contingent workers is their lack of energy or commitment to organizational goals, with lower productivity as the result. The short-term gains of reduced benefits and salary costs must be weighed against the longer-term and less obvious gains derived from an energetic, motivated workforce.

cultures include the ideas that long hours are necessary to get the work done and time at work is an indicator of the extent to which an employee is committed and productive. If values exist that undermine flexibility, they will have to be addressed and changed before a flexible environment can be truly successful.

Concerns About Matters Related to Supervision and Impact on Clients

It is true that supervising in a flexible work environment requires a new set of management skills. Training can help managers learn this style of managing – variously called results-oriented, performance-based or managing by objective – which helps managers feel comfortable supervising people they can't see. Much recent research indicates that the supportiveness of managers is also key to employees being able to manage their work and life conflicts. A growing number of companies are measuring the link between employee commitment and engagement and the bottom line, and they are finding that employee attitudes drive customer satisfaction and revenue.

Role of Middle Management

In the past, while many corporations offered flexible work arrangements, only a limited percentage had written policies, and these policies usually left decisions about FWAs to the manager's discretion. As a result, a very small percentage of employees used FWAs. To be more effective, information must be shared more openly with all involved.

Managers have been rewarded in the past for behaviors that no longer work. They have been taught to treat everyone the same for fear of litigation and to rely on the policy handbook to tell them what to do. Today, managers are expected to use their own judgment and discretion when discussing workplace flexibility. In a time when they are also being asked to do more with less, many managers lack the skills to respond effectively. That's why education and training for managers is a critical component in a successful implementation of workplace flexibility.

Policy, Administration and Systems Issues

The policies and systems of an organization regarding things like headcount, performance evaluations, benefits eligibility and so forth, may serve as invisible barriers to managing work flexibly. Alterations in current practice such as the following may be required:

- The headcount system may need to be changed from the traditional system of counting one person as one employee, regardless of time worked, to a full-time equivalency (FTE) system that counts individuals based on the percentage of time worked. Some companies use a combination of both systems, with a code to indicate who is on what system.

- Encourage managers to use flexibility and reward them when they use it well. Performance evaluations may need to be revised to provide a way to evaluate managers on their use of flexibility and their supportiveness to employees.

- The workweek or workday may have to be redefined to allow for employees working shorter days across a six-day week or longer days in a three- or four-day week.

- Define job descriptions in terms of work requirements rather than in terms of a formal schedule. Client billing systems may need to be adjusted, for example, from billing by the hour to by the job. Work can be spread evenly across the year in some cases.

- Benefits decisions can stall the implementation of flexibility, particularly with regard to reduced-time options. It is important to create equity in benefits around issues such as the company's contribution to the medical plan, the employee's cost of coverage, eligibility for benefits, vacation and holidays. Examine pension policies for possible revision to prevent senior employees from being penalized for reducing their work time.

Work Overload

Many people believe that work overload is the No. 1 barrier to creating a more supportive work environment that includes flexibility. Work overload is a major source of burnout and has a circular effect on both work and personal life. Companies may offer more support, but they also demand more of their employees. There's a growing trend toward 70-hour weeks and working everywhere, all the time, and employers say it is not their fault. They're under pressure to stay lean and improve productivity, they say, and can't find the help they need even when they want it. So they have no choice but to require longer hours of the workers they have.

But workers are getting tired. The cost of absenteeism has jumped and stress is beginning to show up as a significant cause. Personal and family issues have replaced illness as the leading reason for employees' unscheduled absences. People who are giving 110 percent most of the time sometimes feel they need to take a break. Most employees leave the workplace each day burned out and stressed. Most researchers believe if employers want to retain and maximize talented people, they must create an environment that allows them some control over their schedules.

Roles and Responsibilities

To be successful, flexible work initiatives require the cooperation of all involved parties: the organization, human resources, managers and employees. All these partners have roles and responsibilities. It is not enough to provide employees with more flexibility so that they can manage their lives better. In return, employees must be flexible in order to see that their work benefits from the increased flexibility. The company has the responsibility to ensure that the culture of the organization supports this new, flexible environment.

The Role of the Organization

In addition to ensuring that the organization's culture supports a flexible environment, the employer must also provide tools, training and guidelines for managers, supervisors and users of flexible work options. Specifically, responsibilities of the organization include the following:

- Communicate support of flexible work initiatives clearly and often, verbally and in print and online.
- Review and revise policy and/or administrative systems (as necessary) to support flexibility (e.g., headcount policy, benefits eligibility, definition of workday/workweek and so forth).
- Provide guidelines, eligibility criteria and procedures for managers to ensure equity, consistency and clarity.
- Provide guidelines for employees, including sample proposals, sample FWAs and possible manager responses to proposals.
- Provide training in managing flexibility as part of overall manager training. Good training in flexibility should be ongoing — not a one-shot effort — and should include examples and case studies from the company. Examples of successful situations as well as challenging ones should be used and should function as effective learning models.
- Provide information and support for employees to plan, request and work on FWAs, perhaps including an online chat room to connect with others who work flexibly.
- Recognize and reward managers who effectively implement and manage flexible work arrangements.

Responsibilities of Human Resources Managers

Human resources managers provide an interface between the big-picture goals of the organization and the specific needs and goals of individuals and departments. They are often directly involved in developing guidelines and procedures for managers and employees in addition to communicating them. Responsibilities of HR managers include the following:

- Provide guidance and clarification to managers and employees.
- Consider equity and other internal issues.
- Identify training needs.
- Mediate when necessary.
- Foster a positive working relationship between managers and employees.

In addition, HR representatives are often involved in examining all the systems — benefits, policies, technology and so forth — that need to be evaluated and possibly redesigned to support workplace flexibility.

Responsibilities of Managers/Supervisors

Managers and supervisors are vitally important to a successful implementation of flexibility. Managers must consider any reasonable request for flexibility and evaluate its viability based on the needs of the department; the requirements of the employee's job function; the likely impact, if any, on productivity and workload of the department; and an assessment of the employee's skills and ability to work effectively in the new arrangement. Managers must do the following:

- Be familiar with the company's workplace flexibility guidelines.
- Address the business needs of the company and the department.
- Consider each proposal on its own merits.
- Present options to employees/encourage employees to make requests.
- Listen, be open minded and think "outside the box."
- Consider advantages, possible obstacles, resources, customer needs, staffing needs, cost, employees' skills and past performance, and whether eligibility criteria have been met.
- Seek advice from HR and colleagues with experience in managing flexibility.
- Review the plan with the requesting employee and modify, if necessary.
- Accept or reject the proposal (it's OK to reject one for the right reasons).
- Communicate with "flexing" employees, other members of department and peers on a regular basis.
- Pilot the agreed-upon plan.
- Monitor and modify. Assume that fine-tuning will be required.

- Evaluate; give feedback frequently.
- Communicate successes and challenges that result from the new arrangement.

Responsibilities of Employees

It is the employee's responsibility to satisfy all requirements of the job, both in terms of quality and quantity of results, as well as meet the business objectives of his or her job function. Specific employee responsibilities include the following:

- Know what flexible work options are available.
- Analyze personal needs and determine what flexible work option(s) will meet your needs.
- Consider how the arrangement will impact your work, your colleagues and their work, the department and the organization.
- Talk to other employees who work flexibly.
- Talk to your manager.
- Write a proposal and get the manager's feedback.
- Iron out details of the proposal.
- Address your own and your manager's concerns.
- Be flexible. Be willing to compromise. Try new ideas. Pilot programs.
- If a flexible arrangement is initiated, communicate the new arrangement to co-workers.
- Evaluate periodically with the manager and be prepared to change the arrangement, if necessary.

Guidelines for Managers

Don't view FWAs as entitlements. Many managers are relieved when they realize that flexible work arrangements are not an entitlement. Requests for FWAs should be evaluated on a case-by-case basis and decisions based on the business needs of the department, the applicant's ability to perform under the proposed work arrangement, the past performance of the applicant and the employee's ability to meet eligibility criteria. When this is understood, it becomes clear why managing flexibility does not mean losing control over one's workforce.

Be results oriented. Managing by results is consistent with current management goals of flattening the organization and requiring more responsibility and self-management of all employees. This is critical when managing employees who are not on site all the time or not within line-of-sight supervision.

Communicate. Regular communication between employees, managers, co-workers and clients is vital to managing flexibility, and it's as important to communicate about successes and challenges as it is to communicate about concrete details such as schedule changes.

Some 'Do' and 'Don't' Tips for Managing Flexibility

DO

- Reflect flexibility in your management style; communicate and model your support for FWAs.
- Take time to think through your reasons for approving or not approving an FWA request.
- Keep your employee's work goals and tasks and your business goals in mind as you seek ways to support his or her need for flexibility.
- Consult with other HR personnel and managers who have had similar flexibility challenges.
- Encourage employees to form problem-solving support groups with others in similar non-traditional arrangements.
- Reward performance and productivity, not the amount of time spent in the office.
- Inform employees of any potential impact a flexible work arrangement will have on rank, pay and benefits, training and advancement.
- Encourage communication about the need for flexibility and its impact after implementing it.
- Build relationships based on trust and respect.
- Recognize that an employee has a right to a life outside of work.

DON'T

- Limit your thinking about solutions to a flexibility problem; what is proposed is not the only possibility.
- Ask more about an employee's personal reasons for wanting more flexibility than you need to know or that he or she is comfortable sharing.
- Assume that you have to agree to all requests similar to one you have approved.
- Agree to an arrangement that would diminish an employee's rights, violate labor laws or risk safety or security, even if the employee requests it.
- Let your personal biases or values influence your decision. Live by your values and encourage others to live by theirs.
- Use flexibility as a reward to top performers.
- Try to solve problems of competence or irresponsibility by using flexible work arrangements.
- Focus on hours of work time or location rather than output.

Observe, adjust, observe. Because they are new ways of working and managing, FWAs require fine-tuning. They will require further adjustment as situations and demands change. This should be viewed as a normal part of the process.

Nitty-Gritty Issues

When evaluating a proposal for a flexible work arrangement, consider the following:

Work Processes

Certain work processes are critical for achieving business objectives and cannot be compromised. Determine what the business parameters are for your department. Some possible examples include the following:

- Regular department/team meetings that all members must attend

- Ongoing, informal communication among co-workers
- Some travel requirements
- Face-to-face customer interface
- Required telephone coverage
- Extended hours during certain business activities such as financial close
- Availability to customers and co-workers.

Budget/Cost

Salary, benefits, travel and training may require adjustments depending on the proposed FWA. Typically, a compressed work schedule will not affect costs, but other flexible options can either lower costs (e.g., part time) or increase costs (e.g., job share where the total scheduled hours for the two employees exceeds 40 hours/week).

Equipment/Office Setup

Some FWAs require an investment in equipment (e.g., computer, modem, fax, printer, cell phone and so forth). These expenses may be absorbed by the company or the employee, or shared by both. Sometimes a change is also required to the configuration of the office. Such expenses might be one-time costs (such as moving furniture) or ongoing (Internet, phone or fax-line charges).

Vacation, Sick Days, Holidays and Overtime

For part-time arrangements (including job sharing), vacation and sick days are typically prorated. So, a person who works four days a week, if entitled to two weeks of vacation, would be entitled to two four-day weeks. For employees on compressed work schedules, vacation and sick days are calculated according to hours rather than days. For example, two weeks of vacation for a regular full-time employee would be 10 eight-hour days. If working a compressed work schedule, the employee is still eligible to receive 80 hours of vacation, but it might be calculated as eight 10-hour days.

Typically, employees on flexible work arrangements are compensated for holidays when they fall on their regularly scheduled workdays. However, some companies require that employees working a compressed work schedule modify their schedules during holiday weeks so they are working regular schedules and take off the holiday. Work out these details in advance and make sure they are clearly communicated.

Guidelines for Employees

Employees need to understand that flexibility is not an entitlement. Each proposal is evaluated on its own merits, with decisions based on the past performance of the employee, the ability of the employee to work effectively under the proposed arrangement and the ability to continue to meet the job requirements and business needs of the department. Nor are FWAs a cure-all. Employees must carefully assess their own situations and match them up with FWAs that *realistically* can help them meet their needs.

Often employees have misconceptions about flexible work options. Those with young children frequently think that working at home will solve all of their child-care problems. However, it is often necessary to have child-care coverage in order to work at home. Some employers even require it. But, while telecommuting may not solve all child-care problems, it can reduce commuting time significantly, thereby reducing the number of child-care hours needed and increasing the number of hours parents can spend with their children. The important thing is to understand both the advantages and disadvantages of an arrangement so employees know how it will affect them.

Typically, the process for planning a successful flexible work schedule would follow this outline for an employee.

Understand the options. Obtain information from the company that describes options that are available and what their impact is on salary, benefits, vacation, holidays, career advancement and so forth.

Skills Assessment

Part of the evaluation process includes determining whether the employee has the skills and personal characteristics necessary to work effectively in the proposed flexible arrangement. Both the employee and the manager should do the skills assessment. The following questions can be used as a guide.

- Does the employee have the flexibility to adjust the FWA to meet specific short-term business needs should they arise?
- Can the employee work independently? This is particularly applicable to telecommuting or flex-place situations in which the employee must be self-directed and work without a supervisor in close proximity.
- Can the employee be productive when working extended hours? (Applies particularly to compressed work schedules.)
- Does the employee communicate well with others?
- Can the employee document and catalogue information in a way that is accessible to others?
- Does the employee have good organizational and prioritizing skills?
- Can the employee work effectively in cooperation with others?
- Does the employee have the ability to ignore distractions if working outside the work site?
- Can the employee function effectively without having a single, direct influence over outcomes? (Relevant to job sharing.)
- Can the employee accept not being seen at all meetings and social functions?
- Can the employee deal personally with recognition of group performance rather than individual performance?
- Does the employee perform better as part of a group or as an individual contributor?
- Does the employee understand financial cutbacks, if any, that may result? Can the employee's situation tolerate these reductions?
- Will the FWA affect the employee's existing career-development plan? Does he or she understand and accept any changes that are likely to result?

Carefully assess your own situation. What do you want to accomplish by working flexibly? What are your skills and strengths? Do you have the skills to work in this new way?

Make a proposal. The initial request should be prepared like any other business request. It should consider advantages and disadvantages from both management's and the employee's perspective. The proposal also needs to specify a time frame during which the flexible schedule will be followed.

Have an open discussion. There should be an exchange of ideas about the proposal that considers the individual's and the department's needs. Discuss potential advantages and obstacles. Don't think of this first conversation as the time to make final decisions. It is an opportunity to exchange ideas and get more information.

Decide how you will demonstrate that the work is being done. Plan how this will fit in with the department's goals. Is the workload easily measurable?

Problem solve. Use business skills (e.g., negotiation) to work toward a mutually acceptable plan. Explore under what conditions the arrangement might be changed or terminated.

Discuss how you will continue to communicate. Modify the plan as necessary. Be prepared to make changes and adjustments at any time.

Explain plans to other employees. Discuss with co-workers and team members and involve them in decision-making, if appropriate.

Employee Proposal

Although there may be times when a flexible work arrangement might be proposed by the manager, it will generally be the responsibility of the employee to draft a proposal. This is an important process, because it helps the employee organize his or her thoughts, spells out the specifics that can be agreed upon (or negotiated) and allows the employee to address potential problem areas and offer possible solutions. It also provides a written document that can serve as the basis of understanding between the manager and employee, as well as a record to present to senior management if the need arises.

The following guidelines and proposal questions can be used for an employee's request for any flexible work arrangements. Actual proposals may differ, but most should include the following:

- How will your new work arrangement benefit customers/clients, other employees and the company? How will this maintain or improve the business, and how will you overcome any obstacles?

- What is your proposed work schedule? Number of hours per day and per week? Where will work be done? How long do you expect the arrangement to last? Are peak periods adequately covered?

- How will the flexibility affect your work priorities? Will it improve dealing with them, or will it require adjustments to your work and that of others?

- What, if any, job redesign will be necessary? Will all tasks now done continue to be accomplished?

- How will "availability" issues be dealt with? If there is less face-to-face contact, how will you 1) attend meetings, 2) stay in touch with others in the department, including the manager, 3) attend to client/customer needs and 4) handle emergency situations?

- Will working a different schedule affect your dealings with clients? Other employees?

- What impact will the flexible schedule have on salary/benefits?

- What other facts will help your proposal? Provide examples of other successful flexible work arrangements within the company or your division, if possible.

General Checklist for Flexible Work Arrangements

Managers and employees need to consider the same issues when evaluating or creating a proposal for any FWA. The following checklist can be used to ensure that the important issues are being addressed:

❑ **Effect on Department/Company.** How will the change effect the department? Are there business advantages to the department/company? What are they? Do they justify implementation of the plan?

❑ **Coverage/Staffing/Workflow.** What is the proposed arrangement? How will staffing and workflow requirements be affected? Are peak periods covered? Does the plan ensure that minimum employee coverage is provided at all times?

❑ **Job Responsibilities.** What impact, if any, will the new arrangement have on employee job responsibilities? How will problem areas be addressed? How will work continuity be maintained? Does the employee have the skills to handle the proposed arrangement?

• **Communication.** How will employees communicate with management and each other? Clients/customers, other departments and so forth? What time will be set aside for this? How will attendance at meetings and functions be handled? How will the change in schedule/work arrangement be communicated to other employees? Clients? What role will technology play, if any?

❑ **Contingencies.** How will sick days, holidays and vacation be covered? What about increased workloads, seasonal requirements? Can employees be asked to work on days off?

❑ **Compensation, Benefits, Etc.** Will there be any effect on compensation, benefits, overtime and career advancement? Does the employee understand what the effects will be?

❑ **Time Frame.** Is this a time-limited arrangement or open-ended? If time-limited, what is the plan for terminating it? If open-ended, what will happen if it doesn't work out?

❑ **Supervision.** Will the proposed arrangement change the way supervision is handled? In what way? How will employee's performance be evaluated?

❑ **Monitoring and Evaluation.** Will there be a trial period? For how long? How will the arrangement be evaluated? When and how will the success of the arrangement be measured?

Flex-Time Guidelines

Flex time is a schedule that permits employees to choose their starting and quitting times within limits set by management. It requires a standard number of hours (usually 35 to 40) during a five-day week and usually includes core hours when all employees must be present.

Advantages: Flex time is a low-cost employee benefit that raises morale while enabling the organization to improve coverage, extend service hours and reduce or eliminate tardiness.

Compensation and benefits, including vacation, are not affected by flex time since the employee still works the same number of hours per week.

Concerns about Flex Time

For managers, the main concerns that flex time raises have to do with customer service, attendance at staff meetings and supervisory coverage of early and late shifts.

If customer/client service is suffering, then do the following:

- Make sure the prearranged schedule is being respected.
- Review the work schedule: Were needs correctly anticipated? Do changes need to be made, for example, expanding core time?
- Ask employees to solve coverage problems by agreement. If impossible, return to "standard" scheduling.
- Make sure a supervisor or key employee is present at all times to monitor and provide support for customer/client service.

If it is difficult to get staff together for meetings, then do the following:

- Try scheduling several small meetings rather than one large meeting. Explore whether information shared at meetings could be communicated in other ways, such as through electronic mail.

Manager's Checklist for Flex Time

When one employee requests flex time, it can be relatively straightforward to deal with. When several employees or an entire department are involved, the process is more complex. It is important to ensure that enough employees are available to carry out the operational requirements of the department at the optimal level. Points to consider for flex-time arrangements include the following:

❑ What is the earliest time people can start work, and the latest they can leave? This represents the total time frame (total workday) in which flex time can be scheduled.

❑ During what time period is it necessary for all employees to be working (core time)? This represents the work unit's peak period of activity, when it needs to provide a greater level of service or activity than at other times during the day. An example could be 9 a.m. to 3:30 p.m.

❑ To ensure adequate coverage, it might be helpful to chart requested time changes, especially if more than one employee's schedule is affected.

- Make sure all employees receive office communications and announcements. Institute electronic mail, if possible.

- Shift attitudes to get rid of inflexible scheduling habits.

If supervisors sometimes have to work longer workdays to cover all shifts, explore the possibility of having supervisors agree to rotate early and late shifts. For employees, one of the main problems with flex time is keeping up to date on developments within the department and continuing to feel "in the loop" and part of the team. To avoid or solve this problem, employees need to maintain close communication with their managers/supervisors as well as with other employees. It may help to establish a buddy system with a co-worker to share information. And employees must make an extra effort to ensure that all office communications are received. They also need to understand that flex time may not be practical for every job. If you need to constantly interact with other employees or customers, you probably need to work the same hours as they work. If your interaction or direct supervision is restricted to certain times of the day, however, flexible hours should not present problems.

Flex time can be very successful if care is taken to think through the responsibilities and tasks that must be accomplished, and match them with the appropriate skills and experience. Lines of communication must be kept open, including ongoing review and adjustments when necessary.

Compressed Work Schedule Guidelines

A compressed work schedule refers to a workweek (usually 35 to 40 hours long) that is condensed into fewer than five days. The most common formulas are 4/10 (four 10-hour days), 3/12 (three 12-hour days) and 9/80 (nine days over which 80 hours are worked). Sometimes 9/80 is called 5-4/9, referring to the fact that one week of five nine-hour days is followed by a week of four nine-hour days. Summer hours are usually a form of compressed schedules. One of the most challenging aspects of compressed schedules is determining their applicability for exempt employees. How do you compress a job that has no beginning and no end? Care must be taken to address this concern by focusing on output, not time, as the measure of productivity.

Advantages: Compressed work schedules can provide a way to solve business problems such as the need to extend service hours or reduce shift turnover and overtime without increasing labor costs. Employees sometimes prefer them so they can have a day off every week (or every other week) and still get paid a full salary. Compressed work schedules can help employees reduce commuting time and attend to personal needs such as spending time with children, taking classes, developing an avocation, doing community work, helping parents and so forth.

Compensation and benefits will remain the same because the employee is still working a full schedule. In general, overtime will be paid on a weekly basis for employees on compressed work schedules. That is, it will be paid for hours in excess of 40 in a week.

Vacation. If employees are working the same number of hours per week or a full-time schedule, they should be entitled to the same amount of time off. An employee's vacation entitlement is calculated on the basis of working days. For employees on compressed work schedules, vacation is calculated according to hours rather than days. For example, two weeks of vacation for a regular full-time employee would be 10 eight-hour days. If working a compressed work schedule, the employee is still eligible to receive 80 hours of vacation, but it might be calculated as eight 10-hour days.

Concerns about Compressed Work Schedules

In addition to the issue of exempt employees having access to compressed schedules, most concerns about compressed work schedules center around the issues of coverage and stamina. Managers wonder how they can authorize a four-day workweek when they need coverage five days a week. But compressed work schedules

---

Manager's Checklist for Compressed Work Schedules

A proposal for a compressed work schedule may be initiated by one employee, several or an entire department. An individual request will be relatively simple to evaluate, but those involving a number of employees will require careful planning. As with any flexible work arrangement, the manager's primary concern should be the continued efficiency of the department and meeting company goals. Coverage is a particular concern when considering compressed work schedules. The following steps should be taken when evaluating a proposed compressed work schedule:

❑ Is the nature of the work conducive to a compressed workweek arrangement? Will the job be disrupted if there is no one available to perform it for a certain period each week? Will continuity suffer? Will additional costs be incurred?

❑ Can employees work effectively under a compressed workweek schedule? Will it be more difficult to commute? Do employees have the stamina to work longer hours? Can the arrangement be structured to allow it to flex to meet individual needs? Can employees work or rotate shifts?

❑ It may help to create a chart showing the schedules for all employees.

---

are most often used in conjunction with other scheduling arrangements. Some employees may continue to work a standard workweek, or there may be two overlapping compressed work shifts, for example, one Monday through Thursday and the other Tuesday through Friday. Maintaining coverage is not only possible, but is often improved with well-planned compressed schedules.

Some employees are concerned about getting too tired or getting home too late. A compressed workweek may not suit the energy and stamina of every employee. Again, the solution is to integrate several different schedules so employees have the option to work a standard five-day workweek or a modified workweek. This will meet the needs of all employees while assuring ongoing coverage every day of the week. Keep in mind that compressed schedules work best when employees choose them. It also helps to implement compressed schedules on a trial basis so employees have the opportunity to test their stamina and determine if they can work well with longer hours over a shorter period of time.

Most studies indicate that compressed workweeks need careful planning to make sure there is effective coverage and good communication. If the planning process includes employee and management input and encourages modifications to resolve problems in the initial planning, compressed workweek arrangements are more likely to be successful. The key to a successful compressed workweek arrangement is making sure that there is effective communication between members of the department and sufficient coverage by employees to get the job done. Ongoing review is necessary to make sure the arrangement continues to work well.

Part-Time Guidelines

Employees who work part time generally work between 20 and 35 hours per week and receive a prorated salary. There is great variety in terms of the number of hours and days those hours are worked. Regular part-time employment may include job security and all other rights and benefits available to an organization's regular full-time employees. With the increase of women in the workforce and the shift from a production-based to a service- and knowledge-based economy, regular part-time work has become even more important to attract and retain talent.

Advantages for the Company

- Helps retain fully trained and experienced employees
- Provides competitive edge in recruiting quality people
- Helps attract highly skilled individuals who prefer to work on a part-time basis
- Increases productivity: part-timers often bring increased energy to the job and have lower rates of absenteeism.
- Increases loyalty and commitment
- Enhances employment equity by making jobs available to people with disabilities or health problems, as well as those who are unable to work full time.

Advantages for Employees

- Provides a creative solution for employees who need more time or flexibility to meet changing personal needs and responsibilities
- Provides employees with opportunities to continue to develop their skills and abilities on the job
- Provides expanded opportunities for career development if promotions and transfers are offered to equally qualified employees.

Compensation and Benefits

For part-time arrangements, base pay and vacation are prorated. A person who works four days a week, if entitled to two weeks of vacation, would be entitled to two four-day weeks. Holidays and sick days may also be prorated. In some companies, employees are compensated for holidays only when they fall on their regularly scheduled work days. In some cases, medical benefits are also prorated according to the number of hours worked. In others, anyone scheduled to work at least 20 hours per week is entitled to full medical benefits.

Indicators of Need for Part-Time Schedules

The following situations might indicate that an organization has a need for part-time schedules:

- Good employees have left the organization because part time is not an option.
- Some departments or job classifications are experiencing above-average turnover or absenteeism.
- In order to handle the normal workload, some areas have had to overstaff or use an excessive number of substitutes.
- Fifty percent of some departments or job classifications are comprised of women of childbearing age.
- Expanding coverage or extending the company's hours of operation is a business objective.

- Upward mobility to the point of "plateauing" is a problem that might be helped if some mid- or upper-level people wanted to cut back their hours.
- Burnout is a problem for some employees.
- Some senior employees would prefer a part-time schedule.
- There are positions for which it is difficult to recruit good applicants.

Part-Time Options

When employees want to request a reduced work schedule, there are several options they can consider:

- Request a transfer to an existing part-time position within the company.
- Assess with their manager the feasibility of reducing work hours and work volume for the existing position to make the job part time.
- Examine the possibility of job sharing in this position or elsewhere.
- Discuss with their manager the possibility of staffing a vacant position on a part-time basis.
- Propose the creation of a new part-time position in response to a recognized increase in business volume.

These options may be varied, and good communication between the employee and manager is necessary to determine the best alternative.

Manager's Checklist for Part-Time Arrangements

A manager reviewing and assessing a part-time proposal should consider the following:

- ❑ Is the nature of the work conducive to a part-time arrangement? Are there many supervisory responsibilities? How much interaction is required with other departments/clients/customers? How much travel is required? Can the part-time schedule accommodate these requirements?
- ❑ What amount of reduction is being requested and in what form — fewer hours per day or per week, or a block of time during the month? Is this a time-limited or open-ended request for part-time?
- ❑ Is the work plan well thought out in terms of aspects such as what part of the job will continue to be done and what might be reassigned?
- ❑ Has the employee considered the impact on salary and benefits? How can you help the employee analyze the impact of part-time work on salary and benefits?
- ❑ What effect, if any, will working part time have on the employee's career opportunities? Is the employee aware of this?
- ❑ Is any additional equipment, office furniture or space required in order to make the arrangement possible?
- ❑ What do the employee's past work record and performance history indicate about organizational skills and abilities to accomplish tasks within a limited time period?
- ❑ Will I be able to keep my commitment by matching the workload with this part-time schedule. That is, not expect full-time work from a part-time schedule?

Concerns about Part-Time Arrangements

There are some common concerns that managers have about part-time work.

Are all jobs appropriate for part-time work?

Many kinds of work can be done successfully on less than a full-time basis. When identifying part-time opportunities, it is important to consider the nature of the job, the degree of customer contact and the employee's proposed work schedule. Types of jobs that lend themselves to part-time work include project-oriented and specialized jobs that are done independently and other jobs requiring little supervision. If the job requires a lot of communication with other divisions, frequent travel, intense and consistent customer/client contact or extensive supervisory responsibilities, it may be difficult to accomplish on a part-time basis.

Will part-time employees be as committed as full-timers?

Experience shows that because they feel the company has responded to their needs, part-timers sometimes are more committed than the average full-time employees. But, managers should not expect full-time work from part-time employees.

How can I staff a full-time job with part-time people?

You cannot expect a full-time job to be done on a part-time basis. However, the job may be able to be restructured. One option might be to create a second part-time job, either on a stand-alone or a job-sharing basis.

Can managers/supervisors/professionals work part time?

There are many examples of managers/supervisors/professionals successfully working in part-time positions. In these cases, part-time arrangements work best when the following occurs:

• The individual's schedule is scaled back moderately.

• The individual is comfortable delegating work.

- The individual has solid communication skills.
- There are a limited number of employees to manage.
- Management backup is available.

Should the employee's performance be taken into account?

An employee's performance is an important element in the decision-making process. Generally speaking, a strong full-time performer will be just as effective when working on a part-time basis. In some cases, however, an employee's performance may be weak because that person is having difficulty managing a full-time schedule and is suffering from burnout, stress or conflicting work-life obligations. The employee might actually perform better on a part-time basis. Part-time work is not the answer if an employee's performance is weak because of poor motivation, interest, training or ability.

If coverage is inadequate or the employee has difficulty meeting deadlines, do the following:

- Re-examine the job responsibilities to make sure that the workload is appropriate for a part-time schedule.
- Consider using job sharing to meet the requirements of the job or arranging for coverage by co-workers.
- Determine whether further training is required.
- Make sure backup is available.

Part-time employees sometimes receive negative reactions from co-workers.

Negative feelings of co-workers often arise out of not knowing what the part-time employee's schedule or responsibilities are or feeling resentment that they have to cover for the absent employee. Managers must do the following:

- Maintain good communications with everyone involved.
- Make sure the part-time schedule is not causing a staff shortage.
- Make sure that co-workers are aware of the employee's current responsibilities and schedule. Post the part-time worker's schedule for easy reference. Determine what duties must be performed immediately and what can wait for the part-time employee's return.
- Communicate to staff that part-time employees are valuable members of the team.
- Review the part-time situation to see if any modifications need to be made.

From the employee's point of view, feeling left out of the mainstream of the department's functioning and not being advised of new work or changes are the main concerns. Good communication is the key to dealing with these concerns:

- Make sure you receive all office communications and relevant material and are included in important meetings, training programs and so forth.

- Maintain close communication with your manager. Ask him or her to fill you in on projects and assignments of other employees.
- Establish a buddy system with a co-worker who will keep you up to date on important changes.

Job-Sharing Guidelines

Job sharing is a special form of part-time work in which two people voluntarily share the responsibilities of one full-time position.

Advantages

- Helps the company retain valuable employees by allowing them to work part time in positions that cannot be reduced in hours or split into two discrete part-time positions.
- Permits employees and managers to develop a variety of creative work arrangements tailor-made to satisfy the requirements of the job and the needs of the employees
- Pooling the skills and experience of two people usually enhances the range of capabilities that can be applied to the work
- Employees in job-sharing arrangements can often cover for one another during vacations, sick days and perhaps even lunch hours.

Compensation and benefits are the same as for part-time arrangements: base pay and vacation are prorated. A person who works three days a week, if entitled to two weeks of vacation, would be entitled to two three-day weeks. Holidays and sick days may also be prorated. In some companies, employees are compensated for holidays only when they fall on their regularly scheduled workdays. In some cases, medical benefits are also prorated according to the number of hours worked. In others, anyone scheduled to work at least 20 hours per week is entitled to full medical benefits.

Job-Sharing Options

There are several options for job sharing, including the following:

- One week on, one week off. Working an odd-even weekly arrangement, one employee works the first and third weeks and the second employee works the second and fourth weeks each month.
- Half-day on, half-day off. Both employees work four hours a day, five days a week.
- Shared job with half-day overlap on Wednesday. Both employees work two and one-half days a week, with Wednesday overlapping.

Concerns about Job Sharing

The following are common questions that are raised with regard to job sharing:

- **Will job sharing require more supervision?** Typically, after the initial training and coordination are complete, there is less need for close supervision, particularly if the manager has emphasized the job sharers' responsibility for making the arrangement work.

- **What if I do not have room in my department for another person?** Depending on the way the company handles job sharing, it may or may not involve another head count. Some companies have changed to full-time equivalency (FTE) and count not the heads but the job, which means it may take more than one person to do a job.

- **Should job sharers receive the same performance evaluation?** Each job sharer must receive a separate and distinct performance evaluation. Each should be rated on individual performance as well as ability to work as a member of a job-sharing team. Bonuses and merit increases should be given to individuals according to the guidelines for regular full-time employees.

- **How should the work be divided?** Under a job-sharing arrangement, employees may be jointly responsible for all aspects of the job, assigned specific areas of the job responsibilities or have some joint and some specific responsibilities. The key is the partners' ability to effectively meet all requirements of the job.

- **Will job sharing result in higher costs?** In general, job-sharing arrangements can represent added costs in terms of benefits being extended to additional employees

Employee's Checklist for Job Sharing

Each job-sharing situation is unique, and the best way to develop a proposal is to do it jointly with the person with whom you would like to share a job. Things to consider include the following:

- ❑ How will the job-sharing arrangement benefit the company, other employees and the department? Consider factors such as improved scheduling, lack of disruption, better coverage for the position, the added expertise that will be brought to the job and so forth.
- ❑ Who are the job-sharing partners? If you have not identified your partner, how will you go about finding one?
- ❑ What are the strengths of your job-sharing team? What is your combined work history and performance record? Describe the skills and experiences you both bring to the partnership and how your work habits complement each other.
- ❑ What is your work plan? Show how the work will be shared. Will it be 50/50, 70/30 or some other alternative? Will you share the same duties or will you work on different tasks? Will you be working half days, half weeks or alternate weeks? Have you scheduled any overlap time? Show how your work plan will meet the needs of the department.
- ❑ Indicate how you will carry out the responsibilities of the position if you or your partner is sick (including maternity or parental leave), on vacation or needs to exchange time periods.
- ❑ Outline who will be responsible for completing tasks, where overlap might exist and how team members' contributions will be acknowledged.
- ❑ How will the job-sharing arrangement be terminated? Offer suggestions for how the shared job might be carried out if one or both partners are promoted, move to another location or leave the company. Are you prepared to fill in on a full-time basis until a new partner can be found? For how long?

and their families. However, these costs are usually offset by lower turnover, greater coverage and higher productivity.

- **Should job sharers be allowed to informally swap time?** Generally, it is better to permit employees to swap time only with the manager's prior knowledge and approval. It helps to maintain a calendar with the employees' schedules and keep it easily accessible.

- **What if one job sharer appears to be pulling more weight than the other or if one is completing assignments too slowly?** Review the way responsibilities are shared between partners and each employee's strengths and weaknesses. It may be necessary from time to time to adjust assignments to balance the workload.

- **Won't a lot of time be wasted due to duplication of work?** Careful attention should be paid to examining work flow and distributing responsibilities in a way that will avoid duplication. Good communication between job sharers is essential for accomplishing this. Schedules should be arranged with sufficient overlapping time to allow partners to coordinate the work.

Job sharing requires a great deal of effective communication and teamwork. For many people, job sharing is an exciting alternative to full-time work. With careful planning and ongoing effort, both management and employees can benefit from this type of flexible work arrangement.

Telecommuting Guidelines

Next to flex time, telecommuting is probably the best known and most publicized form of flexible work arrangement. Allowing regular employees to work either at home or at a satellite office for at least part of their scheduled work hours is an arrangement that many companies are now using to benefit the company, the employees and the environment. Bolstered by more affordable technology and an explosion of Internet use, telecommuting is expected to continue to grow in popularity. Also called "flex-place," it is especially useful when the nature of the work requires the employee's presence at the office for only brief periods, when the employee regularly commutes between two or more work areas or in situations involving special customer-service requirements. However, the growing use of technology and concerns about the security of company documents and information make it imperative that telecommuting policies carefully consider all aspects of technology and technical support during the planning process.

Advantages

- Decreased operating expenses. With the extremely high cost of office space, allowing employees to work some time off site, combined with some kind of office-sharing program, can significantly reduce operating expenses. Telecommuters can also access busy computers during off-peak hours, thus extending the amount of time equipment is in use.

- Increased productivity. Companies with telecommuting arrangements have cited productivity gains of 5 percent to 20 percent. Employees report that having more quiet time, being able to focus on a particular task without interruption or distraction and working during hours when they have high energy and creativity are among the reasons they often accomplish more off site than working in the office.

- Retention of key personnel. Many sought-after employees like having the enhanced choices telecommuting provides. Thus, telecommuting helps minimize turnover costs and can reduce or eliminate relocation costs.

- Expanded hiring pools. Telecommuting can expand the labor pool to include people who cannot accept on-site jobs, such as those with disabilities, parents of young children, someone caring for an elderly relative, students and retirees. Telecommuting can also include highly skilled individuals who have difficulty traveling long distances to work every day or simply prefer not to travel.

Compensation and benefits are generally not affected by telecommuting unless there has been a decrease in responsibilities and/or hours. Some companies won't pay for overtime; others require that telecommuters get permission in advance to put in overtime.

Telecommuting Options

- **Work at home**

  The employee designates workspace at home to conduct business functions on one or more days per week. This is the most popular form of telecommuting.

- **Satellite office**

  A remote office location — usually placed within a large concentration of employee residences — allows employees at a single company to share common office space and reduce the time and expense of the commute to and from the main office facility.

- **Neighborhood work center or hoteling**

  Workspace is provided for employees of different companies in one location. Each company is usually responsible for administrative and technical requirements of its employees. Hoteling allows an employee to "check in" at a location and work from there temporarily.

Concerns about Telecommuting

Managers frequently express the following concerns:

How can I evaluate someone who works at home/off site several days a week? Whether an employee works on site or off site, it is the manager's responsibility to specify job responsibilities, tasks and objectives as clearly as possible. Emphasis should be placed on output and the quality of results achieved as opposed to face time and the number of hours worked. To make sure that effective communication and feedback with the off-site employee takes place, regular meetings should be scheduled.

Whose insurance covers an accident if an employee is working at home? In most cases, for employees working at home, insurance benefits are the same as if they were working at the office. The company's insurance policy should be checked.

How can I keep an off-site employee in the loop? Communication is key to staying in the loop. Off-site employees should be in regular contact with the office by phone, fax, e-mail and periodic work-review meetings. Scheduling mandatory on-site times can help employees continue to identify with the company's culture and goals. It is sometimes recommended that a minimum of 20 percent of an employee's work time be spent in the office.

Does telecommuting require any special training? Telecommuting requires training for managers and employees. It demands new kinds of management skills. As one expert in telecommuting says, "We need to train managers to focus on whether the budget was completed accurately and on time, rather than to focus on what color pencil was used." Because telecommuting is a novel idea for some managers, many companies are implementing training programs to educate human resources, managers and their employees about the fundamentals of telecommuting.

Manager's Checklist for Telecommuting

Because they may involve off-site locations, additional equipment, telecommunications hookups and new management skills, telecommuting arrangements can be among the more complex arrangements to assess, plan and implement. Managers should consider the following:

❑ Work with HR to establish guidelines, clarify expectations and challenge assumptions regarding telecommuting arrangements. Care must be taken to transition the employee and manager from full time in the office to the telecommuting arrangement. In some cases, the transition period involves working from another floor in the same building to get used to the "remote" arrangement.

❑ Budget for any additional expenses incurred by the purchase of new equipment, insurance or maintenance for employees who are working off-site. What equipment and technical support will be needed? How will this be paid for and maintained? Who will own the equipment? Will the expenses be offset by savings in office-space cost?

❑ Determine which aspects of the job can be done at home or at another location and which must be done working with others at the office. Is the nature of the work conducive to a telecommuting arrangement? Can the employee guarantee a dedicated work space at home or somewhere else?

❑ Set specific quantifiable production and performance goals to measure and gauge employees who work outside of the office.

❑ Strive to maintain a sense of "connectedness" by communicating frequently with off-site employees in order to minimize any feelings of isolation.

❑ Consider ways to protect sensitive company information, if necessary. Will the employee need to access confidential data while working off site? What measures would need to be taken to protect this information?

❑ Determine whether telecommuting will be offered areawide or if it will be restricted to particular job classifications or departments. Will certain jobs be excluded?

❑ Decide which employees will be eligible for telecommuting. Some companies prefer to restrict the arrangement to current employees who are familiar with the company culture and its goals rather than offering it to new hires. Others may recruit and hire people as remote workers because they have highly valued skills.

❑ Develop a screening process to evaluate voluntary in-house applicants. For example, some people cannot deal with the distractions that working at home might present. Others are overwhelmed by the isolation of telecommuting. In addition to analyzing the tasks involved, the work style of employees should be considered, including matters such as the need for self-discipline, motivation and the ability to work on one's own without regular supervision or the social support of co-workers.

❑ Work with HR to plan for the implementation of the arrangement, including preparing and conducting suitable training for managers and employees.

❑ Use "telecommuter's agreement," which can be helpful in documenting agreed-upon procedures and responsibilities. It should include work goals, the length of the arrangement, the daily schedule, special technology needs, methods of communication, expectations about the employee's presence in the office, criteria for performance evaluation and conditions of promotion.

❑ Be prepared to deal with the perceptions and attitudes of co-workers. Colleagues who feel they are burdened with the telecommuter's in-office responsibilities — unless they've agreed to exchange some elements of their job responsibilities — will not be cooperative and may perceive the telecommuter to be a "favored" employee.

Employee's Checklist for Telecommuting

☐ What strengths do you bring to telecommuting? Describe the skills and experiences that will have a bearing on the new work arrangement. What in your past work record would support your ability to work independently at home?

☐ What is your work plan? When will you work in the office? When will you work away from the office? Where will you be at that time? Show how your work plan will meet the needs of the department.

☐ What kind of work space will you use at home? Will it be safe for you and others in the home?

☐ What kind of technology and technical support will be required to do your job?

☐ If you have children or dependent adults at home, what care arrangements will allow you to make sure your work time is dedicated to work?

Unless training is provided, companies will be disappointed in their telecommuting efforts. Training must address those issues likely to produce problems. For example, consider the following: How do managers know telecommuters are working? Flexibility, particularly telecommuting, requires good management skills. Managers should be trained to set good objectives as well as to measure productivity and performance-management skills. Productivity can suffer if telecommuters aren't good at leaving instructions or handing off work to those in the office. Training should be used to enhance those and other communication skills.

Even though many employees, particularly those in professional or management positions, have traditionally taken work home, the idea of formalizing the process and allowing part of someone's regular work schedule to include at-home work days is relatively new. The difference is in the expectations and agreement about the work. It's not just taking extra work home and doing it at night. Employees should be trained so their expectations of telecommuting are realistic. They should be helped with office organization and time management in a remote location and assisted in dealing with technology issues and interruptions by family members and friends. They should also be provided with ways to communicate with managers and co-workers. Telecommuters need to also be made aware of safety and security issues in the home.

For employees, the following situations often occur:

"I feel like I should always be working. I feel compelled to answer the office phone or e-mail no matter what time of day or night." There's a strong tendency to overwork when boundaries are not clear. It is a common reaction, called "tele-workaholic syndrome," which comes from pressure to produce. It usually starts out with telecommuters feeling excited and liberated to be working from home. They feel grateful and think they must always do more work to justify it. With fewer distractions, they usually do get more done. But then the sense of accomplishment gives way to the syndrome, which can lead to burnout and resentment. Employees who telecommute need to learn to set boundaries for themselves, since the boundaries of the office location do not do it for them. It also helps to get clarification from managers about how often one is expected to check/respond to e-mail and voice mail messages.

"I thought being at home would solve my child-care problems, but I can't really focus on work when the children need attention." Telecommuting programs are not a substitute for dependent care. Care arrangements must be made. What telecommuting can do is increase the amount of time available to a parent to be with one's child (or adult relative who needs care) by cutting down on commuting time, by keeping one closer to the care center or by even allowing midday visits to dependents from time to time.

"I miss the structure of having a place to go and the social interaction of working with people." These are some of the more subtle changes that employees who telecommute are not always prepared for. Information about the realities of telecommuting should be available to prospective telecommuters before they make their decisions.

Conclusion

Workplace flexibility is the way work will be done in the 21st century. Flexibility meets the needs of employers, employees and customers, creating a "win-win" situation for everyone. Once shunned by some managers and covered up by others, the use of both informal and formal flexible work arrangements is now recognized as an effective business tool, a competitive advantage and a way to recruit and retain good employees. Flexibility can also relieve the pressures inherent in the struggle to manage the responsibilities of work and personal life. Change is never easy, and creating a flexible workplace requires a lot of changes — in attitudes, in management styles and in the way work is done. Bringing about this change takes commitment and partnership, but it's worth it.

Chapter 4
Child-Care Issues

4

Employers today realize that issues related to child care pose many challenges for working parents and the companies themselves. Child care is an infrastructure in our society. It is necessary for working parents to have child care in order to work. According to the Economic Policy Institute, as of 2002, nearly one-half (45 percent) of employed people were raising children while all the adults in the household were working. In 2001, according to the Federal Interagency Forum on Child and Family Statistics, 61 percent of children from birth through age 6 (and not in kindergarten) spent time in some form of child care; the majority were in child care from infancy onward, often for more hours than their parents spent at work. Despite the importance of child care for working parents, there are many difficulties with the child-care delivery system in America in terms of its quality, convenience and affordability.

Regardless of the age of the child, care can be difficult to find and manage, and in most cases is made up of a patchwork of services that parents have to put together for each child. Typically, young (infant-preschool) children are cared for in their own homes, someone else's home (called family child care), in a child-care center or in some combination of these arrangements. For parents of school-age children, the difficulties don't necessarily disappear. Most school hours don't coincide with parents' work schedules, leaving portions of the day (before and after school) and portions of the year when children must attend another program or take care of themselves while their parents work.

Everyone should be concerned about the lack of quality, affordable child care in our country. Quality of care is directly correlated with a parent's ability to work. When good-quality, reliable child care is not available and parents must work, the result is increased anxiety and absenteeism. A potentially larger concern for employers should be the quality of the future workforce. Recent research has emphasized the importance of the experiences in the early years in terms of brain development. As a nation, we cannot afford the long-term cost of poor-quality child care. Companies can play an important role in educating employees and in reinforcing and enhancing the quality of child care in their communities — not only for their employees, but for their customers as well.

Employers first became aware of the connection between the child-care needs of employees and their ability to work in the late 1970s and early 1980s with the influx of women into the workforce. At that time, the primary response to employees' child-care needs was usually thought to be an on- or near-site corporate child-care center. Although some companies were addressing employees' needs in other ways — typically by providing information through resource and referral services and workshops — in the early 1980s (and now as well, to some extent), the media coverage focused primarily on companies that developed child-care centers.

Today, both employees and management are more aware of the range of issues and options related to supporting the needs of working families. It is now clear that child-care centers are not the only option and may not even be the best way to respond. However, in cases when the development of a new child-care program is appropriate, a child-care center can be a wonderful way to respond to working-family challenges while at the same time meeting business objectives. Such a center should be considered only after careful examination of employees' needs, the company's goals and the community's resources. Companies with child-care centers report an increased ability to recruit and retain employees, a reduction in absenteeism related to child-care issues, increases in productivity, improved morale and loyalty (even among childless employees) and an enhanced public image. However, according to a study by the Families and Work Institute, 2 percent of U.S. companies that offered workers access to day care in 2000 had off-site child care, and 3 percent had on-site child care. Among companies that offered child-care benefits, 24 percent perceive negative return on investment, 36 percent think benefits of the program outweigh its cost and 40 percent perceive child-care programs to be cost-neutral.

When developing a child-care initiative, it's important to consider the broad range of child-care options. These include supporting family child care and/or consortium networks; before- and after-school programs; care for sick children; emergency or back-up care; providing information and support through workshops and counseling and referral services; financial support, including subsidizing the cost of care; a strategic investment in community programs and services; and the option requested most frequently — flexibility and control over time.

A Hewitt *United States Salaried Work-Life Benefits 2003-2004 Survey* of 975 employers found that 95 percent are offering some kind of child-care assistance to employees. The following are the top six types of child-care benefits offered by these companies.

- Dependent-care spending accounts — Allow employees to pay for child care out of their salaries on a pretax basis (94 percent)
- Resource and referral services (42 percent)
- Emergency child-care program (13 percent)
- Child-care centers (13 percent)
- Nursing mother's room; lactation consultant (11 percent)
- Employer-arranged discounts with child-care providers (9 percent).

Direct Child-Care Services

The three main types of child care for young children (infants – preschool) are as follows:

- Child-care centers — care in a facility
- Family child-care homes — care in someone else's home
- In-home care — care in the child's own home.

Any of the three main types of child care might provide the following:

- Full-time child care — care during working hours
- Back-up/emergency care — care when a child's current child care is not available, e.g., the caregiver is sick or schools are closed
- School-age care — care for a school-age child during school holidays, the summer months or before and after school
- Sick care — care for mildly ill children.

The need for affordable, convenient, accessible quality child care for working parents is obvious. However, an employer's decision to provide child care requires careful consideration. Any child care option an employer might support will have advantages and disadvantages that must be carefully weighed in light of specific business, employee and community needs. Care should be taken to not duplicate existing community services. Employers should consider enhancing existing services by improving their quality and increasing the supply of much-needed care for various groups of children, including infants.

While in most cases licensing, quality control, location, possible vendor selection and cost will be factors to consider if the company is interested in developing child care, there are many other issues to consider. Figure 9 on page 114 is an outline of some of the advantages and disadvantages of various corporate child care options.

Assessing Child-Care Needs

The decision to implement child-care options requires a fairly simple needs assessment. Clearly, the most visible work-life option for an employer to support is the development of a child-care center at or near the worksite. Because they are so visible, on- or near-site centers are considered more useful in recruiting and retaining employees than other options. However, the decision to develop a child-care center should not be made lightly. Careful analysis is critical to the success of a company-sponsored child-care center. A decision about whether to implement a child-care program should take into account three important factors:

- Professional investigation of employees' child care needs and preferences
- Clarity about employer's goals and resources
- Knowledge about the supply of and demand for child-care services that already exist in the community.

Direct-Care Program/Description	Advantages
On- or Near-site Child-Care Center Sponsored by an employer or union at the worksite or at another location and operated by the employer or by a nonprofit or for-profit child-care provider. Usually employers subsidize the cost, while cost to users is comparable to community rates.	• Often higher quality than most community programs • Can meet business needs • Visible support and recruitment tool • Reduces absenteeism related to child care • Increases productivity • Improves morale and loyalty (even among childless employees) • Enhanced public image
Consortium Center Groups of employers share the cost and benefits of establishing and operating an on- or near-site child-care center that may be run by a community group or vendor.	• Resources, liability and costs are shared. • Small employers can participate. • The large size of the combined labor force protects the center from long-term underenrollment. • Community children may be included to fill vacancies.
Sick Child Care Program Provides care for children who are mildly ill or recovering from a health problem. Care can be provided in a "sick bay" of a child-care center, in a hospital or by in-home services such as visiting nurses.	• Improves recruitment, employee morale and workflow • Reduces absenteeism • Relieves stress on parents • Enhances company image

A child-care center will not meet the needs of all employees, so it's important to simultaneously consider other programs related to child-care that the organization might implement in addition to or instead of a center. These options might include assisting employees with the cost of child care (through a flexible-spending account

Disadvantages	Other Issues to Consider
• Serves limited population of employees and age group of children • Startup often expensive, and ongoing financial support required to ensure quality and affordability • Equity issues, as use is often limited by tuition, space constraints, commuting patterns, etc. • Not always accessible to all employees, particularly those working for multisite companies • May be open to community children to fill vacancies	• Well-designed needs assessment should be conducted to determine business, community and employee needs/interests • Consideration of type, size and location of facility as they relate to cost, accessibility, etc. • Extent of quality control desired by the employer and how this relates to liability issues • Startup and ongoing management issues • Possible tax advantages
• It may involve complicated negotiations among firms regarding structure, costs, policies and decision-making • The center may be able to serve only a limited number of employees from each participating firm, thus diluting the value for individual companies. • Recruitment/public relations value for individual companies may be reduced. • As needs change, some companies may choose to discontinue participation.	• A well-designed needs assessment should be conducted to determine business, community and employee needs/interests. • The amount of employer control over the program has implications for corporate liability. • Employers often receive tax advantages. • An ongoing subsidy may be necessary to ensure that fees remain affordable for all employees.
• Monitoring quality control may be difficult in a visiting nurse program. • Parents may be reluctant to use a caregiver or program that is unfamiliar to the child. • Usage may be low due to unfamiliarity with the concept or cost. • Employers usually subsidize some of the cost of sick child care programs.	• Well-designed needs assessment should be conducted to determine business, community and employee needs/interests. • Licensing restrictions might preclude employers from providing sick-children services in some states. • Sick children represent a significant cause of absenteeism related to child care among employees. • Hospital-based and visiting nurses are the least expensive to start up.

or subsidies, for example), providing information about community child-care services and educational seminars or partnering with community agencies to help improve the quality and accessibility of existing child-care services.

Direct Care Program/Description	Advantages
Back-Up/Emergency Child Care Program Offers care for employees' children when their regular care is not available, when employees are needed for holiday or weekend work, or when schools are closed. Usually vendor-operated for one company or consortium on site or near site.	• Provides a relief and timely help for employees • Can meet emergency child-care needs of large number of employees • Can provide temporary care for infants as parent transitions back to work from parental leave • Easy to calculate return on investment • Relatively small space and small staff required • Increased productivity • Reduced absenteeism • Enhanced company image.
Family Child-Care Network A network of individual family child care home providers who are connected through a child-care center, agency or association. The network provides support services such as training, equipment, lending libraries and licensing assistance.	• Children can be cared for close to where they live. • Family child-care homes are often more conducive to caring for multiage groups and siblings. • The network can provide infant care, one of the most difficult types of child care to find. • Networks stimulate the supply of community home providers, often the most cost-effective and convenient care for employees.
School-Age Child-Care Program Provides care for children aged 5-14 before and after school, during school holidays and/or during the summer.	• Addresses one of the most critical child-care shortages • Provides comfort to children and reduces their anxiety • Improves morale and reduces parent stress • Contributes to lower absenteeism and higher productivity

A good needs assessment will reveal the following:

• The kinds of child-care needs employees have (or expect to have)

• The groups of employees having the most needs

• The impact of employee needs on their work

• The types of child-care programs that would most effectively address employee needs.

Disadvantages	Other Issues to Consider
• Usage tends to be higher for a single-company, on-site facility. • The purchase of slots in the consortium center may not meet demand. • Care must be taken to assure parents understand the program's "emergency" purpose. • Employers usually subsidize the tuition. • Curriculum and staffing are different from the regular child-care program. • It often provides an example of "quality" child care.	• A well-designed needs assessment should be conducted to determine business, community and employee needs/interests. • For on-site service, consider what ages and child-care needs will be covered. • The cost will vary depending on whether the program is on site or off site, its size, type of facility, etc.
• Much coordination and support are needed to be effective. • Home-care providers may be difficult to recruit and retain; quality control is difficult to ensure. • It's critical to provide incentives/benefits/training for providers. • Insurance can be an issue; the structure of the network may raise tax questions.	• A well-designed needs assessment should be conducted to determine business, community and employee needs/interests • Networks are less expensive to start up than on-site or consortium centers. • Ongoing financial support is generally advisable. • Quality is closely akin to the availability of support services.
• It requires transportation if the program is not housed at the child's school. • Programs for older children may be hard to develop, because these children may feel that they are too old for child care.	• A well-designed needs assessment should be conducted to determine business, community and employee needs/interests. • Location is critical because employees' children are likely to come from a variety of locations. • The availability of organizations and/or sites for the development of such programs can be an issue.

Methods for collecting data include an employee survey and one-on-one interviews with senior management, employee focus groups, human resources focus groups and so forth.

The decision-making and planning process is considerably more complex for building a child-care facility than for other work-life benefits; therefore, working with an expert is critical. Child care is a regulated industry, and the consultant can help you conduct a feasibility study and develop a request for proposals (RFP) when you are ready to select a company to develop and manage the child-care center.

Some of the things to consider in terms of feasibility are the availability of a site and the financial resources that will be required. Is an appropriate location for a child-care center available? Is it zoned for child-care use? Do you have the financial resources to develop and *maintain* a high-quality center? Also, it is important to have a realistic projection of utilization. As a rough guideline, a majority of experts predict that between 2 percent and 4 percent of the employee population is likely to enroll their children in an employer-sponsored child-care center. If you are using an employee survey to predict utilization, the survey should have a high return rate (50 percent to 70 percent of employees with children) in order to increase accuracy. Results of employee surveys must be carefully interpreted. Typically, only about 50 percent of those parents who say they will enroll their children in a corporate-based center actually do so. Accurate prediction of utilization numbers is critical, because centers have closed because of miscalculations about utilization.

When conducting a child-care feasibility study, care should be taken to determine current child-care difficulties experienced by employees, including cost, location, quality, convenience of hours and so forth. It is extremely important when a company considers developing its own child care to have the feasibility study conducted by an objective third party. Child-care center developers often conduct such studies, but they have a vested interest in the outcome. A child-care counseling and referral service vendor may also provide consulting services or may be able to refer you to an independent consultant who can conduct an objective assessment.

On-Site and Near-Site Child-Care Centers

On-site or near-site centers can be for primary care — the ongoing daily care of a child — or for back-up care that is provided on a temporary basis when primary care arrangements are unavailable. Some centers provide both types of care, but many do not. Back-up care has grown in popularity during the past five years, particularly in urban areas where transporting a child to the work site on a regular basis is impractical for parents. Employees who are able to use an on-site or near-site child-care center usually appreciate the high quality and convenient location.

Additional *advantages* of on-site or near-site centers include the following:

- Absenteeism and lateness related to child-care issues is reduced because of the reliability of the child-care arrangement.
- Morale is improved because employees appreciate the convenience of having child care at or near the worksite.
- A parent is close by to handle unusual upsets and respond in case of an emergency.
- The company can closely monitor the quality of the child-care program.
- The hours of operation can be adjusted to meet the needs of the company and the employees.

- The visibility of a child-care center can help attract and retain employees, can heighten the morale and loyalty of employees who use the center and can offer positive employee relations opportunities.
- Greater parental involvement in the center's activities is encouraged. Frequent contact between parents and a center can result in better center-parent relationships.
- Employees are able to enjoy a higher quality of child care at a fee typically comparable to fees associated with community-provided child care.
- Employers are eligible for tax incentives.

Disadvantages of on-site or near-site centers include the following:

- The startup and operating costs can be high, and there is usually a need to subsidize the ongoing operating costs of the center.
- The number of employees who indicate interest will likely be greater than the number who actually sign up once the center is open.
- If the center is not fully enrolled, staff and space may be underutilized.
- There may be equity issues as out-of-office workers, including sales and those working at other locations, may find an on-site center less convenient than other forms of care.
- Waiting lists for a center may cause friction among employees.
- A full-time child-care center that is on site may not be practical for employees who travel long distances or use public transportation.
- A child-care center is highly visible and may contribute to a sense of inequity in a multisite company if the center does not serve all locations.

Consortium Child-Care Centers

Consortium child-care centers are developed for several employers who want to function as partners with one another and share resources, liability and the cost of the facility. They offer a way for smaller companies to provide child care while not taking on all the responsibility, and they also offer a way for multisite companies to possibly address the child-care needs of employees in a variety of locations. A consortium center can be developed to serve employers in the same industry or to serve different industries that are in the same geographic area.

Developing a consortium center requires that the companies involved be able to cooperate in planning and operating the center. They must trust each other and share similar points of view in order for the collaboration to be successful. Often a child-care vendor develops a consortium center and solicits companies to participate. Some possible prerequisites for gaining cooperation among members of a consortium include the following:

- After a proposal has been initiated, a period of time ("stew time") must be built in to the process to allow the potential members to carefully consider how great their commitment to the center is.
- Vendors can provide information on the general benefits of employer-supported child care and those benefits that are specific to consortium ventures.
- Probable costs, potential problems and consortium participation should be discussed during stew time.
- Most company officials will need to be educated about the requirements for quality child care and about how a consortium operates.
- Vendors should assist participants in clarifying both individual company and joint consortium goals, and they should point out contradictory or conflicting goals.
- When the financial and contractual commitments for each company are large, prospective members must determine whether the costs to their individual organizations are outweighed by the benefits expected from consortium participation.
- Cooperation is influenced by the shared history of the participants. A history of competition can adversely affect the ability of participants to work together.

The interests of the various corporate members of a child-care center consortium may not be equal. This may be the case when a small company with limited child-care needs enters into a consortium with larger companies that have substantial child-care needs. Spaces for children are usually divided according to the employer's estimated percentage of participation in the consortium. To avoid misunderstandings, partners should work out agreements at the outset that deal with procedures for handling management, liability and withdrawal from the consortium. A consortium can be initiated by a community group or a private developer, or by a group of companies. In the case of a vendor, the service is usually marketed to corporations on a per-slot basis.

Advantages of a consortium center include the following:

- Because the costs are divided among partners, they may be lower than comparable costs per participant employee in a center sponsored by a single company. When a developer assumes the cost of creating the center, the costs may be even further reduced.
- Liability is shared. Because the consortium is often established as an independent entity, participating companies may be legally distanced from claims that may arise out of a damage or injury suit.
- Community relations and intercompany employee relations can be strengthened.
- A decline in use by one company can be offset by use by other participating companies.
- Multisite companies have the possibility of replicating the consortium model in other locations.

Disadvantages of a consortium center include the following:

- The financial stability of the consortium depends on the financial stability of all of the partners.
- The demand for spaces in the center may be greater than the supply, and the consortium may not have the flexibility to expand.
- Rules for who may use the center and how much they must pay (or how much employees must co-pay) may differ widely among the partners in the consortium. Policy setting, paperwork and procedures for handling problems may become complex and difficult for staff to manage.
- Public relations advantages, although still significant, may be somewhat diluted, because no single company gets full credit for the center.

In addition to regular, full-time care, consortium centers are a popular way to provide back-up care and emergency child care.

Back-Up (Emergency) Child Care

Parents must have some form of child care in place so that it's possible for them to go to work. But, because of the nature of the child-care delivery system in this country, parents must often rely on a patchwork of arrangements. And, it is not unusual for something to go wrong — a caregiver gets sick or takes time off, a center or school is closed and so on. When care breaks down, parents often have no alternative but to take time off and stay home with the child, which is estimated to cost American businesses more than $3 billion a year in lost productivity. Realizing the stress involved and the enormous cost in lost productivity, employers are addressing the need for back-up or emergency care in a variety of ways. Employers can establish or reserve slots in an on-site or near-site back-up child-care center, or they can contract with a service that provides in-home care. Typically, employee use of these services is fully or partially subsidized by the employer.

Hewitt's *2004-2005 U.S. Salaried Work/Life Benefits Report* shows that of 936 employers surveyed, 97 percent offer some type of child-care benefit and 12 percent offer sick/emergency child care. State regulations, or the lack of them, don't seem to be a barrier to growth. Back-up care allows companies to provide services to a larger number of employees than a full-time child-care center can, and back-up child care's clear-cut effect on productivity (through reduced absenteeism) makes it easy to quantify savings. Back-up care, which is used occasionally, also makes a lot of sense in urban areas where it may be impractical for employees to bring their children to a worksite child-care center on a daily basis. Most back-up centers are facilities built specifically to care for children when their regular care is not available, although some permanent child-care centers also provide back-up care. Some companies offer back-up care in addition to permanent or full-time care; others offer only back-up care. Back-up care requires less space and a different staffing pattern than full-time child care. The registration and reservation processes must be carefully established and handled so that when there's a need, employees can use the facility.

Care for Sick Children

For all working parents and their employers, care for a sick child is another major problem. The overwhelming majority of employees must change their child-care arrangements when their children become ill. The American Medical Association estimates that children become sick between six and 10 times a year, and studies indicate the rate of absenteeism due to sick children ranges from four-and-a-half to eight days per year.

Sick-child day care is a complex problem for employers. Even if parents are able to attend work when their children are sick, they are often stressed and less productive. Most prefer to stay home at the beginning of an illness or if their child is very sick and to use their paid sick leave to care for a sick child. In worksite focus groups, parents frequently talk about how torn they feel when they have to choose between staying home or leaving a sick child. Often they feel forced to lie to their employers, calling in to say they are sick in order to get a paid sick day off, when it is really their child who is ill. It is a no-win situation for most parents. In using sick days for their child's illness, employees may not have any leave left for their own illness. They often go to work even when they're not well themselves, because they're afraid they will not have any sick days left if and when their child becomes sick. In some cases, new technology has allowed employees to work from home when their child is sick, and some companies are changing their sick-leave policies by creating time-off "banks" to help employees avoid this problem.

Most child-care programs do not now permit enrollment of sick children. However, regulations are being developed in most states to allow child care for sick children. Options for care generally include freestanding centers dedicated to the care of sick children, hospital-based centers, "sick bays" attached to regular centers, family child care homes and in-home care. Although pediatricians have traditionally been opposed to child care for sick children, in the last few years pediatricians have changed their position and are now becoming involved in child care for sick children in a variety of ways — from providing advice to actually running centers. At an average cost of $40 to $50 per day (in addition to the cost of regular child care), most child care for sick children cannot exist without employer subsidies. Many companies are becoming more comfortable with the concept of child care for sick children and are accepting the cost because they recognize that what they save by reducing absenteeism more than offsets the cost.

Hospital-based child-care centers for sick children have historically had the longest lives. Free-standing centers have difficulty surviving financially but have been known to work, especially when they have enough corporate support. Some full-time child-care centers are adding "sick bays" where specially trained caregivers provide care to mildly ill children in specifically allocated and designed space.

School-Age Child Care

There are many times during the year when schools are closed and school-age children require additional care. This can include daily before- and after-school care, summers and school holidays. There are approximately 1,000 hours in the year when school-age children are not at school or with their parents. Employees whose children care for themselves before and after school miss an average of 13 days of work per year.

Research has documented the fear, loneliness and boredom children who are left home alone ("latchkey kids") feel and the stress this causes their working parents. Research indicates there are other reasons to help employees who need school-age child care. School-age programs might be located in the child's school, in a Family Child Care home, a child-care center, a church or synagogue, a recreation center or a community center. The key point is that these programs must supplement the normal school schedule in order to meet the working parent's schedule.

Corporate support for the care of school-age children can take many forms, including training in self-help skills. Employer-supported programs for school-age children generally fall into one of the following categories:

- On- or near-site programs for employees' school-age children, including before- and after-school programs and vacation/holiday activities

- Information and resources for employees who have school-age children, including resource and referral services, a homework helpline, tax-free salary set-asides for dependent care and flexible work arrangements

- Support for community programs that serve school-age children, including financial contributions and participation in community partnerships.

24-Hour (Odd-Hour) Care

It is difficult for most working parents to find affordable and high-quality child care, but the problem becomes even greater when care is required during nonstandard hours. The issue of 24-hour or odd-hour child care is growing due to the following trends:

- More employers operate around the clock. The long-term trend toward a service-based economy has led to the operation of more businesses during early mornings, evenings, nights and weekends.

- The global nature of the economy, which has people doing business with people all over the world at all hours of the day and night, has also contributed to this 24-hour trend.

- Employers in all sectors are changing their schedules for reasons ranging from increased flexibility to enhanced customer satisfaction to reduced air pollution.

Shift workers have been found to struggle with huge obstacles in fulfilling family responsibilities. These obstacles often severely impact shift workers and are costly to their employers in terms of absenteeism, tardiness, safety infractions and —

ultimately — productivity. Due to the lack of regular child care that fits their schedules, these workers are more likely to rely on relatives, neighbors or friends for child care. They often have a hard time finding care, and their children are frequently left alone before and after school.

Other Child-Care Options

Providing Information and Support

Working parents are often unaware or unsure of where to turn for answers to questions about child care and parenting. To help employees become more effective and educated consumers, employers can provide information to their employees using a resource and referral service through a vendor and/or conducting workshops on topics of interest. Resource and referral services typically provide employees with information and counseling on child-care issues and help employees find and manage child-care arrangements. The service often includes education (telephone counseling, print material, online information and/or workshops) about a broad range of child-care issues, including quality care, adoption, information and support for nursing mothers, finding colleges and so forth.

Policies and Customized Work Arrangements

In trying to manage work and family responsibilities, time and scheduling problems often arise. Parents' work schedules may be frequently interrupted by breakdowns in child care, illnesses and other family needs that cost employers in lost work time. The ability to customize a work schedule to fit with personal needs is one of the most cost-effective supports an employer can offer. Companies typically have policies regarding scheduling options such as flex time, part time, compressed schedules, job sharing, flex place or telecommuting and sabbaticals. Both employers and employees benefit when these options are made available, and when employees and managers are educated about them, encouraged to use them and suffer no penalty for using them.

Many companies offer parental leave for fathers and mothers for birth and adoption, with some portion paid. Allowing new parents time to bond with their child and establish comfortable routines helps avoid absenteeism and unnecessary stress. In addition, leave policies that allow employees a specified number of days (with or without pay) to care for a sick child assure parents that they won't need to choose between a sick child and their jobs. Many employers also realize that providing support for nursing mothers can be an advantage for both the employee and the employer in terms of reduced absenteeism and stress. Providing a lactation room for nursing mothers is another way to demonstrate that support.

Providing Financial Assistance

Child-care expenses can place severe financial stress on a family. The cost for child care can range from $1,500 to $15,000 per year depending on the child-care fees and the number of children in the family. Many families spend at least 10 percent of their income on child-care services, with lower-income families paying a larger percentage, sometimes as much as 25 percent. The cost of care prevents some families from choosing the highest quality of care. As a result, they may select less stable and less expensive care, which creates even greater stress and reduces effectiveness at work. Employers can help by offering a Dependent Care Spending Assistance Plan (DCAP) that allows employees to use pretax dollars to pay for care; by offering a flexible benefits plan or "cafeteria plan" that allows employees to choose from a range of benefits and customize their benefit package; by providing a subsidy through vouchers or reimbursement for a portion of the cost of care; and by financially supporting local child-care programs through grants and/or in-kind services.

Companies can support community child-care programs by underwriting training, by providing equipment and supplies and/or by offering volunteers to help with purchasing, bookkeeping, marketing and so forth. This type of support can be a valuable way of connecting with the community and customers while effectively addressing employees' needs. In some cases, companies are leveraging their corporate contributions to focus on early child-care needs in communities in which the companies have operating units and/or residing employees. Even a small contribution can often go a long way in the child-care industry. In some communities, companies are joining forces to improve the quality, quantity and accessibility of child care. By combining corporate volunteer efforts with services that meet the child-care needs of employees and the community, employers can make a dramatic difference in the lives of their employees, their customers and their future workforce.

Child care is a complex issue, but there are many ways an employer can help. Companies that address the child-care needs of their employees find that the investment can have enormous benefits.

Chapter 5
Elder-Care Issues

5

During the last decade and primarily because of the aging population and the dual-focus workforce, the time one adult spends caring for another has emerged as a workplace issue. Finding and coordinating elder-care services is no easy task, especially for an employed caregiver. It requires an in-depth knowledge of complicated systems such as health care, insurance and housing options.

Holding a job and providing elder care at the same time frequently causes stress, depression and burnout that can lead to increased absenteeism and turnover. The study *Overwork in America: When the Way We Work Becomes Too Much* (Families and Work Institute, 2004) found that employees with elder-care responsibilities tend to be more overworked than employees without these responsibilities. And, the study reports, only 25 percent of organizations offer elder-care benefits.

In addition, elder caregivers who are working may also be dealing with the stress of long-distance care giving and financial hardship. Though concentrated among older employees, a surprisingly large percentage of younger employees are reporting elder-care responsibilities. The number of employees with both child-care and elder-care responsibilities, the so-called "sandwich generation," is evolving into a rather large "club sandwich."

According to a 2003 study by ComPsych Corporation, workers who care for both children and elderly relatives put in enough caregiving hours to make it a second job. Of the employees polled, 8 percent are part of the sandwich generation. These individuals reported spending an average of 36 hours per week on caregiving duties, as follows:

- 10.4 hours per week on child-care tasks such as bathing, feeding or making care arrangements
- 9.6 hours per week on extracurricular activities for children
- 4.5 hours per week driving children to school
- 4.1 hours per week on caregiving tasks for an elderly relative
- 2.6 hours per week traveling to the elder's residence
- 4.7 hours per week on making arrangements (financial, legal, social or health-related) for the elder.

These caregivers reported getting only six hours of sleep per night and needing to take off 18.9 vacation and sick days per year to deal with personal and caregiving issues. Although elder care should not be considered a woman's issue, the role of women as traditional caregivers and the increase in their participation in the labor force have become major factors in the evolution of the need for elder-care support.

Several other studies have also documented how widespread elder-care responsibilities are among the American workforce. According to the *National Study of the Changing Workforce*, published by the Families and Work Institute, 25 percent of the U.S. labor force has elder-care responsibilities. *The Wall Street Journal* reported in 2001 that elder care was becoming as big an issue in the United States as child care, and that quite possibly it would loom even larger in the near future, with almost two-thirds of employees under age 60 believing they'll have elder-care responsibilities in the next 10 years. The *Journal* cited a survey sponsored by Metropolitan Life Insurance Co. that found that as the nation's workforce ages, employers can expect to lose between $11 billion and $29 billion annually because of work-schedule conflicts traced to elder care.

The *Journal* report noted that by 2006, nearly 40 percent of the population will be older than age 45, and many will face elder-care situations. In company-sponsored surveys, in addition to those currently providing elder care, another 20 percent frequently predict they will have elder-care responsibilities in the next one to five years. In fact, the National Council on Aging estimated that between 30 percent and 40 percent of all employees will assist their elderly parents in 2020, compared with 12 percent today.

Employers have begun to offer a variety of programs to help their employed caregivers, but in many cases that support has not reached the same level of assistance offered for child care. According to a July 30, 2001, *USA Today* report, many employers don't know whom elder-care issues affects. Citing a survey by The Human Resource Institute and Boomerang of 150 large employers, *USA Today* reported that most companies don't have accurate data on the number of caregivers among employees. Additionally, 80 percent of the survey respondents either didn't know or had to guess at the percentage of caregivers in their workplace.

With greater numbers of workers expected to be caring for elderly relatives in the future, it's critical for employers to find ways to help employees cope with those demands. Recommended employer actions cited in the report were as follows:

- Support the caregiver by providing counselors who are ready to let the employee talk about what is going on.
- Educate the workforce so it knows what it may face in the near future. Let it know that the average duration of caregiving is about four years, but that the time period is likely to increase as medical advances prolong life.

- Ensure that supervisors understand what caregivers experience and how to help them manage the stress.

Description of Elder Care

Unlike child care, which typically involves finding services primarily for healthy children who live with the employee, elder care requires a set of services to respond to a wide range of often unpredictable medical, emotional, physical and financial possibilities. These services are frequently required to be delivered some distance from the employee. Elder care takes many forms, including meals, transportation to medical appointments, food shopping, financial assistance, assisting with housework or emotional support. When elder-care needs occur, they tend to be unpredictable and involve many unknowns. These needs often cause anxiety about things such as the ability to find and pay for immediate care or ways to take preventative measures like withholding car keys away from an elderly parent. Employees with elder-care responsibility are often called upon to assist in making costly financial decisions around issues of long-term care. In many cases they have very little information and little confidence in their ability to get comprehensive information on public and private benefits, service and financial options, and risks of needing extensive care over time. Adult children usually want to respect the autonomy and decision-making capability of their older adult relatives. However, most people are not proactive when it comes to elder care, and critically important discussions about "what to do if" rarely take place in advance.

Cost of Elder Care and the Needs of Working Caregivers

Elder care is estimated to cost employers $1,141 per employee per year in absenteeism, turnover and lost productivity, according to a 1997 study by MetLife. Based on this data, the cost for a company with 10,000 employees, of which 20 percent (2,000) have caregiving responsibility, would be about $2,282,000 ($1,141 x 2,000) per year.

Employed caregivers need help obtaining the comprehensive information, guidance and support required to make complex financial, service and care-management decisions. The needs of working elder caregivers typically fall into the following categories:

- Time — Flexibility to schedule work and caregiving activities in ways that allow effective management of the two sets of responsibilities, along with respite time that offers time away from both work and caregiving responsibilities
- Information — Access to accurate, up-to-date information about community-based services, community-based resources, and legal and financial issues
- Financial Assistance — The ability to pay for services needed to appropriately care for an older adult relative; payment may require combining the financial resources

of the elder, the working caregiver, other family members and government or private-sector programs

- Emotional Support — An understanding and caring support network that includes family members, friends, co-workers, supervisors and perhaps advisory professionals.

Employers' Responses to Employees' Elder-Care Needs

The National Study of the Changing Workforce (Families and Work Institute, 2002) shows that 24 percent of employees have access to elder-care resources and referral services, as compared to only 11 percent in 1992.

In 1998, a Mercer and Bright Horizons Family Solutions study found that the elder-care services most frequently offered by companies were as follows:

- Consultation and referral (81 percent)
- Long-term care insurance (35 percent)
- Counseling (14 percent)
- Financial support/other (4 percent).

Companies providing elder-care benefits report that employee utilization of these programs is growing but still relatively low, usually for the following reasons:

- General discomfort on the part of workers when discussing issues related to elder care, perhaps rooted in the feeling that addressing such an issue is a private family matter
- Corporate cultures where it's still not acceptable for employees to admit they have outside family demands that impact their work time and priorities
- Ineffective communication techniques for reaching workers who need the information and assistance most (i.e., the working caregiver in a crisis situation), and a lack of awareness on the part of employees as to the actual range of elder-care benefits provided
- Demographic bulge in the number of working elder caregivers is just beginning to be felt as baby boomers enter their 60s.

Elder-care experts agree the objective of any company elder-care initiative should be to help employees plan ahead. Continual marketing is necessary to make sure employees know about available resources and to increase utilization of elder-care services. Communication should stress a positive, long-range planning approach. Human resources, benefits, wellness and work-life areas can all share responsibility for the elder-care initiative and find ways to publicize the issue and resources. When employees are able to plan ahead and prepare for elder-care responsibilities, their employers also benefit.

See Figure 10 on page 133 for a comprehensive list of potential employer-sponsored elder-care supports.

Flexible or Customized Work Arrangements
- Informal or occasional flexibility
- Part time and job sharing
- Voluntary reduced time
- Phased retirement
- Compressed schedule
- Flex time
- Telecommuting or flex-place

Paid Time Off
- Sick days
- Vacation
- Sabbatical
- Personal days
- Paid time off bank

Paid or Unpaid Time Off
- Family leave
- Medical or emergency leave
- Personal leave
- Bereavement leave

Policies
- Time off
- Relocation policies

Insurance Coverage
- Health insurance
- Dental insurance
- Life insurance
- Unemployment insurance
- Workers' compensation insurance
- Long-term care insurance

Financial Assistance
- Publicizing federal or state tax credits
- Dependent-care reimbursement plan
- Subsidized dependent-care reimbursement plan
- Subsidized care or vouchers
- Discounts for care

Access to Information
- Distributing educational materials
- Resource library, possibly online
- Workplace caregiver fairs
- Workplace caregiver workshops and support groups
- Elder-care counseling and referral
- Elder-care locator
- Elder-care counseling through employee assistance program

Direct Service Programs
- Geriatric case or care management
- On-site adult-care center
- Near-site adult-care center
- Intergenerational program
- Community resource development

Information and Support

According to a September 23, 2003, report by the U.S. Department of Health and Human Services' Administration on Aging, family and friends informally provide 80 percent of the care needed by elders. These caregivers, many of whom are working, need a great deal of information and support to be most effective. The programs that most companies offer include resource and referral services, elder-caregiver fairs or expos, elder-care material in a resource area or online, and workshops and support groups on elder-care issues. According to the Families and Work Institute's *2002*

National Study of the Changing Workforce, elder-care resource and referral services are one work-life program that has increased significantly. In 1992, only 11 percent of employees had access to this service, while nearly a quarter (24 percent) have access today. More employees also need elder-care services as the population ages: 35 percent of workers, men and women alike, say they have provided care for a relative or in-law who is 65 years old or older in the past year. The purpose of providing information and support is to offer accurate, time-saving access to information so that the best care available can be provided. Knowing they have access to this information can help those employees interested in planning ahead and can relieve stress levels in those individuals who would not know where to start without this assistance.

Elder-Care Consultation and Referral

About 7.7 million employees working today for employers of all sizes have access through their employers to elder-care resource (or consultation) and referral services. Approximately 3 million employees receive the services in-house, and 4.8 million receive them through a third-party vendor. IBM was the first U.S. company to provide such services.

Many companies offering elder-care consultation and referral services find the utilization rate typically ranges between 5 percent and 10 percent annually. However, once employees use the elder-care consultation and referral service and are more knowledgeable about the range of services provided, they are likely to be repeat users. The company typically pays for employees' use of the service. In a recent focus group, a senior manager shared her anxiety over the need to move her elderly mother with Alzheimer's Disease into a facility. The manager was not aware that her company offered a service to help find and manage this type of care. Upon hearing this, the manager began to cry, saying how relieved she was to know help was available; it would not only save time away from work, but would give her peace of mind.

The purpose of contracting for elder-care consultation and referral typically is as follows:

- Relieve stress and anxiety by providing employees with access to expert counseling that can help them identify concerns and make informed decisions based on detailed knowledge of local community and national resources.
- Provide consumer education through counseling and written materials to help employees select appropriate care.
- Provide individually researched referrals for a broad range of providers and help employees manage their elder-care needs.

Such a service can save employees a great deal of time and aggravation, and thus the company reduces lost productivity. For example, if an employee's parent needs frequent transportation to and from the doctor's office to receive treatment for a chronic illness, and the doctor's office hours conflict with the employee's work hours, the employee will either have to take several hours off every week, eating up precious vacation time, or take unpaid time off to accommodate this need. However, by calling the consultation and referral service, the employee can get access to community-based resources that could provide the necessary transportation.

Most elder-care consultation and referral services include the following:

- A toll-free number for employees to call. A professional takes each employee through a screening process to clarify the reason for the call.

- A variety of print, video, audio and online educational materials. Regardless of the format, educational materials cover relevant elder-care topics and can be sent to the employee directly, or to the older adult dependent.

- Referrals to appropriate resources in specific communities, often cited as the greatest time-saving aspect of the service. After identifying the reason for the employee's call, a list of resources that meet the criteria is sent to the employee.

- Access to the service through the Internet. Many employers link their intranet benefits sites to a national vendor's online version of the consultation and referral services. In general, employees can access and download educational materials, can e-mail elder-care specialists or consultants a question, can order additional elder-care materials and can perform their own searches within the vendor's database.

- On-site seminars on elder-care topics and follow-up customer satisfaction phone calls and/or surveys.

Companies are increasingly adding new specialized services to enhance their offerings.

Elder-Care Workshops/Support Groups

Networking is one of the best ways to discover resources that address elder-care concerns. Many employees caring for older adult relatives build support systems that include their older adult's neighbors, clergy, friends, doctors, accountants and other advisors. Employed elder caregivers can expand their networks to include their co-workers at various company workshops that may be offered throughout the year. These workshops tend to focus on health, medical, financial, legal and emotional issues specific to elder care. Such issues include wills and trusts, Medicare and Medicaid, housing options, long-term care choices, communication with older relatives and understanding the normal aging process. These sessions, usually facilitated by an elder-care expert, can be an important component of a company's support.

Since elder care is frequently a long-term commitment, elder-care support groups may evolve out of the workshops or be established independently by employees themselves. The main purpose of a support group is to give elder caregivers a chance to share experiences and to know that they are not alone in facing the challenges and dilemmas of caring for an older relative. Support groups are usually small groups of employees that meet regularly to deal with one issue. The success of support groups relies heavily on the commitment of their members and having access to resources to help manage the process. In some cases, resource and consultation or employee-assistance services may provide occasional facilitators for support groups. Such support can make the difference between an employee who is able to cope with work and family during an emotional time and an employee who is not able to function effectively.

Elder-Care Resource Expo

An expo or fair can highlight community resources that deal with elder-care issues. Local and national organizations involved in elder care might come to the worksite during an expo to publicize the services they offer. At such an event, which may be part of a larger health-care or benefits fair, employees can obtain literature on topics of interest and talk directly to an organization's representative. Some companies ask employees who attend the expo to fill out a short survey so they can gather more specific information about the elder-care needs of their employee population. An expo can be an effective way to encourage employees to be more proactive regarding elder-care issues.

Work-Life Resource Area

Material on elder-care issues can easily be included in a work-life resource area. Providing books, magazine articles, newsletters and visual media on issues of concern to employees dealing with elder care extends the potential audience for the resource area. Some companies sell products or services that are directed to the older population — medications, health aids, vacation packages and so forth that might be included in the employee resource area.

Another way to provide employees with information on elder-care issues is to produce a booklet on the subject. The guide can contain information about the normal aging process, physical and mental health, and how to find help with elder-care issues.

End-of-Life Supports

End-of-life care may occur in three phases:

- Providing care in advance of the death of a loved one
- Dealing with the practical and emotional issues surrounding the death itself
- Mourning and recovery.

In many cases, the workplace doesn't know how to respond to these events. Program policies or services specifically targeted to mourning and recovery (which may take an extended period of time) seem to be less common than those targeting the practical and emotional issues surrounding the death itself. Possible workplace responses for employees dealing with end-of-life issues include flexible work arrangement policies, personal and bereavement leaves, consultation and referral services, geriatric case management services, seminars, support groups or resource libraries.

Policies

Employees dealing with elder-care issues will probably encounter difficult personal situations that will impact, temporarily or permanently, the way they work. They may need a respite from work. Some companies let employees use sick time, vacation and personal days with or without pay. If caregivers don't rest, they will burn out at some point, and the company will also lose. Sometimes, because the person who's ill gets so much attention, we forget that the caregiver needs help to maintain health, handle stress and battle exhaustion.

Elder-care needs are often sudden and unpredictable and require flexibility and responsiveness from the employee caregiver. Working for a company that understands the unpredictable nature of the elder-care challenges facing employees allows employees to feel dedicated to both their jobs and their families. Employed elder caregivers can benefit greatly from having flexible, customized work arrangements. Some companies recognize that employees often need more than personal or vacation time to deal with family-related crises, especially those related to elder care. In response, some employers include policy language allowing employees to use sick leave to care for sick children and other family members. Many companies combine personal sick days with family sick days, giving employees a certain number of days off each year that can be used for either personal sick time, when a family member is sick or some combination of both. However, there is typically no increase given in actual number of days off, with the majority of companies allowing three to 12 days off per year for family illness.

Financial Assistance/Financial Planning

Subsidized Emergency or Respite In-Home Elder-Care Services

Elderly relatives occasionally need emergency care in their homes or in employees' homes, either because of illness or accident or because of some other disruption in their regular schedules. A few companies offer employees help in finding and paying for emergency in-home elder care. Emergency elder-care services are usually subsidized by employers as a way of ensuring that employees will be able to use the program, resulting in reduced absenteeism. Employers often stipulate limits or a maximum number of days or hours that an employee can use this service during a year or some other specified period of time.

In rare instances, an employer, or a consortium of employers, may subsidize full-time in-home elder-care services. This has occurred because employees frequently rely on community-based services, like a home health aide, to care for their older adult relative during the hours they are at work. Without this care option, many employed elder caregivers would not be able to work. Unfortunately, home health aides are typically underpaid and many have no certification, which creates care arrangements that at best may be unpredictable. In response to this need, some employers are subsidizing employees' home health aide expenses.

Direct Elder-Care Services

Although still relatively rare, some companies have established breakthrough direct service programs to meet the elder-care needs of their employees. Currently not used by large numbers of employees, these programs are charting new ground and will likely become more common in the future. They could include geriatric care managers, support for community-based services, adult-care centers, intergenerational care and life design programs.

Geriatric Care Managers

Geriatric care managers are doing the job families used to do, helping move their elders through a system that is increasingly complex. Geriatric care managers specialize in understanding the complex maze of services available to older adults. These professionals assess an older adult's specific needs, link the older adult to resources that will address those needs and follow up to make sure the older adult is getting the best possible care available. By using a geriatric care manager to connect to the most appropriate resources specific to an elder's need, long-distance caregivers can extend their reach into the older relative's community. This also gives the older relative a local advocate and the family an educator on a variety of geriatric issues. The services of a geriatric care manager may be subsidized by the employer, and in some cases are offered through the resource and referral vendor.

Supports for Community-Based Services

Some companies are investing in community programs that provide services for older adults as a way to expand the supply and improve the quality of elder care around the country and in areas where employees work and live.

Adult-Care Centers

Some older adults need care during the day but are otherwise healthy enough to stay in their own homes. These centers are typically staffed by physical therapists, nurses, occupational therapists, geriatric aides and support workers. Adult day-care centers can meet the needs of employees and their elderly relatives and are an option a few companies have chosen to develop.

Intergenerational Care Programs

In some cases, companies that are presently supporting on-site or near-site child care may consider adult or intergenerational day care as appropriate add-ons. There are a few state governments that encourage the development of elder-care facilities. Michigan has provided tax incentives to companies developing intergenerational day care.

The goal of intergenerational programming is typically to do the following:

- Provide children with accurate information and knowledge about the elderly that will enable them to form positive, realistic concepts of and attitudes toward the elderly.

- Expose children to an unbiased look at the diversity of older people, teaching them to value the many and varied characteristics, attributes and qualities of the elderly.
- Enable children to feel positively about their own aging and about the elderly, and offer the elders planned interaction with young children.

Implementing a New Elder-Care Program

There is no one way to proceed when developing a corporate elder-care program, and there are many opportunities to experiment. In order to plan effectively, the organization should consider the following:

- Who will be covered or eligible under the program/policy - usually the parent, in-law or spouse of an active employee.
- What types of programs and policies to offer.
- Where to provide services - near the workplace, where employees live or where elders live.
- Frequency of services — an ongoing program or an intermittent program.

Before approaching the development of new programs, the company should assess existing programs and policies. Most companies have some programs and policies in place that would be helpful to employees with elder-care concerns. However, in many cases, the programs and policies have not been packaged to reflect the assistance they provide for elder care. The first step in creating an elder-care program is to take a look at existing programs and policies and see how they might be organized as part of an elder-care program. Some programs and policies might not currently have an elder-care component but could easily be adapted. For example, if the company currently conducts wellness seminars that focus on medical issues, the topics might be extended to include issues of concern to employees dealing with elder care.

The methods used to determine elder-care needs can be similar to those used to assess child care or other work-life needs. Some companies choose to undertake an employee survey just to assess elder-care concerns. The assessment can be useful when companies are determining the most pressing needs of working caregivers; analyzing the company's current policies, benefits and services; and identifying the gap between employees' needs and existing policies. An assessment will make it easier to identify and create a list of recommendations for new programs or policies that will address specific employee caregiver needs.

It can be extremely beneficial to involve an expert on elder-care issues in the assessment and planning process. The elder-care expert should understand both the viable options for support and the special issues of employed caregivers and corporate involvement.

Evaluating an Elder-Care Program

Some companies run into difficulty when evaluating the effectiveness of elder-care programs. One of the first questions usually asked is, "How many employees use the program or policy?" Although this question provides an interesting measure, answers to the following additional questions may produce a more accurate evaluation of the program's impact than can utilization figures alone:

- Did the program or policy address employees' need? If not, why not?
- What is the overall objective of the program?
- How well does the program or policy meet its objectives?
- How well was it communicated?
- How would employee caregivers change the program or policy to make it more helpful?
- What other kind of support do employee caregivers report needing?

Such questions provide qualitative data that can be most helpful in determining if a program has met its objectives and how best to modify it in the future. Programs might be evaluated by tracking utilization using a questionnaire, an evaluation or feedback form, focus groups and individual interviews.

The Future of Corporate Elder Care

Based on the demographics, elder care will be an issue of increasing importance to workers in the future. Additional research is needed. Centers such as the new Boston College Center on Aging & Work, created with a $3-million grant from the Sloan Foundation, will help explore the impact of elder caregiving on the workplace and will help shape the corporate response to the issue.

It seems clear, given the magnitude of elder-care concerns, that responsibility for addressing employees' elder-care issues cannot be handled by individual corporations by themselves. This responsibility must be a cooperative effort on the part of government, employers, local colleges, advocacy organizations, senior centers, adult day-care programs and other organizations. Companies can play an important role in actively encouraging public-private partnerships. Collaborative partnerships, perhaps, offer the most promise for innovation and new resource development.

Chapter 6
Work-Life Effectiveness as a Catalyst for Organizational Change

6

What Is Organizational Change?

There is no single definition of organizational change. Much of the change that's occurred as a result of work-life efforts in the past might be considered change with a small "c" or "tinkering around the edges." However, much of the work that's needed today is focused on creating enduring change that truly challenges the assumptions, beliefs and behavior of companies and changes them. This type of change may be considered transformational, or change with a capital "C."

At the beginning of the 20th century, ideas about organizational change presumed that people were motivated exclusively by money, that any change should aim to improve how managers could control employees and lower costs, and that all corporate environments were basically the same. Organizational change was used in command-and-control workplaces where management wanted to maximize control and minimize risks and costs. In these situations, organizational change is done "to" employees with the expectation that they will comply with whatever changes they are told to implement. In reality, people — and thus organizations — rarely change because they are told to do so. In our current human-capital environment and knowledge economy, we know that people are motivated by a range of complex variables. We recognize that organizational change is most successful when it is based on empowering employees and involving them in making their own decisions. In today's world, organizational change involves whole systems and requires shared learning, information and leadership.

In this chapter, we will explore concepts of organizational change as well as some of the more recent developments in work-life that relate to diversity, health and wellness, and the concept of the importance of people, or human capital, as an asset.

Organizational Change Today

Today's economy of globalization and rapid change has produced a new paradigm of organizational change. This paradigm is based on the concept that change takes place by looking at the organization as a whole system. According to Peter Senge, organizational change can be accomplished by using the interrelationships among structure, processes and people within an organization. Also involved are learning and reflecting on one's assumptions and beliefs, interpreting and understanding these assumptions and beliefs, and then designing new ways to work.

This approach to internal organizational change presupposes that since an organization is made up of people, change happens when these people change the way they think, which in turn leads to changes in how they make decisions and act. With this approach to organizational change, people themselves change. Organizational change of this nature is capital "C" change, a genuine transformation, and is sometimes called "organizational transformation." An organizational-transformation approach means involving people at all levels of the organization in participating in the visualization of the future, assessing the current state and generating solutions to move toward the future. Organizational transformation works best in workplaces characterized by high involvement and shared decision-making.

The main challenge associated with organizational transformation is that it's a long, time-consuming process that requires constant attention and commitment from people, especially leaders. Since most of today's organizations are still hierarchical, organizational transformation means that leaders must guide the change. Yet the demands of shareholders and financial institutions may cause leaders to bow to short-term pressures at the expense of longer-term change processes. Additionally, organizations often inadvertently stifle examination of assumptions and the questioning of decisions by making such actions too risky, by imposing sanctions or penalties for challenging the status quo. Current attempts at organizational transformation include matrix organizations, reengineering and quality efforts. However, to date, many of these efforts have not been successful. This is because, for example, matrix organizations represent the creation of teams from different functions that work together on particular projects to foster greater collaboration and systemic integration, yet these people still protect their own territory, rely on short-term quantitative measures, and focus on daily operations and short-term planning. A possible reason for this behavior is that the majority of executive-leadership styles conform to the traditional pyramid style, which reflects the type of organization in which most executives have spent their careers.

Effective leadership in the Information Age needs to be very different from the leadership of the Industrial Age. Leaders need to reflect on and be willing to challenge the assumptions that guide their decisions and actions, yet they often appear to be the most reluctant group within any organization to engage in reflection among themselves and across their peer group. Senge describes today's leader as a designer, a steward and a teacher. As a designer, a leader helps build a foundation of purpose and articulates core values. As a steward, a leader puts the needs of others, including employees, first. As a teacher, a leader surfaces people's beliefs, assumptions and prejudgments in order to help people envision new views of reality and see many possibilities. Some organizations today are providing experiences that encourage managers to consider how their own decisions and actions can be changed. Such changes include those that foster an environment where engagement, commitment, diversity and flexibility can flourish. Managers who are able to implement such changes are rewarded, and their successful implementation of goals related to work-life encourages ongoing organizational transformation.

The main premise behind organizational transformation is that change is everyone's business and that real, sustainable change is only possible by involving people at all levels in the organization, including those involved with customers and suppliers. The most effective way to transform an organization is through honest, open dialogue among different people connected to the organization who are willing to look inward and examine their own beliefs and actions. This learning and sharing of information — often promoted by work-life and diversity professionals — generates an understanding of the need for change and highlights where the change champions and opportunities are.

Work-Life Perspective on Organizational Change

What's the connection between organizational change and the work-life movement? As research has shown, companies with happy employees perform better. Human resources professionals have long based their careers on that assumption; however, it took Sears to prove it with a classic study showing quantitatively that a 5-percent increase in employee satisfaction resulted in a 1.2-percent increase in company sales. In order to accomplish this goal, what's needed is a holistic approach to work-life effectiveness that includes diversity, health/wellness and a human-capital approach that can be the catalyst to increase employee satisfaction, commitment, engagement and productivity. Consider these findings:

• One in three American employees is chronically overworked, while 54 percent have felt overwhelmed at some time in the past month by how much work they had to complete, according to *Overwork in America: When the Way We Work Becomes Too Much*, a 2004 study by Families and Work Institute.

The more overworked employees are:

- More likely to make mistakes at work. Twenty percent of employees reporting high overwork levels say they make a lot of mistakes at work, versus none of those who experience low overwork levels.

- More likely to feel angry at their employers for expecting them to do so much. Thirty-nine percent of employees experiencing high overwork levels say they feel very angry toward their employers, versus only 1 percent who experience low overwork levels.

- More likely to resent co-workers who don't work as hard as they do. Thirty-four percent of employees who experience high overwork levels versus only 12 percent of those experiencing low overwork levels say they *often* or *very often* resent their co-workers.

- More likely to have higher levels of stress, using a standardized measure of stress that has been correlated in other research with physical health problems. Only 6 percent who experience low overwork levels are highly stressed, compared with 36 percent of those who are highly overworked.

- The number of full-time or part-time employees who reported high job stress rose to 45 percent in 2002, up from 37 percent the year before, according to a National Institute of Occupational Safety and Health study. An estimated 40 percent of U.S. workers reported their jobs were very or extremely stressful, with 25 percent calling their jobs the greatest stress factor in their lives.

- An estimated 70 percent of the more than 1,500 participants felt they didn't have a healthy "balance" between their work and their personal lives, according to a 2002 survey on work-life by online job board TrueCareers.

- In a 2001 national study by PricewaterhouseCoopers, three out of 10 employees reported chronic overwork and said they are more likely to do the following:

  - Look for another job (49 percent vs. 30 percent).

  - Feel anger toward their employers (43 percent vs. 3 percent).

  - Experience work-life conflict.

  - Report high levels of stress, poor coping skills and sleep problems.

  - Report making mistakes at work (17 percent vs. 1 percent for nonoverworked employees).

- The United States leads in long work hours and in hours of work increasing, with the highest hours for U.S. managers and professional workers, according to a 2003 study by Jerry Jacobs, University of Pennsylvania. A WFD Consulting study found that long work hours (>50/week) correlate to increased burnout and intention to leave, not employee commitment.

- Stress costs American employers approximately $300 billion per year in lost productivity and health-care and replacement costs, according to the Stress Institute of America's latest findings, with 200 million lost days and costs of treating depression and anxiety greater than $50 billion annually. Eighty-eight percent of employers report stress-related issues harm productivity and retention according to studies by Bill Ortbals, Magellan Behavioral Health (2001); · International Labor Organization's Mental Health in the Workplace (October 2000); and Roper Starch Worldwide Inc.

- A 1999 study of a random sample of 1,000 Americans conducted by the John J. Heldrich Center for Workforce Development at Rutgers University and the Center for Survey Research and Analysis at the University of Connecticut found that, compared with 88 percent who express concerns about working conditions and 71 percent who are concerned about job security, a whopping 95 percent of employed Americans are worried that their work takes away too much time from their families — making this the leading concern of American workers (Austin American Statesman, March 18, 1999).

- Staff with work-family conflicts are three times more likely to consider quitting (43 percent vs. 14 percent), and over one-third of employees frequently experience negative spillover from the job to their personal lives (e.g., bad mood, low energy level, poor quality of time for family and friends) (Source: *National Study of the Changing Workforce*, Families and Work Institute, 1997).

- Spherion's 2004 *Emerging Workforce Study* shows a workforce that is surprisingly confident and self-reliant, poised to walk out on employers at the first opportunity. The survey sliced across all industries, age groups, demographics, geography, sexes and job levels. The response was the same across the board. While being successful at work and moving up the career ladder were top priorities for 35 percent of those surveyed, 86 percent said work fulfillment and work-life "balance" were their No. 1 career priority.

With indicators like these, it makes sense that focusing on work-life issues can yield positive business results. In fact, multiple studies have proven that creating a more supportive work environment benefits not only employees but also their colleagues and their employers.

- Deloitte & Touche found that senior-management support and formal introduction of flexible schedules resulted in $20.6 million in savings due to reduced turnover in 2001.

- A collegial, flexible workplace is associated with a 9-percent increase in market value, according to a 2001 Watson Wyatt *Human Capital Index Study*.

- Workers in companies with high flexibility are absent less than half as often as those in low-flexibility companies. Workers in these companies also experience less stress, fewer time-management problems and less work interference with family (Duxbury, Conference Board presentation, March 1998).

- A 2003 study by Towers Perrin and consultant Gang & Gang found that more than half of the employees surveyed feel negative. One-third feel "intensely" negative because of excessive workload, concerns about management's abilities to lead, anxiety about the future, lack of challenge and insufficient recognition, including feeling that pay is not commensurate with performance. Among those who are intensely negative, 28 percent are actively looking for a new job or are poised to leave at the first opportunity, and 25 percent plan to stay in their current job, suggesting a large group of disaffected workers hanging on to their jobs and potentially adversely affecting both colleagues and customers. Their ideal workplace, say employees, is one that gives them a sense of self-worth — a feeling of confidence, competency and control, results (the contributions they could make to the success of the business) and rewards.

In its 1996 study, *Relinking Life and Work: Toward a Better Future*, the Ford Foundation argued that a dual agenda in the workplace — one that considers both the employer's and the employee's needs — not only eases employees' lives but also leads to enhanced productivity and other tangible business benefits. The study was based on six years of research in three major companies (Corning, Tandem Computers and Xerox) and created a new work-life frontier. According to the research, the process of challenging old assumptions and cultural beliefs that underlie work and work-life frees employees to think more creatively about work in general and provides companies with a strategic opportunity to achieve a more innovative workplace.

The study also found that rigidities — in scheduling, in roles, in processes — that impede work-life effectiveness also (and probably not coincidentally) impede efficient business functioning. It recommended that managers and employees be evaluated and rewarded not only based on possessing and applying skills in their work, but also based on the way in which they interact with one another as supervisors and colleagues. If a manager is evaluated on effectively planning a project, it could begin to change a culture where overtime is assumed and expected to a culture that sees overtime as unnecessary and unrealistic, resulting in more personal time for team members. The way performance is measured and the way employees are compensated can drive and shape new employee behaviors and values. According to the research, an organization will begin to transform all areas of itself when it evaluates and rewards managers for support of work-life effectiveness and encourages appropriate attitudes, capabilities and actions within all areas of job responsibilities.

As Randall Tobias, former chairman of the board and chief executive officer of Eli Lilly and Company, said in his 1996 Conference Board presentation, "Eli Lilly is addressing work-family concerns because — to the people on whom we depend — these issues are as important as ensuring that our facilities have lights that enable them to see, that our PCs are positioned so they're least likely to get carpal syndrome and that they get their paychecks on time." Tobias explained his company's position on managing work and personal life responsibilities as follows:

> Let me give you an example of the cultural barriers we must overcome. We all know people who regularly work 12, 13 or more hours a day and rarely take much, if any, of their vacation time. When we ask why these people behave that way, and frequently expect others to do the same, the answer, in most cases, is that they've been rewarded for this work style or they've seen others rewarded for it.
>
> In many cases, these employees are striving to create and reinforce an image of heroic commitment. All too often, I might add, this work style may deflect their management and their colleagues from focusing on their actual results. What's more, this style not only leads to imbalances in the employee's personal and professional lives, but can also create similar problems for colleagues whose schedules are controlled or affected by this employee's work style.

When I observe that people are consistently working late into the night and on weekends, I frequently question them directly about their personal effectiveness and ask them point-blank about the reasons why they can't do a better job of managing their time and working more efficiently. It's a critical part of our commitment to make sure that people stop doing things that are no longer important, start doing things that are important, and do those right things as effectively and efficiently as possible.

It's clear that future management practices need to place more emphasis on "people skills." Consider these thoughts from *Ideas That Will Shape the Future of Management Practice* (Donald L. Bohl et al., Organizational Dynamics, 1996):

Real world organizations and their management continue to give priority to — and to do quite well with — the functional and technological sides of the organization. But the human side continues to be "downsized" — in importance as well as head count. The fact of the matter is that human resources do make a difference. As successful real-world organizations and startup companies have discovered, people may be the only sustainable competitive advantage that an organization has in our global, informational world.

Human resources management practices of the future will have to be considered as a package of practices. All these practices send signals on what employees should do, what is rewarded and what is not. The boundaryless, virtual, networked, horizontal and learning organizations all require a transfer of decision-making to those employees closest to the customers. Moving decision-making authority down requires that top managers trust employees at lower levels to make accurate and informed decisions. These forms of organizations provide the advantage of internal flexibility, while at the same time adapting to changes in their environment. There is closeness between members of the organization and their customers and suppliers. These designs require managers to listen to customers and change their products and distribution systems to meet customer needs, rather than telling customers what to expect.

Despite all the experiments with reengineering, it has become clear that reengineering has not met expectations. Even promoters like Hammer and Champy have admitted disappointment. Part of the problem with current efforts to create a new strategy for improving profitability and competitiveness is that work and personal life issues have rarely been used as levers for change and are rarely thought to be integral to business strategy. Most companies think of work-life issues as diversions from the real strategic aims of the organization, or as some simple add-ons that can boost morale for downsizing survivors, win awards or help achieve "employer of choice" status. This resistance must be met with a more holistic, integrated approach that incorporates a human capital approach that includes diversity and health and wellness agendas.

Organizational Change: Work-Life and Diversity, Health/Wellness and Human Capital

Organizational change can be influenced by a close connection with work-life and diversity and health and wellness initiatives and a clear focus on the importance of human capital.

Work-Life and Diversity

Work-life is fundamentally a diversity issue, and not just because it impacts women or has different significance in different geographies around the world. The life and career cycle of each employee is unique. We can no longer generalize about the needs of a particular employee or even a group of employees because they are women, live in a certain country or have just begun or are nearing the end of their careers. Everyone's definition of work-life effectiveness is personal and changes as life and work change. This requires that the individual, not just the organization, eventually come to terms with where the boundaries between work and personal life should be. The company will always want as much time and effort as the employee is willing to give, even when we can document that being a workaholic may not be good for the employee's health or the organization's ultimate success.

In today's Information Age, with limitless accessibility and the opportunity to work all the time, everywhere, it is up to individual employees to challenge their own assumptions and set limits on work. In the past, the organization provided those limits and articulated its own assumptions, and that's still important. But, for most employees, the days when the company provides strict rules about when to work (or when work stays in a building and employees leave work behind when they leave the building) are over. We need to find ways to turn off all the connectivity and enjoy life, to find ways to help employees transition successfully from high-work times to lower work times or to take time out from work all together. Until employees are encouraged, and in fact rewarded, for setting their own limits and finding "a life" outside of work, the worker, workplace, families and communities will continue to suffer.

Work-Life and Health and Wellness

Many health issues have been documented to be work-related, not just in the obvious areas where workers are exposed to dangerous materials and so forth, but in such situations where employees don't have control over time and are forced to make impossible choices between their work and their families. With rising health-care costs, employers are beginning to "connect the dots" and are trying to understand some of the health-related issues that can be addressed by creating a more supportive work environment. Healthier employees can be more productive and engaged. In fact, research has shown that the lack of "presenteeism" — being able to bring one's whole self to work and not be distracted by other pressures — costs employers a great deal in lost productivity because employees may bring their "bodies, but not their brains" to work.

Today's work challenges demand a fully engaged workforce. When employees don't feel well, come to work sick so they can save their sick days for their child's illness, and are stressed because they have to choose between a personal need and work, their productivity and creativity suffers. Companies are developing wellness programs to address some of these issues, but as long as these initiatives are "siloed" and not integrated as part of a holistic strategy, they will have limited results. Data must be collected from a variety of sources — turnover, absenteeism, health records and so forth — and analyzed over time along with other work-life related information in order to fully understand and address health and wellness issues and be able to plan cross-functional, long-term interventions from a work-life perspective.

Work-Life and Human Capital

In many ways, the work-life field has reached a crossroad. There is sufficient data available to document the need for work-life effectiveness and its importance to the success of the company. However, resistance persists. It is only with a human-capital perspective that we can begin to understand why that resistance has not been addressed, and find the right framework to create the changes that are necessary to truly have work-life effectiveness. I believe the new human capital framework, as described by Dr. Sandy Burud in her award-winning book, *Leveraging The New Human Capital*, points us in the right direction. Work-life no longer needs to try to be the "tail wagging the dog." With a human-capital perspective, it becomes obvious and necessary. The human-capital perspective defines people as assets — not costs — that have value to the organization and must be treated as any asset, that is, nurtured and invested in over the long term. It requires the examination of core beliefs regarding people, business and the role of work, as well as a new definition for the principles and practices that are the operational guidelines for the organization. It is only by working from this new perspective that work-life can assume its new role in changing organizations so people can be productive and also have a life.

Where Do We Go from Here?

The promotion of corporate attention to work-life issues needs to be made on the basis of what's good for business. For the most part, employees have been expected to fit their lives into the workplace rather than the workplace acknowledging the human side of the enterprise. While this emphasis from a business perspective may have been understandable, it ignores the impact on employees, their families, customers and the society at large. Few organizations have questioned whether their policies are actually good for families or personal well-being, and if they aren't, how they can expect to meet business objectives. If work hours are strictly defined, do people feel trusted and will they still exhibit the initiative necessary for competitive advantage? If rewards and recognition are linked strongly to the number of hours worked, how is output valued? If a woman on maternity leave is encouraged to come back to work before she or her baby are ready, what is the impact on health, productivity and morale? For the most part, companies don't account for these costs to organizations, individual employees or their families and communities.

Most workplace policies have been designed to encourage employees to work more hours and be more productive, which results in an ironic definition of what's "family-friendly." Many companies with part-time arrangements penalize those who work part time. Success in firms that allow part-time work is often defined as 50-hour instead of 70-hour workweeks. In the end, what is created is an awkward value structure that gives priority to the organization's perceived needs and devalues those of the individual. This structure doesn't take into account the fact that the organization's needs cannot be met when the individual's needs have been ignored or sacrificed.

A traditional perspective views the relationship between the organization and the individual as one-directional. Addressing work and personal life issues from this perspective, therefore, means removing any distractions or inconveniences that might get in the way of work. It is assumed that work and life coexist, but not that they are linked — or fundamentally reciprocal. From the individual's perspective, work and personal life are parts of a whole. While both the organization and the individual would agree that "bringing the whole person" to the job is important in order to achieve full utilization of workers, the organization's concept of "person" is often only as "worker."

The current terminology in the work-life field may not be adequate to describe the new perspective. The new paradigm is not about tinkering at the margins of the organization and doing something "nice" for employees. It is not about restructuring and moving boxes around. It is about real transformational change. And it is time to challenge the long-held beliefs about the ways of doing business that are out of synch with the needs of a workforce primarily made up of knowledge and service workers in the Information Age.

Unless there's a real appreciation for the complexities of the relationship between work, family, community and personal life, and a concern for the sources of conflict deep within the organization, or what Dr. Sandy Burud calls "core beliefs," solutions will continue to be of limited help to individuals and organizations. Research and company experience have begun to reveal that effective solutions call for fundamental changes in the way people are recruited, valued, managed, trained and promoted. The new focus must be on trying to understand the relationship between the work environment (cultural norms, managerial practices and work processes) and the factors that have been shown to be the strongest predictors of work-life conflict, stress and negative work behaviors.

In challenging economic times, with job security declining and workloads increasing, the importance of transforming organizations has increased. In addition to removing inconsistencies in the organization and finding ways to support real flexibility and employee engagement, the focus needs to shift to how employees are treated. We need to consider issues such as the impact of work-life on production and service delivery, customer needs and expectations, team effectiveness, community relations, security and business continuity. We must also examine the connections between employee, family and community health and well-being and the success of the organization. Where once work-life seemed to be concerned only with employee needs and services, now the field must also focus on true organizational change if its mission is to be achieved.

Appendix

Flexible Work Schedules Survey Brief
State of the Work-Life Profession 2005
Employee Work-Life Survey Sample
The Seven Categories of Work-Life Effectiveness

Flexible Work Schedules Survey Brief

WorldatWork, the Alliance for Work-Life Progress and the Regional Research
Institute for Human Services at Portland State University
October 2005

Introduction & Methodology

In August 2005, WorldatWork, The Alliance for Work-Life Progress (AWLP) and the
Regional Research Institute for Human Services at Portland State University
conducted a survey to identify trends in work-life policies and practices. Survey
participants were asked about the prevalence and use of flexible work arrangements,
as well as their level of knowledge about various work-life and dependent-care issues.

For the purposes of this survey, "flexible work arrangements" refer to choices
about the time and/or location that work is conducted (Rau, 2003)[1]. For example,
altering starting and quitting times or working from home are both considered
flexible work arrangements. Here, a "formal" flexible work arrangement is written
into organizational policy and the employee and supervisor must follow organizational
procedure, while "informal" flexible arrangements are based on supervisory discretion
and can be undocumented (Eaton, 2003)[2].

Surveys were emailed to 4,645 WorldatWork and AWLP members, and 552
participants completed the survey. Results of individual questions are presented in
the "Detailed Survey Results" section. Please note that totals may not always equal
100 percent due to rounding differences.

Executive Summary

Flexible work schedules and work-life supports create opportunities for both
employees and employers. Employers appreciate the boost in productivity and morale
while employees reap the benefits of structuring work around their lives instead of
the other way around. Although flexible work scheduling can be a win-win situation
under the right circumstances, it goes against the traditional Western work culture.
In the United States specifically, the customary work ethic has always boasted long
hours and face time at the office as essential ingredients of the recipe to success.

How much has the modern Western work culture welcomed flexibility as a viable business strategy, and how far do we still have to go?

While results of this study indicate workplace cultures in the United States are trying to incorporate flexibility and enhance work-life integration for some employees with particular needs, there are more steps to take before flexible schedules evolve beyond isolated, individual perks. Employees who disclose a personal reason for a flexible work request are more likely to have it approved in three out of four organizations, although something more than "I would like more control over my schedule" appears necessary. Requests due to medical, child-care or other urgent personal matters are likely to be approved, perhaps because a "good enough reason" is required to trump the traditional presumption about when, where and how we work.

A mounting awareness of the need for work-life balance is beginning to erode the traditional business adage that counseled employees to leave their personal lives at home. Over half of participants regard their organizational cultures as receptive to handling personal issues on company time, although 40 percent say the attitude is highly dependent on individual supervisors, suggesting the potential for multiple cultures to exist in one workplace. In order for organizations to fully capitalize on the benefits of flexible work, employees will need visible acknowledgement and encouragement from organization leaders.

Other highlights of the survey include the following:

- Nine in 10 organizations participating in this survey offer a flexible scheduling program, and more than half of flexibility programs operate informally. Forty-four percent have a formal policy, while about 5 percent do not have a flexible work program.

- About one in three participants maintain their work culture does not encourage employees to work flexible schedules, even though they are offered.

- The most common way for employees to request a flexible work arrangement in nine out of 10 organizations is to verbally contact the immediate supervisor.

- What factors are most important to employers when considering a flexible work request? Most frequently, employers weigh the impact on coverage, the ability of the employee to complete his or her duties and the impact on customers most heavily when deciding whether to grant a flexible work request.

Detailed Survey Results

Flexible work arrangements operate on an informal basis in more than 50 percent of organizations, although only 44 percent have implemented formal policies and procedures (See Figure 1 on page 159.) Only about 5 percent do not have either type of policy.

Formal flexible work policies are fairly new to most organizations. About one in four organizations created their programs in the last five years, and another

16 percent added them in the last six to 10 years. (See Figure 2.) Only about 7 percent of policies have aged more than 10 years, and a full 45 percent still have no formal policies regarding flexible work.

Which employees are eligible for flexible work schedules? Salaried employees have the widest array of flexible arrangements at their disposal, at least on an informal basis. (See Figure 3 on page 160.) About half of the organizations surveyed report their salaried employees can exercise flex time on a daily basis, and slightly more than half can telecommute. Hourly employees have somewhat more restricted access to flexible work. About one in three organizations offer flex time to hourly employees, including daily flex time, on an informal basis. Telework, defined as working from home on a full-time basis and rarely visiting the worksite, is not available for any employees at a majority (60 percent) of organizations. Employees also lack access to job sharing either formally or informally in 61 percent of the organizations surveyed.

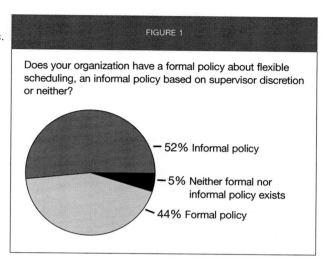

FIGURE 1

Does your organization have a formal policy about flexible scheduling, an informal policy based on supervisor discretion or neither?

- 52% Informal policy
- 5% Neither formal nor informal policy exists
- 44% Formal policy

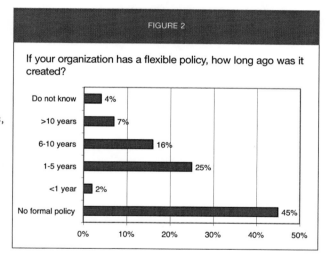

FIGURE 2

If your organization has a flexible policy, how long ago was it created?

Do not know	4%
>10 years	7%
6-10 years	16%
1-5 years	25%
<1 year	2%
No formal policy	45%

Although salaried employees have an edge in exercising flexible work schedules, a majority of organizations make flexible benefits available to different types of employees. (See Figure 4 on page 160.) Eight in 10 employers offer flexible arrangements to professional employees. Clerical/administrative, technical and managerial employees can access flexible work arrangements in three out of four organizations.

FIGURE 3

Which of the following flexible work arrangements is available in your organization? (Check all that apply.)[3]

	Salaried		Hourly		Not Available
	Formal	Informal	Formal	Informal	
Flex time	37%	49%	29%	31%	15%
Daily flex time	13%	53%	8%	30%	33%
Compressed workweek	24%	23%	23%	16%	46%
Telecommute	28%	54%	15%	19%	19%
Telework	18%	16%	9%	6%	60%
Part-time work schedules	36%	27%	32%	20%	28%
Job Share	19%	10%	14%	9%	61%

FIGURE 4

Which of the following types of employees have access to and/or use flexible work arrangements in your organization? (Check all that apply.)

	Accessible	Used by more than 50% of employees	Not applicable
Clerical/Administrative	73%	13%	19%
Technical	74%	14%	16%
Professional	84%	15%	10%
Managerial	78%	14%	14%
Sales/Customer Service	54%	11%	28%

Asking whether flexible arrangements are accessible and whether more than 50 percent of employees in the category exercise flexible scheduling are two different questions. Indeed, access is more typical than majority practice. (See Figure 4.) Only a small percentage of employers report that flexible schedules are used by more than 50 percent of employees in each category. For example, 15 percent of organizations report that more than 50 percent of their professional employees actually flex their schedules.

Flexible work arrangements may be accessible, but workplace culture can play a huge role in determining whether employees actually make use of the opportunity. About 56 percent of organizations report their culture is supportive of employees taking time at work for personal issues, although a sizable minority (40 percent) say the level of support is highly dependent on individual supervisors. (See Figure 5.) Given the potential number of departments, a schism within organizations may exist where some employees feel flexibility and work-life supports are acceptable while others believe the practices are frowned upon. Only 5 percent acknowledge that their organizations do not support employees taking time at work for routine personal or family issues.

Although flexible work arrangements exist within a majority of organizations, employees may not feel free to utilize the option. Employees may perceive a gap between the offer of flexibility and the acceptability of actually practicing it. About one in three HR professionals report that their cultures do not encourage the use of flexible work arrangements. (See Figure 6.)

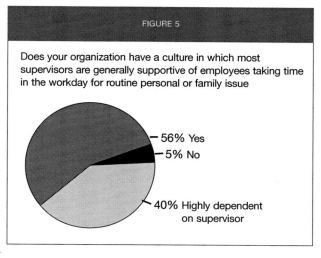

FIGURE 5

Does your organization have a culture in which most supervisors are generally supportive of employees taking time in the workday for routine personal or family issue

- 56% Yes
- 5% No
- 40% Highly dependent on supervisor

Supervisors play an important role in arranging flexible schedules. As depicted in Figure 7 on page 162, almost 90 percent of survey respondents cite contacting the immediate supervisor as the most common way to plan a flexible schedule. Less than half ask employees to e-mail their direct supervisors, and 36 percent request that employees verbally contact human resources.

Establishing policies and practices related to flexible work resides with HR departments in the majority of organizations surveyed. (See Figure 8 on page 162.) While HR professionals may be responsible for formal policies and practices, many flexible programs operate on an informal level, with supervisors approving and implementing the schedules. About one in three respondents indicate that their flexible work program is decentralized, with decisions made at the line or supervisor level.

Employees who discuss why they need a flexible schedule increase the likelihood of securing approval for the request in three out of four organizations.

FIGURE 6

From your perspective, what is the primary reason employees do not use flexible work arrangements?

Even though the organization offers them, the culture doesn't encourage the use of flexible work arrangements	34%
Flexible work arrangements do not meet employee needs	11%
Employees don't know about flexible work arrangements	5%
Do not know	13%
Not applicable	19%
Other	18%

(See Figure 9 on page 163.)
Flexible scheduling may not
be such an acceptable option
that it can be secured
automatically or without any
particular reason, although
about 15 percent of
organizations indicated
disclosure has no bearing on
the decision. Nearly one in
10 do not want to hear the
personal reasons behind the
request out of concern for
potential liability.

Flexible scheduling has
practical implications for
both the employee and
the employer. We asked
participants how much
weight they assign certain
factors when evaluating a
flexible work proposal.
The results are shown in
Figure 10 on page 163.
The most dominant
considerations involved
the employee's ability to
meet job responsibilities,

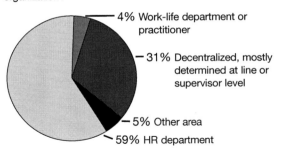

FIGURE 7

Which of the following are ways employees can request flexible work arrangements? (Check all that apply.)

Verbally contact immediate supervisor	89%
E-mail direct supervisor	49%
Verbally contact human resources	36%
E-mail the HR department	23%
Complete standardized paperwork	22%
Verbally contact co-workers	5%
File a request form online	5%
Verbally contact work-life department	4%
E-mail work-life department	3%

FIGURE 8

Where does the primary responsibility for policies and practices related to flexible work arrangements reside in your organization?

4% Work-life department or practitioner

31% Decentralized, mostly determined at line or supervisor level

5% Other area

59% HR department

impact on customers and impact on coverage. The nature of the job duties was afforded significant weight in 78 percent of organizations. A majority also heavily weighs the supervisor's recommendation and the employee's past performance.

Disclosure of the personal reasons prompting a flexible work request helps many employees secure their employer's approval. Does disclosure of any reason make approval more likely, or are employers likely to respond more favorably to certain types of reasons than others? Survey participants were asked how likely they were to grant flexible work requests given a variety of different reasons. (See Figure 11 on page 164.) Granting a flexible schedule request due to terminal illness of a family member was "very likely" to be approved in 56 percent of organizations, and short-term child-care difficulties would "likely" earn approval in 50 percent of organizations. Employees who ask to work flexible schedules so they can seek drug or alcohol treatment would "likely" be granted permission in eight out of 10 organizations, while asking for flexible work to support a family member's drug rehabilitation would "likely" receive approval in about six out of 10 workplaces.

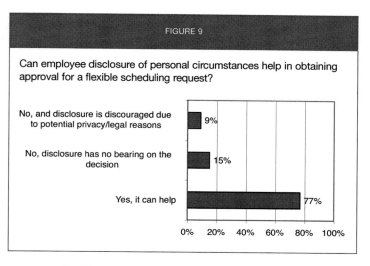

FIGURE 9

Can employee disclosure of personal circumstances help in obtaining approval for a flexible scheduling request?

No, and disclosure is discouraged due to potential privacy/legal reasons	9%
No, disclosure has no bearing on the decision	15%
Yes, it can help	77%

Parents whose children are experiencing behavioral difficulties at school may find their employers somewhat ambivalent about granting a flexible work schedule on that justification. About 44 percent of employers were neither "likely" nor "unlikely" to grant a flexible schedule for a parent whose child was acting out at school, and 43 percent were swayed in neither direction for a parent whose child was expelled from school. Employers were least likely to grant flexible schedules for employees training for a marathon — six in 10 participants said their organizations would be "unlikely" or "very unlikely" to grant such a request. Employers also would be less likely to approve a flexible schedule so an employee can care for a sick animal.

Flexible work schedules can make good business sense for an organization. A variety of outcomes can result from implementing a flexible work program, and

FIGURE 10

In your organization, how much weight is given to the following factors when the average employee's proposal for flexible work is being evaluated?

	Little Weight	Some Weight	Significant Weight	Not Applicable
Employee's ability to continue job responsibilities	<1%	6%	90%	4%
Impact on customers	<1%	8%	86%	5%
Impact on coverage	2%	9%	85%	4%
Employee's job duties	2%	17%	78%	3%
Supervisor's recommendation	3%	24%	68%	5%
Employee's past job performance	5%	30%	60%	5%
Length of time employee needs arrangement	12%	38%	43%	6%
Reason for request	12%	39%	41%	8%
Employee retention	12%	49%	34%	5%

FIGURE 11

The following are some reasons employees give when requesting flexible work arrangements. Please rate how likely it is that approval would be granted for each reason.

	Not likely at all	Unlikely	Neither likely nor unlikely	Likely	Very likely to request grant
Short-term child-care difficulties	2%	4%	13%	50%	32%
Short-term child illness	1%	1%	7%	40%	50%
Family member with health issues	<1%	1%	13%	45%	41%
Terminal illness of family member	<1%	<1%	9%	34%	56%
Ongoing chronic health condition of employee	<1%	2%	13%	40%	44%
Child with ongoing chronic health condition	<1%	2%	16%	43%	38%
Elderly parent needing care	<1%	5%	22%	47%	26%
Child acting out at school	4%	12%	44%	29%	11%
Training for a marathon	23%	35%	30%	9%	3%
Child's therapy appointment	3%	4%	22%	46%	25%
Physical therapy for employee injury	2%	2%	11%	40%	46%
Child expelled from school	6%	13%	43%	25%	13%
Drug or alcohol treatment for self	2%	2%	15%	37%	44%
Drug or alcohol treatment for family	3%	7%	32%	39%	19%
Care for sick animal	20%	25%	36%	14%	5%
Child with disability needing care	1%	2%	18%	44%	35%
Mental health treatment for self	2%	2%	15%	38%	44%
Mental health treatment for family	3%	5%	26%	41%	26%
Self-development (courses, education, lessons)	5%	9%	33%	38%	15%

survey participants were asked to anticipate how their leadership would weight the significance of various business results. (See Figure 12 on page 165.) Three out of four organizations said improving employee satisfaction would be given at least strong consideration, and 72 percent strongly value employee retention. More than half found increasing employee productivity persuasive. Given the effect of stress on productivity, it was surprising that 60 percent of employers perceived declining employee mental health as weak, or holding no weight one way or the other. Perception of fairness among employees also did not sway employers for, or against, implementing flexible work schedules.

Flexible work arrangements operate informally in a majority of organizations. An assumption that flexible work can be worked out on a case-by-case basis with individual supervisors may explain the lack of formal inquiry about employees' flexibility needs. If employee needs are handled at the line or supervisor level, a formal survey of employee needs may be identified as unnecessary and duplicative. As shown in Figure 13 on page 165, 86 percent of organizations in this study do not regularly ask employees about their flexible scheduling needs.

FIGURE 12

From the perspective of your organizational leadership, how strong are the following business reasons for allowing employees to have flexible work schedules?

	Very weak	Weak	Neither strong nor weak	Strong	Very strong
Improves employee retention	3%	5%	21%	45%	27%
Improves employee productivity	4%	8%	31%	37%	21%
Improves employee job satisfaction	3%	3%	17%	52%	25%
Decreases employee stress	3%	8%	31%	42%	16%
Decreases employee mental-health problems	3%	11%	46%	29%	10%
Improves employee commitment	2%	5%	22%	50%	22%
Improves quality of life for employees and families	2%	4%	21%	47%	26%
Improves recruitment of a diverse workforce	4%	11%	31%	36%	19%
Improves employee engagement	3%	7%	29%	44%	18%
Improves employee work-life balance	2%	5%	21%	46%	27%
Improves employee morale	2%	4%	18%	52%	25%
Decreases employee absenteeism	2%	7%	29%	45%	16%
Improves perception of fairness among all employees	4%	15%	42%	28%	10%
Increases the public image of being an employer of choice	5%	8%	30%	40%	17%
Increases social responsibility	6%	13%	42%	28%	11%

Where do HR professionals go to learn about their employees' dependent-care needs? Figure 14 on page 166 demonstrates that most often, they reach out to organizations that are familiar to them, such as HR professional organizations (20 percent) and employee assistance providers (EAPs) (28 percent.) About 16 percent cite child- and elder-care resource services as the best informants. Very few HR professionals turn to professional training or rely on continuing education, both of which were marked by less than 1 percent of participants.

HR professionals also feel fairly comfortable in their level of knowledge about various dependent-care issues. For example, three out of four survey respondents believe they are at least "knowledgeable" about parenting, and 68 percent believe they are at least "knowledgeable" about child development from

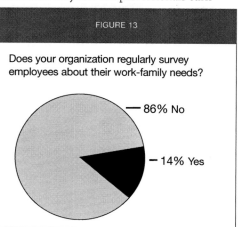

FIGURE 13

Does your organization regularly survey employees about their work-family needs?

— 86% No

— 14% Yes

birth through age 12. (See Figure 15.) They report being less informed about child disabilities and mental health (38 percent each) and adult disabilities (39 percent.)

Employees with questions about benefits are often directed to their HR department. Knowledge about local resources, especially as they relate to employee benefits, seems to be comfortable ground for survey participants. (See Figure 16 on page 167.) Eight in 10 respondents state they are "familiar" or "very familiar" with health-care resources, 63 percent with child care and 61 percent with employee stress management resources. Respondents felt most familiar with child mental-health care options (43 percent), elder care (47 percent) and work-life integration (49 percent).

FIGURE 14

Figure 14: What is the single best resource for information regarding employees' dependent-care issues? (Check one response only.)

EAPs	28%
HR professional organization	20%
Child- and elder-care resource/ referral service	16%
Colleagues	8%
Personal experience	5%
Parent/employee advisory group	3%
World wide web/Internet	3%
Continuing education	<1%
Professional training	<1%
Not applicable	10%

High perceptions of comfort with dependent-care and flexible scheduling needs may account for the relative lack of training that is offered to managers or supervisors. As shown in Figure 17 on page 167, 81 percent of organizations have not offered training about flexible work arrangements for HR professionals in the last two years, and three out of four have not trained HR employees on work-life issues. Supervisors have not been offered training about flexible scheduling or work-life matters in about three quarters of organizations surveyed.

FIGURE 15

Please rate your personal level of knowledge about the following topics related to dependent care.

	Almost no knowledge	Not much knowledge	Neither knowledgeable nor not knowledgeable	Somewhat knowledgeable	Very knowledgeable
Child development, birth-12	9%	10%	13%	44%	24%
Adolescent development, 13-21	10%	14%	21%	42%	13%
Parenting	7%	8%	12%	46%	28%
Elder-care responsibilities	6%	17%	19%	43%	15%
Adult disabilities	11%	21%	29%	33%	6%
Child disabilities	12%	22%	29%	33%	5%
Adult mental health	9%	18%	26%	40%	8%
Children's mental health	12%	22%	29%	33%	5%

FIGURE 16

Please rate your level of familiarity with resources in your community addressing the following work-life issues of employees.

	Very unfamiliar	Unfamiliar	Neither familiar nor unfamiliar	Familiar	Very familiar
Employee stress management	5%	12%	22%	48%	13%
Child care	4%	13%	20%	47%	16%
Parenting	4%	15%	26%	43%	12%
Work-life integration	5%	15%	30%	37%	12%
Health care	2%	6%	11%	48%	33%
Adult mental-health care	5%	17%	25%	41%	12%
Drug and alcohol treatment	5%	15%	25%	43%	12%
Children's mental-health care	6%	21%	29%	35%	8%
Elder care	6%	17%	30%	35%	12%

In order to get a sense of the workplace culture regarding dependent-care needs, participants were asked how much they agreed or disagreed with a series of statements reflecting attitudes toward personal issues. (See Figure 18 on page 168.). The results indicate that respondents believe their workplaces are fairly sympathetic to dependent-care needs and flexible work. For example, 84 percent of respondents reject that their organization has an "unwritten rule" forbidding employees to deal with personal issues at work. Another 75 percent dispute the statement that their organizations look unfavorably on employees who put family needs ahead of their job.

Somewhat inconsistently, 39 percent also indicate that employees are reluctant to ask for flexible work arrangements. What accounts for this perceived hesitation? As shown in Figure 6 on page 161, one in three participants believes employees do not exercise flexible scheduling because the culture ultimately does not support it.

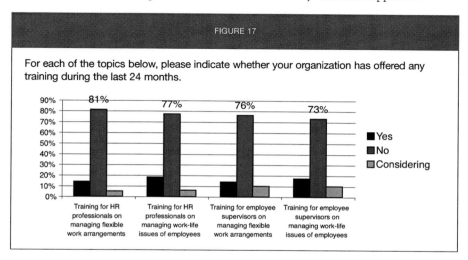

FIGURE 17

For each of the topics below, please indicate whether your organization has offered any training during the last 24 months.

FIGURE 18

For each statement below, please indicate the extent to which you agree or disagree, when you think about your organization[4].

	Strongly Disagree	Somewhat Disagree	Agree Somewhat	Strongly Agree
There is an unwritten rule at my place of employment that you can't take care of family needs on company time.	49%	35%	13%	3%
At my place of employment, employees who put their family or personal needs ahead of their job are not looked on favorably.	37%	38%	22%	4%
If you have a problem managing your work and family responsibilities, the attitude at my place of employment is, "You made your bed, now lie in it."	51%	34%	13%	2%
At my place of employment, employees have to choose between advancing in their jobs and devoting attention to their family or personal lives.	30%	40%	24%	7%
In this organization, parents are encouraged to take time off work to care for their children with ongoing health issues.	7%	31%	45%	17%
In this organization, employees are reluctant to ask for flexible work arrangements.	26%	36%	32%	7%
In this organization, it is OK for parents to receive phone calls at work regarding their children with ongoing emotional or behavioral challenges.	4%	8%	47%	41%
Supervisors in this organization are supportive of the needs of employees who have children with disabilities.	3%	8%	54%	35%
Co-workers in this organization are not supportive of parents of children with emotional or behavioral challenges.	36%	45%	16%	4%

It's possible that while organizations are theoretically amenable to flexible scheduling and other work-life supports, employees may be waiting on acknowledgement from organizational leadership of their genuine acceptability. If key leaders do not openly vocalize their dedication to work-life integration and flexible scheduling, or practice it themselves, employees may remain reluctant to take the initiative.

Respondent Demographics

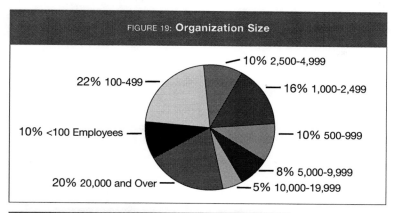

FIGURE 19: **Organization Size**

- 10% 2,500-4,999
- 22% 100-499
- 16% 1,000-2,499
- 10% <100 Employees
- 10% 500-999
- 20% 20,000 and Over
- 8% 5,000-9,999
- 5% 10,000-19,999

FIGURE 20: **Type of Industry**

Manufacturing	16%
Finance and insurance	16%
Other	16%
Professional, scientific and technical	12%
Health care and social assistance	6%
Information	6%
Other services (except public administration)	6%
Utilities	5%
Public administration	4%
Retail	4%
Educational services	2%
Transportation and warehousing	2%
Accommodation and food service	1%
Arts, entertainment and recreation	1%
Administrative support, waste and remediation	<1%
Agriculture	<1%
Construction	<1%
Management of companies and enterprises	<1%
Mining	<1%
Real estate, rental and leasing	<1%
Wholesale trade	<1%

Footnotes

1 Definition adapted from Rau, B. (2003). Flexible work arrangements: A Sloan work and family encyclopedia entry. Retrieved May 20, 2003, from http://wfnetwork.bc.edu/encyclopedia_template.php?id=240.

2 Formal v. Informal Definition taken from Eaton, S. (2003). If you can use them: Flexibility policies, organizational commitment, and perceived performance. Industrial Relations, 42 (2), 145-167.

3 Items adapted from the Workplace Flexibility Index. Bond, J.T., Thompson, C., Galinsky, E., & Prottas, D. (2003). Highlights of the National Study of the Changing Workforce. New York: Families & Work Institute.

4 First four items are the work-family culture scale, Families & Work Institute, National Study of the Changing Workforce.

State of the Work-Life Profession 2005
An AWLP Member Survey Brief — March 2005

Introduction and Methodology
This report summarizes the results of a 2005 survey of Alliance for Work-Life Progress (AWLP) members and conference attendees. Because the survey was designed to examine the current state of the profession from the practitioner perspective, it intentionally screened out service providers, vendors and academics after a few initial questions. The results below represent the views and practices of current practitioners in the field.

In January 2005, surveys were electronically sent to 549 AWLP members. In February, attendees of the AWLP Annual Conference & Exhibition were offered an additional opportunity to participate in the survey via hard copy. Through both of these channels, 191 nonduplicated completed surveys were received, a response rate representing 31 percent of the total AWLP membership[1]. A high response rate and a similar demographic profile between survey respondents and the general AWLP membership as a whole provide a high level of confidence regarding the validity of the data contained in this report.

Key Findings

Are the ranks of work-life practitioners dwindling, static or increasing?
The number of work-life practitioners appears to be either static or increasing. Seventy-five percent of the survey's respondents continued past the initial screening question, meaning they are practicing in the work-life profession as either a full- or part-time work-life practitioner, or an HR professional with some work-life effectiveness responsibilities (the remaining 25 percent in the survey serve the profession in another way).

When asked what has happened in the past year to the number of full-time equivalent (FTE) employees dedicated to work-life effectiveness programs in their organization, a combined 91 percent indicated that the number has either remained static (69 percent) or increased (22 percent). Only 9 percent said the number of work-life FTEs has decreased in their organization during the past year

Who are the champions of work-life effectiveness programs today?

According to respondents, top management (CEO or top HR professional) is leading the way today when it comes to championing work-life effectiveness programs. When asked who was the champion for work-life in their organization five years ago vs. today, the number of respondents who believe that employees were (and are) the primary champions for work-life decreased substantially.

Who has responsibility for work-life programs within organizations?

Almost two-thirds of respondents indicated that a "work-life specialist" — not an HR or other generalist — is currently responsible for implementing work-life effectiveness programs within their organizations. In addition, the majority of those organizations had a work-life specialist role one year ago. About 30 percent have organizational work-life effectiveness under the responsibility of a generalist.

What are the common areas of focus for work-life professionals?

The time allocation by work-life related employees within organizations appears to be fairly well-balanced among the seven categories presented in the AWLP model of organizational work-life effectiveness, which lends significant credence and validity to the model. The single largest amount of time spent by work-life professionals today is in the health and well-being category, followed by a cluster of three other categories: culture-change initiatives, workplace flexibility and caring for dependents. The final three categories of the AWLP model also created a cluster around the 10-percent range.

When presented with the same list of categories and asked about their organizational emphasis for 2005, respondents indicated that the workplace flexibility category would be a focus this year to attract, retain and motivate employees.

Detailed Survey Results

In early 2005, the AWLP administered a survey to its entire membership with the primary goal of examining the state of the work-life profession. A secondary goal of the survey was to test and validate the AWLP seven-category model of organizational work-life effectiveness. The AWLP model contains seven broad "buckets" or areas of potential organizational focus for employee work-life effectiveness programs. The seven categories are as follows:

- Workplace flexibility
- Paid and unpaid time off
- Health and well-being
- Caring for dependents
- Financial support (e.g., adoption assistance, financial planning, etc.)
- Community involvement (e.g., volunteering, philanthropy, etc.)
- Culture-change initiatives (e.g., diversity/inclusion, work redesign, etc.).

Although vendors, academics, service providers and consultants who serve the work-life profession are a critical component of the field, this survey was specifically designed for practitioners. An initial screening question on the survey allowed all respondents to self-identify their current status in the profession, such as "practicing work-life professional" or "academic/researcher," etc.

To ensure clarity of the results, those that did not indicate whether they were full- or part-time work-life professionals were asked to skip to the end and submit because of the possibility that they could significantly skew the results of certain lines of inquiry. For example, on a question such as how time is allocated within an organization to certain work-life programs, a respondent from a work-life consulting firm might answer quite differently from a practitioner in a manufacturing company. The first survey question served to separate current practitioners from those who serve the field in other ways.

Respondents' Status in the Work-Life Field

More than three-quarters of the survey's participants indicated they are either a currently practicing work-life professional or HR professional with at least some current work-life responsibility. About 14 percent identified themselves as consultants, vendors or academics serving the work-life field, and a small group of "other" respondents included a handful of non-HR directors, employee assistance program (EAP) managers and a few people that described themselves as currently "in transition." (See Figure 1.)

As noted above, following this first screening question, all respondents who indicated they were nonpractitioners were asked to skip to the end for two opportunities to offer open-ended comments about the state of the profession. Those who indicated they were practitioners were asked to continue on through the rest of the survey.

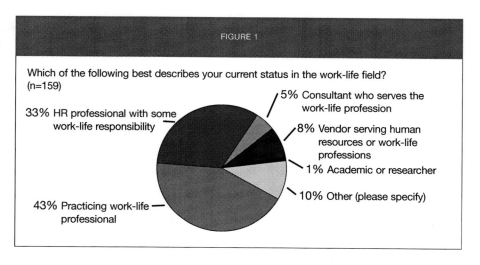

FIGURE 1

Which of the following best describes your current status in the work-life field? (n=159)

33% HR professional with some work-life responsibility

5% Consultant who serves the work-life profession

8% Vendor serving human resources or work-life professions

1% Academic or researcher

10% Other (please specify)

43% Practicing work-life professional

Staffing: Current FTEs

The survey's second question used the seven-category AWLP model of organizational work-life effectiveness to ask respondents how many FTE employees worked on these issues within their organization. Eighty-two percent of respondents reported that their organization has at least one FTE position dedicated to work-life effectiveness (as defined by the categories). (See Figure 2.)

A somewhat surprising 21 percent indicated that their organization employs five or more FTEs dedicated to work-life. A closer look at these specific organizations indicates that they are predominantly large companies. Additionally, because "health and well-being" is specifically listed as a component of the AWLP work-life model, it is possible

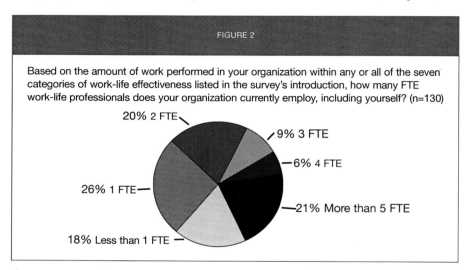

FIGURE 2

Based on the amount of work performed in your organization within any or all of the seven categories of work-life effectiveness listed in the survey's introduction, how many FTE work-life professionals does your organization currently employ, including yourself? (n=130)

20% 2 FTE
9% 3 FTE
6% 4 FTE
26% 1 FTE
21% More than 5 FTE
18% Less than 1 FTE

that some respondents counted their benefits staff that works on employee health care in this calculation.

Staffing: Change in the Number of FTEs

The presence of work-life professionals within organizations seems to be stable — and in more than a fifth of respondent organizations (22 percent), it is

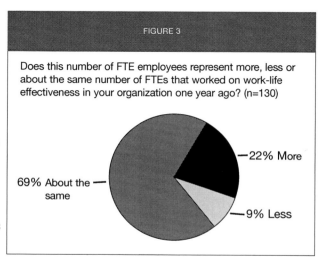

FIGURE 3

Does this number of FTE employees represent more, less or about the same number of FTEs that worked on work-life effectiveness in your organization one year ago? (n=130)

22% More
69% About the same
9% Less

increasing. Fewer than seven out of ten organizations (69 percent) say their organization has about the same number of FTEs today on work-life as it did one year ago. Only 9 percent of respondents say that the number of full-time employees dedicated to work-life effectiveness has decreased during the past year. (See Figure 3 on page 174.)

Respondents' Own Time Allocation Across the Seven Work-Life Categories

Figure 4 illustrates how respondents reported their personal time allocation on the job among the seven work-life effectiveness categories presented at the beginning of the survey (whether the respondent indicated full time or only part time on work-life programs). In aggregate, the data in Figure 4 paints a picture of how the typical work-life professional today spends his or her time on the job, and the picture is rather balanced, In other words, it is not dominated by any single area of work-life effectiveness. The single largest allocation of time is 24 percent on health and well-being, meaning the average work-life professional spends about a quarter of his or her job on organizational health and well-being initiatives. This is perhaps not surprising, given the focus in recent years in virtually all organizations on containing health-care costs.

Behind health and well-being were three categories that all came in roughly the same in terms of time spent, between 17 percent and 18 percent: culture-change

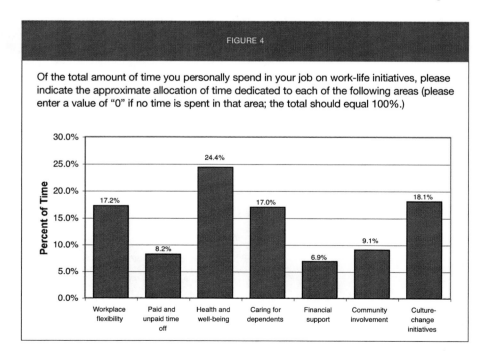

FIGURE 4

Of the total amount of time you personally spend in your job on work-life initiatives, please indicate the approximate allocation of time dedicated to each of the following areas (please enter a value of "0" if no time is spent in that area; the total should equal 100%.)

initiatives, workplace flexibility and caring for dependents. Finally, at the bottom end of the scale was another cluster of three categories, all hovering in the 7 percent to 9 percent range: community involvement, paid and unpaid time off, and financial support.

Respondent's Competency Self-Assessment Across the Seven Categories

While Figure 4 indicated that respondents spend the most time on health and well-being programs within the work-life function, this category is not where respondents feel most competent. On average, by a slight margin, respondents believe their competence level in workplace flexibility is the highest, followed closely by health and well-being, and caring for dependents. Consistent with the time allocation, financial support was rated as the category in which respondents felt least competent. (See Figure 5.)

Organizational Time Allocation Across the Seven Work-Life Categories (All FTEs)

Figure 6 on page 177 shifts the focus of a previous question regarding time allocation away from the individual answering the survey and asks about time allocation for the entire group of FTE employees working on work-life issues within the respondent's organization.

The graphic representation of Figure 6 is nearly a mirror image of Figure 4, with the most time being allocated to health and well-being programs within the organizational work-life framework — although this category increases from 24 percent to nearly 33 percent of all work-life FTE time allotted within organizations to health and well-being. There is also significant consistency between personal allocation of time and the allocation of time among all work-life FTEs on the second and third clusters of categories. The second cluster of workplace flexibility, caring for dependents and culture-change initiatives all came in a range of about 15 percent to 20 percent each, similar to the results in Figure 4. The third cluster (community involvement, paid and unpaid time off and financial support) also remained fairly constant.

FIGURE 5

Please assess your personal competency on each of the categories below (even if your organization does not offer any programs in that area) by ranking the categories from one to seven, with one being "most competent" and seven being "least competent"

Rank	Work-Life Effectiveness Category	Mean	n
1	Workplace flexibility	3.09	128
2	Health and well-being	3.15	126
3	Paid and unpaid time off	3.57	127
4	Caring for dependents	3.55	127
5	Culture-change initiatives	3.80	127
6	Community involvement	4.19	126
7	Financial support	4.62	126

Strategic vs. Tactical Nature of Work-Life

When asked about the strategic and/or tactical nature of the work-life function in their organization during the last year, the single largest block of respondents (roughly 45 percent) said that nearly equal amounts of time were spent on strategy and tactics. Eighteen percent of respondents indicated that discussions have moved from tactical back to strategic. Another 18 percent reported that they are still in the initial stages of development of their work-life function. The relatively small number of respondents within the "other" category talked about diminishing resources and budget cuts, the allocation of work-life initiatives among various departments, and how discussions are limited because the work-life programs are already quite mature. (See Figure 7 on page 178.)

Who Serves the Work-Life Function: Generalist or Specialist?

When the survey turned to a question about whether the organizational work-life function was occupied by either a generalist or a specialist during the past year, roughly half of all respondents (51 percent) said that their organization had a work-life specialist in the role. (See Figure 8 on page 178.) In addition, about one in 10 (10 percent) indicated that the responsibility for implementing work-life effectiveness programs moved from a generalist to a specialist role within the past year. Thus, a combined six in 10 organizations in the survey reported they have a specialist, as opposed to a generalist, working on work-life issues.

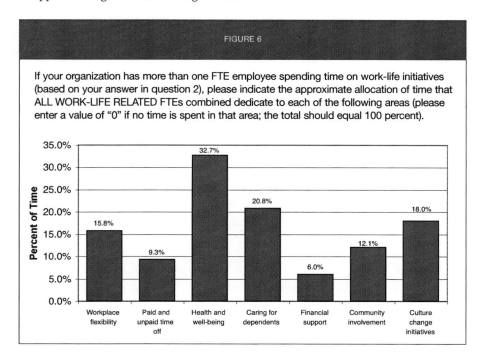

FIGURE 6

If your organization has more than one FTE employee spending time on work-life initiatives (based on your answer in question 2), please indicate the approximate allocation of time that ALL WORK-LIFE RELATED FTEs combined dedicate to each of the following areas (please enter a value of "0" if no time is spent in that area; the total should equal 100 percent).

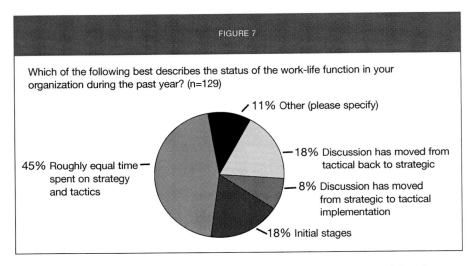

FIGURE 7

Which of the following best describes the status of the work-life function in your organization during the past year? (n=129)

- 11% Other (please specify)
- 18% Discussion has moved from tactical back to strategic
- 8% Discussion has moved from strategic to tactical implementation
- 18% Initial stages
- 45% Roughly equal time spent on strategy and tactics

About 30 percent said that an HR generalist was either given responsibility for implementing work-life effectiveness programs in their organization during the last year or already had the responsibility. Some of those in the "other" category said that implementation is a joint effort between generalist and specialist roles. One respondent mentioned the formation within the past year of an employee-based, work-life "action team" to handle implementation of work-life effectiveness programs.

Work-Life Budgets

Only one in five organizations (21 percent) have a specific, "work-life" budget or line item within their organizational budget, while the largest percentage

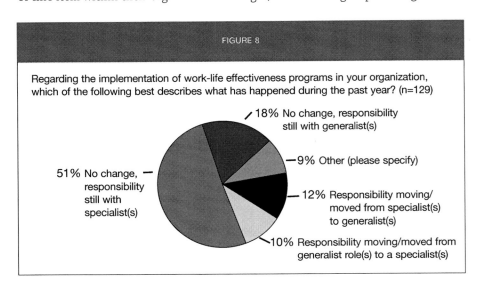

FIGURE 8

Regarding the implementation of work-life effectiveness programs in your organization, which of the following best describes what has happened during the past year? (n=129)

- 18% No change, responsibility still with generalist(s)
- 9% Other (please specify)
- 12% Responsibility moving/moved from specialist(s) to generalist(s)
- 10% Responsibility moving/moved from generalist role(s) to a specialist(s)
- 51% No change, responsibility still with specialist(s)

of respondents reported that work-life initiatives are funded through various line-items and departments. Another 39 percent of respondents said their organization's funding for work-life is a combination of specific work-life line items and parts of other budgets. (See Figure 9.)

Who Advocates for Work-Life Effectiveness?

Figures 10 and 11 on page 180 show a comparison of who the survey's respondents believe was the primary champion of work-life effectiveness five years ago vs. today. The results show a slight shift toward more involvement from the top organizational leader or CEO, and movement away from employees as the primary champion. Today, a combined 48 percent of respondents say that the primary champion is either the top organizational leader/CEO (15 percent) or top HR leader (33 percent). While these figures are comparable to what respondents believed to be the situation five years ago, the shift away from employees as champions is a suggestion that work-life effectiveness programs are more valued today by organizational leadership.

Most of the respondents that chose "other" for today said that the work-life effectiveness champion within their organization now runs the gamut from various directors and managers to a combination of all levels. Those who answered "other" regarding the organizational champion five years ago commonly said that a work-life effectiveness champion did not exist five years ago.

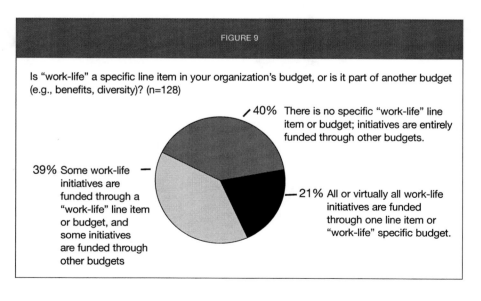

FIGURE 9

Is "work-life" a specific line item in your organization's budget, or is it part of another budget (e.g., benefits, diversity)? (n=128)

40% There is no specific "work-life" line item or budget; initiatives are entirely funded through other budgets.

39% Some work-life initiatives are funded through a "work-life" line item or budget, and some initiatives are funded through other budgets

21% All or virtually all work-life initiatives are funded through one line item or "work-life" specific budget.

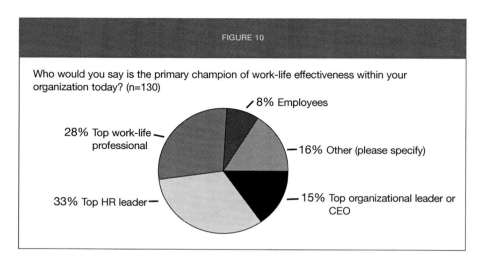

FIGURE 10

Who would you say is the primary champion of work-life effectiveness within your organization today? (n=130)

8% Employees

28% Top work-life professional

16% Other (please specify)

33% Top HR leader

15% Top organizational leader or CEO

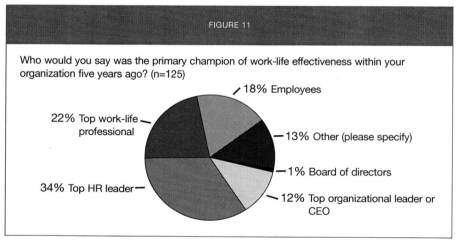

FIGURE 11

Who would you say was the primary champion of work-life effectiveness within your organization five years ago? (n=125)

18% Employees

22% Top work-life professional

13% Other (please specify)

1% Board of directors

34% Top HR leader

12% Top organizational leader or CEO

Primary Areas of Focus for 2005

During 2005, respondents indicated that their organizations would be placing the greatest emphasis on the workplace flexibility facet of work-life effectiveness for employees (34 percent). Health and well-being finished second (29 percent) among the seven categories of work-life effectiveness, and culture-change initiatives came in a distant third place at just over 16 percent. (See Figure 12 on page 181.)

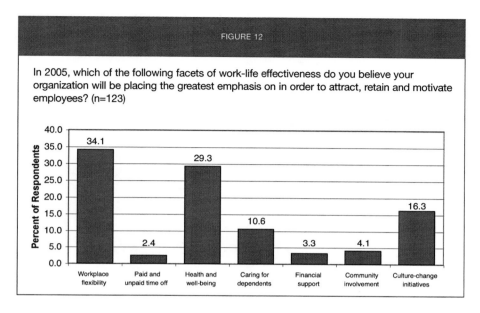

FIGURE 12

In 2005, which of the following facets of work-life effectiveness do you believe your organization will be placing the greatest emphasis on in order to attract, retain and motivate employees? (n=123)

Respondent Demographics

Number of Employees	
Less than 100	12.1%
100 - 499	3.4%
500 - 999	8.6%
1,000 - 2,499	8.6%
2,500 - 4,999	12.1%
5,000 - 9,999	15.5%
10,000 - 19,999	13.8%
20,000 or more	25.9%

Industry	
Health Care & Social Assistance	17.4%
Professional, Scientific & Technical Services	15.7%
Finance & Insurance	13.9%
Manufacturing	7.8%
Educational Services	6.1%
Other Services (except Public Administration)	6.1%
Retail Trade	3.5%
Utilities	2.6%
Public Administration	2.6%
Transportation & Warehousing	1.7%
Information	1.7%
Other	20.9%

Footnote

1 Ten questionnaires were completed without any identifying information, and although these responses were included in the individual question data and analysis, they are not represented in the demographic information contained in this report.

Appendix A: Sample: Employee Work-Life Survey

EMPLOYEE WORK-LIFE SURVEY

X COMPANY is committed to helping you manage your work and personal responsibilities by creating a supportive work environment. In order to better understand employees' work-life concerns and make decisions about how to respond, we are conducting an assessment to explore work-life needs and values.

In participating in this project, you can be assured of complete anonymity and confidentiality. Nowhere on this questionnaire will you be individually coded, named or otherwise identified. Your specific answers will only be seen by _____. Data from this study will be reported in aggregate form, representing the views of all employees.

Thank you for participating in this survey.

DIRECTIONS: This survey is composed of multiple-choice questions. Please respond to all statements by checking the appropriate box. Please read each question, marking only one answer per question unless otherwise directed.

SECTION 1 — Life Events
1. Which of the following describe life events you are currently experiencing or will likely experience within the next six months? (Please check as many as apply.)

Please check all that apply.

a.	Getting married/committing to a lifelong relationship	1- ☐
b.	Returning to school/taking a course – technical/college/graduate	1- ☐
c.	Buying or selling a home/moving/relocating	1- ☐
d.	Pregnancy or pregnancy of wife/partner	1- ☐
e.	Adopting a child or children	1- ☐
f.	Enrolling a child in child care/primary school for the first time	1- ☐
g.	Managing single parenthood	1- ☐
h.	Addressing significant loss of household income	1- ☐
i.	Addressing a child's special needs	1- ☐
j.	Coping with teenagers	1- ☐
k.	Blending families	1- ☐
l.	Making health/wellness a priority	1- ☐
m.	Sending a dependent off to college	1- ☐
n.	Significant marital stress and/or getting divorced/separated	1- ☐
o.	Legal entanglements	1- ☐
p.	Becoming a grandparent	1- ☐

q.	Caring for an ill or aging loved one	1- ☐
r.	Coping with a major illness/injury	1- ☐
s.	Losing a loved one	1- ☐
t.	Losing your job/spouse or partner loss of job	1- ☐
u.	Being promoted	1- ☐
v.	Retiring	1- ☐
w.	Major financial issues – dealing with extensive debt, credit issues	1- ☐

SECTION 2 — Work Schedule

2. I am regularly scheduled to work: (Please check one box indicating your primary schedule.)
1- ☐ Weekdays: during the day   3- ☐ Weekends: during the day
2- ☐ Weekdays: evenings/nights   4- ☐ Weekends: evenings/nights

3. How many hours are you scheduled to work in a typical week?
1- ☐ 20-25 hours   4- ☐ 36-40 hours   7- ☐ 51-55 hours   10- ☐ 66-70 hours
2- ☐ 26-30 hours   5- ☐ 41-45 hours   8- ☐ 56-60 hours   11- ☐ 70+ hours
3- ☐ 31-35 hours   6- ☐ 46-50 hours   9- ☐ 61-65 hours

4. How many hours do you actually work in a typical week?
1- ☐ 20-25 hours   4- ☐ 36-40 hours   7- ☐ 51-55 hours   10- ☐ 66-70 hours
2- ☐ 26-30 hours   5- ☐ 41-45 hours   8- ☐ 56-60 hours   11- ☐ 70+ hours
3- ☐ 31-35 hours   6- ☐ 46-50 hours   9- ☐ 61-65 hours

SECTION 3 — Health and Wellness

5A. How often do you make your health/wellness a priority? (Please check only one box.)
1- ☐ Never
2- ☐ Seldom
3- ☐ Sometimes
4- ☐ Often
5- ☐ Always

5B. Which of the following would you like to do to make your health and wellness more of a priority? (Please check all that apply.)
1- ☐ Exercise two to three times weekly.
2- ☐ Receive annual physical checkup(s) (such as: evaluating weight, cholesterol, blood pressure, and obtaining recommended screening tests).
3- ☐ Eat a healthy diet.
4- ☐ Reduce stress in a way that works for me (yoga, massage, walking, time with friends, etc.).
5- ☐ None of the above.

5C. What would help you make your health and wellness more of a priority? (Please check all that apply.)
1- ☐ More time
2- ☐ More energy
3- ☐ More financial resources
4- ☐ More information
5- ☐ Better community services

SECTION 4 — Family

6. Do you currently have daily responsibility for children under 15 years of age?
   1- ☐ Yes   2- ☐ No (skip to question #9)

7. For parents with children under 15 years of age: Based on your own experience raising children while working, what are the TOP three challenges you currently face regarding child care, if any? (Please check only three boxes.)

Top 3 Challenges

a.	Finding child care that is convenient to work or home	1- ☐
b.	Paying for my child-care arrangement(s)	1- ☐
c.	Finding quality child care	1- ☐
d.	Finding child care with hours/days that match my work schedule	1- ☐
e.	Excessive time spent managing child-care arrangements	1- ☐
f.	Finding back-up child care when my usual arrangement is not available	1- ☐
g.	Arranging for summer/vacation care for elementary school-age children	1- ☐
h.	Finding child care for before and after school hours	1- ☐
i.	Arranging care for a child who is sick	1- ☐
j.	Finding supervised arrangements for children ages 12-15 yrs.	1- ☐
k.	Worrying about the affect on my child due to caregiver turnover/changes/inconsistencies	1- ☐
l.	Worrying about the safety of my child	1- ☐
m.	No current child-care challenges (If this row is checked, please do not check any other boxes in Question #7.)	1- ☐

8. How many times, if ever, during the last three months have you experienced each of the following because of a child-care conflict? (For items a and b, please check only one response.)

	None	1-3 Times	4-6 Times	7-10 Times	More Than 10 Times
a. Missed days at work	1- ☐	2- ☐	3- ☐	4- ☐	5- ☐
b. Missed time during work (arrived late, left early, left and returned)	1- ☐	2- ☐	3- ☐	4- ☐	5- ☐

9. Are you responsible for the care of an elderly or disabled adult?
   1 - ☐ Yes, on a regular basis (primary responsibility and/or weekly care)
   2 - ☐ Yes, on an occasional basis (biweekly/monthly/bimonthly care)
   3 - ☐ No, not now, but expect to be within the next three years (skip to question #13)
   4 - ☐ No, not currently (skip to Question #13)

10. On average, how much time do you spend each week caring for an elderly/disabled adult(s)? (Please include direct and indirect time spent, including phone calls.)
   1 - ☐ Less than 1 hour   4 - ☐ 11 - 15 hours each week
   2 - ☐ 1 - 5 hours each week   5 - ☐ 16 - 20 hours each week
   3 - ☐ 6 - 10 hours each week   6 - ☐ More than 20 hours each week

11. Which of the following statements do you feel most accurately describes your situation? (If you care for more than one elderly/disabled adult, please check the box for the person who requires the most care.)

    1 - ☐ The elderly/disabled adult(s) I care for lives in my home.
    2 - ☐ The elderly/disabled adult(s) I care for lives elsewhere in my community.
    3 - ☐ The elderly/disabled adult(s) I care for lives outside my community (more than a 60-minute one-way drive/commute).

12. How many times, if ever, during the last three months have you experienced each of the following because of an elderly/disabled adult-care conflict? (For items a and b, please check only one response)

	None	1-3 Times	4-6 Times	7-10 Times	More Than 10 Times
a. Missed days at work	1 - ☐	2 - ☐	3 - ☐	4 - ☐	5 - ☐
b. Missed time during work (arrived late, left early, left and returned)	1 - ☐	2 - ☐	3- ☐	4 - ☐	5 - ☐

SECTION 5 — Emotional Well-Being

13. Overall, how important to you is the ability to effectively manage your work and personal life?

Very Important	Moderately Important	Not very Important	Not at all Important	Important
1 - ☐	2 - ☐	3 - ☐	4 - ☐	5 - ☐

14. Indicate the overall level of stress you have felt within the last three months as a result of conflict between your work and personal life responsibilities.

Very Stressed (90-100%)	Stressed (75%)	Moderately Stressed (40-50%)	Not very Stressed (20-30%)	Not at all Stressed
1 - ☐	2 - ☐	3 - ☐	4 - ☐	5 - ☐

15. To what extent does workplace stress adversely affect the following personal activities? (For each item, please check only one response.)

	To a great extent	Somewhat	Not at all	Does not apply
a. Time with family	1 - ☐	2 - ☐	3 - ☐	4 - ☐
b. Parenting children	1 - ☐	2 - ☐	3 - ☐	4 - ☐
c. Caring for elders/disabled/sick adults	1 - ☐	2 - ☐	3 - ☐	4 - ☐
d. Social time with friends	1 - ☐	2 - ☐	3 - ☐	4 - ☐
e. Personal development (learning, reading, training)	1 - ☐	2 - ☐	3 - ☐	4 - ☐
f. Volunteer work, civic and community activities	1 - ☐	2 - ☐	3 - ☐	4 - ☐
g. Spiritual or religious activities/development	1 - ☐	2 - ☐	3 - ☐	4 - ☐
h. Personal interests/hobbies	1 - ☐	2 - ☐	3 - ☐	4 - ☐
i. Health-related maintenance activities such as doctor's appointments	1 - ☐	2 - ☐	3 - ☐	4 - ☐
j. School activities with child or children	1 - ☐	2 - ☐	3 - ☐	4 - ☐
k. Extracurricular activities with child or children	1 - ☐	2 - ☐	3 - ☐	4 - ☐
l. Activities with spouse/partner	1 - ☐	2 - ☐	3 - ☐	4 - ☐
m. Exercise, recreation and physical activities	1 - ☐	2 - ☐	3 - ☐	4 - ☐

SECTION 6 — Financial/Legal

16. Which of the following, if any, will be your TOP three critical financial/legal concerns over the next year?

Program/Description		Top 3 critical financial concerns
a.	Financial/estate planning/tax services	1 - ☐
b.	Legal services	1 - ☐
c.	Automotive expenses	1 - ☐
d.	College/private primary-school tuition and expenses for minor dependents	1 - ☐
e.	Child-care expenses	1 - ☐
f.	Heath-care expenses	1 - ☐
g.	Home-improvement expenses	1 - ☐
h.	Recreational/travel expenses	1 - ☐
i.	Moving/relocation expenses	1 - ☐
j.	Debt consolidation/management/payoff	1 - ☐
k.	Pet care expenses	1 - ☐
l.	First home purchase	1 - ☐
m.	Elder-adult-care expenses	1 - ☐
n.	Education/training for self/spouse/domestic partner	1 - ☐
o.	No legal/financial concerns over the next year (If this row is checked, please do not check any other boxes in Q16.)	1 - ☐

SECTION 7 — Work

17. To what extent do these factors interfere with your ability to manage your work and personal life responsibilities? (Please check only one box per row.)

	To a great extent	Somewhat	Not at all	Does not apply
a. Amount of work	1 - ☐	2 - ☐	3 - ☐	4 - ☐
b. Number of hours I'm expected to work	1 - ☐	2 - ☐	3 - ☐	4 - ☐
c. Control over work schedule	1 - ☐	2 - ☐	3 - ☐	4 - ☐
d. Work-related travel	1 - ☐	2 - ☐	3 - ☐	4 - ☐
e. Regularly bringing work home on weeknights/weekends	1 - ☐	2 - ☐	3 - ☐	4 - ☐
f. Staying late/coming in early to work	1 - ☐	2 - ☐	3 - ☐	4 - ☐
g. Not being able to leave work when a personal problem arises	1 - ☐	2 - ☐	3 - ☐	4 - ☐
h. Length and time of commute	1 - ☐	2 - ☐	3 - ☐	4 - ☐

18. Overall, what impact do your family and personal responsibilities have on the following aspects of your work? (For each item, please check only one response.)

	Negative	Somewhat negative	No impact	Somewhat positive	Very positive
a. My morale	1 - ☐	2 - ☐	3 - ☐	4 - ☐	5 - ☐
b. My work performance	1 - ☐	2 - ☐	3 - ☐	4 - ☐	5 - ☐
c. My productivity	1 - ☐	2 - ☐	3 - ☐	4 - ☐	5 - ☐
d. My relationship with my supervisor	1 - ☐	2 - ☐	3 - ☐	4 - ☐	5 - ☐
e. My relationship with my co-workers	1 - ☐	2 - ☐	3 - ☐	4 - ☐	5 - ☐
f. My absenteeism	1 - ☐	2 - ☐	3 - ☐	4 - ☐	5 - ☐
g. My tardiness	1 - ☐	2 - ☐	3 - ☐	4 - ☐	5 - ☐
h. My stress	1 - ☐	2 - ☐	3 - ☐	4 - ☐	5 - ☐
i. The amount of work-life conflict	1 - ☐	2 - ☐	3 - ☐	4 - ☐	5 - ☐

19. Please indicate your agreement with the following statements.

My manager:

	Strongly disagree	Disagree	Neither agree or disagree	Agree	Strongly agree
a. Recognizes the importance of work-life issues to business success	1 - ☐	2 - ☐	3 - ☐	4 - ☐	5 - ☐
b. Respects me as a whole person and recognizes that I have a life outside of work	1 - ☐	2 - ☐	3 - ☐	4 - ☐	5 - ☐
c. Trusts me to do my work effectively	1 - ☐	2 - ☐	3 - ☐	4 - ☐	5 - ☐
d. Tries to reduce unnecessary work	1 - ☐	2 - ☐	3 - ☐	4 - ☐	5 - ☐
e. Regularly expects employees to take work home at night and/or on weekends	1 - ☐	2 - ☐	3 - ☐	4 - ☐	5 - ☐
f. Consistently reallocates work to single, childless workers when other employees with family obligations must leave	1 - ☐	2 - ☐	3 - ☐	4 - ☐	5 - ☐
g. Is flexible when I need to work in nontraditional ways (place, time, etc.)	1 - ☐	2 - ☐	3 - ☐	4 - ☐	5 - ☐
h. More favorably views those individuals who constantly put their jobs ahead of their families and/or personal life	1 - ☐	2 - ☐	3 - ☐	4 - ☐	5 - ☐
i. Treats everyone equitably when responding to employees' work-life issues	1 - ☐	2 - ☐	3 - ☐	4 - ☐	5 - ☐
j. Is held accountable for supporting employees/implementing work-life policies and practices	1 - ☐	2 - ☐	3 - ☐	4 - ☐	5 - ☐
k. Receives support from the organization to implement/manage work-life policies and practices	1 - ☐	2 - ☐	3 - ☐	4 - ☐	5 - ☐
l. Consistently asks me to rearrange my work hours or extend my work hours on short notice	1 - ☐	2 - ☐	3 - ☐	4 - ☐	5 - ☐
m. Values the quality of my work more than the amount of time I spend working at the office	1 - ☐	2 - ☐	3 - ☐	4 - ☐	5 - ☐

20. In the past year, have you done any of the following because of your family/personal responsibilities?

		Yes	No	Not applicable
a.	Turned down travel	1 - ☐	2 - ☐	3 - ☐
b.	Turned down overtime or extra hours	1 - ☐	2 - ☐	3 - ☐
c.	Turned down work assignments	1 - ☐	2 - ☐	3 - ☐
d.	Produced lower-quality work	1 - ☐	2 - ☐	3 - ☐
e.	Rearranged work hours	1 - ☐	2 - ☐	3 - ☐
f.	Reduced work hours	1 - ☐	2 - ☐	3 - ☐
g.	Made errors in your work	1 - ☐	2 - ☐	3 - ☐
h.	Been distracted so that productivity declined	1 - ☐	2 - ☐	3 - ☐
i.	Used the telephone more than appropriate	1 - ☐	2 - ☐	3 - ☐
j.	Turned down promotion	1 - ☐	2 - ☐	3 - ☐
k.	Turned down relocation	1 - ☐	2 - ☐	3 - ☐
l.	Thought seriously about quitting your job	1 - ☐	2 - ☐	3 - ☐

21. Overall, how satisfied are you with your current job?
   1 - ☐ Very dissatisfied
   2 - ☐ Somewhat dissatisfied
   3 - ☐ Somewhat satisfied
   4 - ☐ Very satisfied

22. How important is your ability to manage work and personal life responsibilities in your decision to continue working at your current organization?

Very important	Moderately important	Not very important	Not at all important	Important
1 - ☐	2 - ☐	3 - ☐	4 - ☐	5 - ☐

23. To what extent do you agree with the following statements regarding your organization's work-life programs, policies and practices? (Please check only one box per row.)

	Strongly disagree	Disagree	Neither agree or disagree	Agree	Strongly agree
a. I am aware of the work-life programs, policies and practices available to me.	1 - ☐	2 - ☐	3 - ☐	4 - ☐	5 - ☐
b. My immediate supervisor is knowledgeable about work-life programs, policies, benefits and practices.	1 - ☐	2 - ☐	3 - ☐	4 - ☐	5 - ☐
c. My organization's total work-life and life-event package meets my needs.	1 - ☐	2 - ☐	3 - ☐	4 - ☐	5 - ☐
d. The work-life programs, policies, benefits and practices in my organization are as good as those in other organizations.	1 - ☐	2 - ☐	3 - ☐	4 - ☐	5 - ☐
e. Employees with dependents/families receive more benefits than those without dependent's family obligations.	1 - ☐	2 - ☐	3 - ☐	4 - ☐	5 - ☐

24. Please indicate the three items that would be most useful in helping you effectively manage your work and personal life responsibilities:

Indicate up to three most useful items.

a.	More control over when/where I work	1 - ☐
b.	Better (more supportive and flexible) management	1 - ☐
c.	More rewarding work	1 - ☐
d.	Less work	1 - ☐
e.	More counseling and information to reduce stress	1 - ☐
f.	More supportive co-workers	1 - ☐
g.	More dependent-care (child and/or elder/disabled adult) services	1 - ☐
h.	More benefits that address life-event issues across: life span/life cycle, family style, economic level, etc.	1 - ☐
i.	Greater career opportunities	1 - ☐
j.	More financial information and services	1 - ☐
k.	More wellness/fitness information and services	1 - ☐
l.	More education/training opportunities	1 - ☐
m.	No additional resources required (If this row is checked, please do not check any other boxes in Q24.)	1 - ☐

25. Given the following factors, would you recommend your current employer to a friend as a good place to work? (Please check only one box per row)

		Yes	No	Maybe
a.	Company's work-life programs, policies, benefits and practices	1 - ☐	2 - ☐	3 - ☐
b.	Workplace environment/culture	1 - ☐	2 - ☐	3 - ☐
c.	Flexible work environment	1 - ☐	2 - ☐	3 - ☐
d.	Career opportunities: training/development	1 - ☐	2 - ☐	3 - ☐
e.	Pay/compensation	1 - ☐	2 - ☐	3 - ☐
f.	Overall benefits package	1 - ☐	2 - ☐	3 - ☐
g	Quality of management	1 - ☐	2 - ☐	3 - ☐
h.	Commitment to community/social responsibility	1 - ☐	2 - ☐	3 - ☐

26. What are the chances that you will be at this organization one year from now?

90-100%	70-89%	50-69%	49% or less
1 - ☐	2 - ☐	3 - ☐	4 - ☐

GENERAL INFORMATION

27. Gender:
    1 - ☐ Female
    2 - ☐ Male

28. Age:
    1 - ☐ Under 21 years old   4 - ☐ 41 - 50 years old
    2 - ☐ 21 - 30 years old   5 - ☐ 51 - 60 years old
    3 - ☐ 31 - 40 years old   6 - ☐ 60+ years old

29. How long have you worked at your organization?
    1 - ☐ Under 1 year   4 - ☐ 5 - 10 years
    2 - ☐ 1 - 2 years   5 - ☐ 10 - 20 years
    3 - ☐ 2 - 5 years   6 - ☐ 20+ years

30. Which of the following best describes your job classification?
    1 - ☐ Executive (president, CFO, CEO, etc.)
    2 - ☐ Senior management (director, AVP, VP, etc.)
    3 - ☐ Manager/supervisor
    4 - ☐ Salaried, nonmanager, nonunion
    5 - ☐ Hourly, nonmanager, nonunion
    6 - ☐ Hourly, nonmanager, union

31. I am located at: _____(business unit, division or location)

32. Which of the following best describes your primary geographic work location:
    1 - ☐ U.S. - New England   10 - ☐ Canada
    2 - ☐ U.S. - Middle Atlantic   11 - ☐ Latin America
    3 - ☐ U.S. - East North Central   12 - ☐ Australia
    4 - ☐ U.S. - West North Central   13 - ☐ Europe
    5 - ☐ U.S. - South Atlantic   14 - ☐ Middle East
    6 - ☐ U.S. - East South Central   15 - ☐ Africa
    7 - ☐ U.S. - West South Central   16 - ☐ Asia/Pacific
    8 - ☐ U.S. - Pacific
    9 - ☐ U.S. - Mountain

Write-In Comments: Please share any other thoughts related to this survey and/or topic.

Thank you for taking the time to complete this survey.
Please return using the enclosed envelope by _____, 200_.

The Seven Categories of Work-Life Effectiveness

Successfully Evolving Your Organization's Work-Life Portfolio

Defining Work-Life Effectiveness

Alliance for Work-Life Progress (AWLP) defines work-life effectiveness as a specific set of organizational practices, policies and programs as well as a philosophy that actively supports efforts to help everyone who works to achieve success within and outside of the workplace.

Using the Work-Life Effectiveness Categories to Build a Successful Portfolio

Building a multifaceted work-life portfolio for your organization is both an art and a science. At its best, a successful work-life portfolio can result in tangible increases in productivity, employee engagement, retention and attraction. The process of effectively engineering your work-life portfolio will require a variety of skills in planning the outcome, implementing the plan and controlling the desired results.

The work-life effectiveness categories below have a proven track record in helping organizations create a collaborative relationship between employers and employees in order to optimize business outcomes. These pillars of support for work-life effectiveness address the most important intersections between the worker, his or her family, the community and the workplace. They include the following:

- Caring for dependents
- Proactive approaches to health and wellness
- Creating a more flexible workplace
- Financial support
- Creative uses of paid and unpaid time off
- Community involvement
- Managing change and cultural challenges.

Planning and Work-Life Portfolio-Building Decisions

Without a model for successful work-life effectiveness, your portfolio may be received as the following:

- Uncoordinated
- Nonintegrated
- Disorganized
- Not measurably impactful or equitably accessible to either the business or the employee.

Applying the Categories to Build a Work-Life Portfolio

First Phase: Assessing your present work-life situation

Clarify which products and programs exist within each section of your organization's portfolio. Ideally, each is performing optimally to meet your organization's values and the needs of your employees.

Second Phase: Coordinating your work-life portfolio components

Evaluate gaps and identify areas needing improvement so that each category is harmoniously coordinated with your organization's strategic goals.

Using the categories to renew or engage your work-life efforts should result in a work-life portfolio that is as follows:

- Coordinated
- Integrated
- Based on sound planning decisions
- Strategic
- Organized
- More accessible (has something for everyone in your organization)
- Measurably impactful on the organization and employee morale.

Caring for Dependents

Work-life programs began in most organizations in response to the growing need of dual-income parents for child-care resource and referral services. This service has greatly expanded over the past decade to include elder-care support, long-term care insurance and emergency backup dependent-care services for both children and elderly relatives.

This category may contain, but is not limited to, the following services:

Child care:

- Child-care resource and referral services
- Child-care discount program at national providers
- Emergency backup child-care service (two options: center-based and in-home care).

Elder care:

- Elder-care resource and referral services
- Long-term care insurance
- Emergency backup elder-care service.

Business Impact of Support for Dependent Care

In the 2004 *Kids at Work — The Value of Employer-Sponsored On Site Child Care Centers*, 1,000 manufacturing employees were interviewed and were willing to pay $225 a year out of their own pockets to help employers provide child-care centers. The same study revealed that two companies who provide centers were saving at least $150,000 by offering child care. Also, employers offering child-care benefits report positive impacts of child-care programs on workers' performance as well as reductions in turnover, absenteeism and recruitment costs.

Employees of Bristol Myers Squibb perceived that they had a better relationship with their supervisor and felt more positively about company policies as a result of being users of the on-site child-care centers. (Gibson, Stacey. Interview by Sloan Work and Family Research Network Newsletter. *The Network News*. Winter 2004.)

A 2003 study, *Cost Benefits of Child Care for Extended Hours Operation* by Circadian Technologies, found that when child care is offered, absenteeism, turnover and overtime are reduced. Absenteeism costs went down by $300 a year per employee.

A 2001 General Services Administration study found that child-care subsidies offered to low-income workers resulted in 55 percent who were better able to concentrate on work, 19 percent who reported fewer days absent from work and 75 percent who felt the subsidy program had improved their job performance.

Proactive Approaches to Health and Wellness

Stress reduction is a central premise of work-life effectiveness. Because the negative impact of stress-related illness has been shown to eclipse the combined annual profits of the *Fortune* 100 companies, focusing on this category of work-life support holds the most promise of contributing to the reduction of escalating health-care costs. Employee assistance programs (EAPs), fitness center affiliations, workplace convenience services, on-site stress-reduction seminars and proactive wellness strategies all fit here.

This category may contain, but is not limited to, the following programs:

- Employee Assistance Programs (EAPs)
- Concierge service
- Workplace convenience services
- Fitness center affiliations
- On-site work-life seminars (e.g., stress reduction, financial planning, parenting, etc.).

Business Impact Implementing Proactive Approaches to Health and Wellness

A March 2005 Gallup research survey showed that 62 percent of engaged employees felt their work lives positively affected their personal health.

According to *The National Report on Work & Family*, a Jan. 7, 2003, study of hospital workers in Finland found "attention to interpersonal treatment" decreased the risk of ill health. In addition, male employees who felt they were treated unfairly were 41 percent more likely to take sick leave, and women were 12 percent more likely to take sick leave than those who felt respected.

A long-term evaluation of the financial and health impact of a large-scale corporate health and wellness program for Johnson & Johnson has shown that participating employees had significantly lower medical expenses and achieve overall improvements in several health-risk categories, such as high cholesterol, hypertension and cigarette smoking. The Medstat Group Inc., of Ann Arbor, Mich., conducted the two-part study for Johnson & Johnson. The evaluation included a financial analysis of medical insurance claims for 18,331 Johnson & Johnson domestic employees who participated in its health and wellness program from 1995 to 1999. Reduction in medical-care costs amounted to a savings per employee of $225 annually. The savings came from reductions in hospital admissions, mental-health visits and outpatient-service use. Savings grew over time, and most came in the third and fourth years after the program began. Employee medical expenditures were evaluated for up to five years before and four years after the program started. Johnson & Johnson's savings averaged $8.5 million annually for the same four-year period after the program began, primarily due to lower administrative and medical utilization costs.

DuPont saw a 14-percent decline in disability days over a two-year period. The company also saw an increase in savings due to lower disability costs, which offset program costs during the first year. The savings provided a return of $2.05 for every dollar invested. (Bertera R. "The Effects of Workplace Health Promotion on Absenteeism and Employee Costs in a Large Industrial Population," *American Journal Public Health*, Vol. 80, Issue 9 1101-1105, 1990.)

Creating a More Flexible Workplace

This category includes, but is not limited to, the provision of a variety of flexible work arrangements that enable greater customization over when, where and how work gets done. The three most common full-time options are flextime, telecommuting or telework (working remotely) and compressed workweek. The three most common less-than-full-time options include job sharing, phased return from leave (maternity or other) and regular part-time work.

The workplace flexibility category may contain, but is not limited to, the following programs:

Full-Time Options:

- Flex time

- Telecommuting

- Compressed workweek.

Part-Time Options:

- Part-time schedule

- Job sharing

- Phased return from leave.

Business Impact of Creating a More Flexible Workplace

The August 2005 *Flexible Work Schedules* study by WorldatWork and AWLP showed nine out of 10 organizations offer flexible scheduling, more than half of which operate informally.

According to a 2001 article in *The Scotsman*, a study by the London School of Economics and the Policy Studies Institute, control is the key to both stress and retention. The amount of pressure, stress, motivation and enjoyment of the job is influenced more by how much control employees feel they have over their time rather than by long hours worked.

Finding an Extra Day a Week: The Positive Influence of Perceived Job Flexibility on Work and Family Life Balance, a 2001 study of IBM employees by Brigham Young University researchers, showed that workers who believe they have flexibility are able to work eight hours more a week and still feel they have work-life balance. This study is unique in that it quantifies the relationship between flexibility and work-life balance.

A 2001 Watson Wyatt *Human Capital Index* study showed companies that support flexible work arrangements such as flex time, telecommuting and job sharing had a 3.5 percent higher market value than companies with no workplace flexibility.

At Bell Atlantic, productivity among telecommuters increased 27 percent, while Illinois Bell experienced a 40-percent increase in productivity from telecommuting as reported in the 1997 study, *Creating High Performance Organizations — The Bottom Line Value of Work/Life Strategies*.

Financial Support

Providing financially for oneself and loved ones from now through retirement is basic to work-life effectiveness. Benefits and compensation professionals provide critical strategies and programs to ensure work-life effectiveness.

The financial support category may contain, but is not limited to, the following benefits:

- 401(k) plan

- Personal financial-planning service

- Pension plan
- Adoption reimbursement
- Tuition reimbursement (student aid/loan programs)
- Dependent-care flexible spending account
- Health-care flexible spending account
- Voluntary benefits (e.g., auto, home, pet insurance)
- Mortgage-assistance program
- Vision-discount plan
- Pretax parking and transit benefits
- Accident insurance
- Cancer insurance
- Legal-assistance plan.

Business Impact of Financial Support

According to the Watson Wyatt Worldwide and the Washington Business Group on Health (WBGH) *Staying@Work 1999/2000 Fourth Annual Survey*, the total cost of disability can average nearly 15 percent of a company's payroll, including sick pay, worker's compensation, short-term disability and long-term disability.

CF Industries, a Long Grove Illinois manufacturer, has been offering financial classes and counseling for seven years. Employees who have the ability to make personal financial choices are more productive, have more ownership and have minimal absenteeism. (Work & Family Connection, *Work & Family Newsbrief*, Dec.1, 2000.)

Creative Use of Paid and Unpaid Time Off

Time to spend with loved ones and in one's community is the most fundamental element of work-life support. Some newer policies in this category include paid family leave for new fathers as well as mothers, and paid or release time for community service.

This category may contain, but is not limited to, the following programs:

- Personal days/vacation
- Paid holidays
- Paid family leave for new parents (fathers as well as mothers)
- Sabbaticals
- Paid leave bank and buy-back programs
- Extreme travel comp-time policies

- After-hours e-mail and calling policies
- Responsive shift-work policies.

Business Impact of Using Paid and Unpaid Time Off Creatively

The 2002 *CCH Unscheduled Absence Survey* revealed that work-life practices help cut absences, and organizations with more work-life initiatives had better morale.

The 2000 study, *Life's Work: Generational Attitudes Toward Work and Life Integration*, by the Radcliffe Public Policy Center, surveyed 1,008 male workers between the ages of 20-39 and found that spending more time with their families was more important to them than challenging work or earning a high salary. In fact, 70 percent of respondents indicated that they would be willing to give up some pay in exchange for more family time.

The 1993 *Evaluation of Johnson & Johnson's Balancing Work and Family Program* conducted by Families and Work Institute revealed that employees who used the company's work-family benefits (especially on-site child care and flexible work arrangements) were absent for less than half a day in a three-month period, compared to one day for other workers not using work-life programs.

Community Involvement

This is one domain in which employers' and employees' interests are spontaneously in close alignment, because both the workforce and customers come from the community in which the organization operates. Corporate responsibility is expanding to include not only new types of external community outreach, but also a renewed internal focus on building a strong internal sense of community. Formal ethics programs, shared (or catastrophic) leave banks and disaster-relief funds are some creative new ways of taking care of each other.

This category may contain, but is not limited to, the following programming:

External outreach:
- Community volunteer program
- Matching-gift program.

Internal sharing:
- Shared-leave program (donating personal/vacation time to others facing emergency situations, such as a child with a terminal illness or other family catastrophe)
- Disaster-relief fund.

Business Impact of Community Involvement

A 2002 DePaul University study compared the "100 Best Corporate Citizens of 2001" with organizations listed on the S&P 500 and revealed that companies that are socially responsible were found to have more than a 10-percent higher sales growth, profit growth and return on equity than companies that do not make the list.

A 1997 New York University Stern School of Business study revealed that *Fortune* 500 companies with a good reputation are more profitable, based on the finding that stock prices were relatively higher among 216 companies known for being socially responsible.

The General Mills' Corporations in the Community study reported that supervisors noticed an improvement in teamwork and other interpersonal skills for employees who participated in the company's volunteer program.

Managing Change and Cultural Challenges

Creating genuine support for work-life effectiveness at all organizational levels usually requires strong leadership in the areas of culture-change management, new types of management training to create an optimally collegial, flexible work environment and work redesign. Additionally, in order to eliminate any residual barriers to the full engagement and productivity of every contributor, it is sometimes necessary to launch specific interventions to eliminate gender inequity or other existing cultural barriers to full productivity. Thus, there is a growing link between work-life effectiveness, diversity initiatives, women's advancement, mentoring, networking and other change-management endeavors not elsewhere classified.

This category may contain, but is not limited to, the following:

- Diversity/inclusion initiatives
- Women's-advancement initiatives
- Work redesign (efforts to reduce work overload and burnout)
- Team effectiveness
- Work environment initiatives

Business Impact of Managing Change and Cultural Challenges

The 2002 National Study of the Changing Workforce, by Families and Work Institute, revealed that 77 percent of workers who experience their culture as being supportive say it is highly likely they will stay, compared with 41 percent who don't describe their culture as supportive. This study also finds the importance of supportive work-life policies and practices, such as flexible work arrangements, is clear — when they are available, employees exhibit more positive work outcomes, such as job satisfaction, commitment to the employer and retention, as well as more positive life outcomes, such as less interference between job and family life, less negative spillover from job to home, greater life satisfaction and better metal health.

In a 2000 Gallup Study, 2 million employees at 700 companies rated having a caring boss higher than money or fringe benefits. This study confirms findings by a 1999 Lou Harris Association/Spherion study that found that 40 percent of employees who rated their supervisors as poor were likely to leave their company, compared to 11 percent who rated them as excellent.

Selected References

Selected References and Resources

Articles

Aitken, Sandi and Cherwitz, Nancy. 2001. "Getting a New Perspective." *workspan*, October, 40-43.

Apgar, IV, Mahlon. 1998. "The Alternative Workplace: Changing Where and How People Work." *Harvard Business Review*, May-June.

Arnott, Dave and Russo, David. 2001. "Looking for Love — Are Employees Too Dependent on Employers for Happiness?" *workspan*, June, 50-53.

Belliveau, Paul L. 2004. "Feeding the Sandwich Generation." *WorldatWork Journal*, Fourth Quarter, 24-31.

Benefitslink.com 2001. "Europe's Employers Beginning to Address Work/Life Issues." *workspan*, February, 10.

Blizinsky, Ellen. 2000. "Good Things Come In Small Packages." *ACA News*, February, 19-21.

de Valk, Penny. 2004. "The Global Mobile Workforce: Building Productive Expatriate Assignments." *workspan*, December, 40-43.

dol.com. 2001. "DOL to Focus on Work Issues for Women." *workspan*, June, 14.

Drizen, Mark. 2005. "Let's Get Engaged: Benchmarks Help Employers Drive Results." *workspan*, April, 46-51.

Evans, Elaine. 2002. "Regaining Employee Loyalty: Tools to Win the Fight." *workspan*, November, 38-41.

Federico, Richard F. 2004. "When Silence is Not Golden: Eldercare Communications Can Enhance Productivity." *workspan*, January, 44-47.

Friedman, Stewart D., Christensen, Perry and DeGroot, Jessica. 1998. "Work/life: The End of the Zero Sum Game." *Harvard Business Review*. November-December.

Giancola, Frank. 2005. "Flexible Schedules: A Win-Win Reward." *workspan*, July, 52-54.

Greenhaus, Jim. 2002. "Increase Productivity with Work-Life Benefits." *workspan*, March, 8-10.

Healey, Andrea. 2001. "Keeping Work-Life and Your Sanity Intact." *workspan*, April, 50-52.

Johnson, Ryan M. 2002. "What Matters Now: Town Hall Meetings and Surveys Explore the Profession in Changing Times." *workspan*, January, 44-46.

Kruger, Pamela. 2001. "Jobs for Life." *Fast Company*. May.

Landsberg, Richard D. and Williams, Flora L. 2000. "Financial Planning for the Workforce — The Time Is Now." *ACA News*, January, 11-12.

Lingle, Kathleen M. 2005. "Employer of Choice Is in The Eye of the Beholder." *WorldatWork Journal*, Third Quarter, 26–31.

Lingle, Kathie. 2004. "Assessing Work-Life Effectiveness." *workspan*, October, 20-27.

LoJacono, Stephen. 2001. "Back-up Care: The New Benefits Tie Breaker." *workspan*, January, 16-20.

McCracken, Douglas M. 2000. "Winning the Talent War for Women: Sometimes It Takes a Revolution." *Harvard Business Review*. November-December.

Meleliat, Judy. 2001. "Shaping Up With A Total Web Workout." *workspan*, March, 16-20.

Meyerson, Debra E. 2001. "Radical Change the Quiet Way." *Harvard Business Review*. October.

Newton, Christopher C. 2001. "Getting Personal." *workspan*, November, 46-49.

Novelli, William D. 2001. "Opening the Dialogue to Elder Care." *WorldatWork Journal*, Fourth Quarter, 25-28.

Offutt, Steve. 2005. "Best Workplaces for Commuters." *workspan*, October, 45-47.

O'Neal, Sandra. 2005. "Total Rewards and the Future of Work." *workspan*, January, 18-26.

O'Toole, Robert E. 2001. "Providing Resources for Working Elder Caregivers." *workspan*, November, 50-53.

Parus, Barbara. 2004. "Pump Up Your Flexibility Quotient." *workspan*, August, 48-53.

Parus, Barbara. 2004. "Who's Watching Grandma? Addressing the Eldercare Dilemma." *workspan*, January, 40-43.

Parus, Barbara. 2003. "Workplace Stress: How Do Employees Get Relief?" *workspan*, June, 40-43.

Parus, Barbara. 2003. "Adoption Benefits: Employers Promote Family Ties." *workspan*, March, 40-43.

Parus, Barbara. 2000. "Measuring the ROI of Work/Life Programs." *workspan*, September, 50-54.

Pascoe, Robin. 2005. "Enriching Work and Life in the Global Workplace." *workspan*, October, 40-43.

Piktialis, Diane. 2004. "Bridging Generational Divides to Increase Innovation, Creativity and Production." *workspan*, August, 36-41.

Richman, Amy. 2006. "Everyone Wants an Engaged Workforce. How Can You Create It?" *workspan*, January, 36-39.

Scott, Carol. 2005. "Helping Employees Become Wellness CEO." *workspan*, May, 76-83.

Svoboda, Catherine. 2001. "Senior Female Execs Happy with Work/Life Balance." *workspan*, January, 12-13.

Verma, Nidhi. 2005. "Making the Most of Virtual Working." *WorldatWork Journal*, Second Quarter, 14-23.

Vincola, Ann. 2001. "Helping Employees Balance Work-Life Issues." *workspan*, June, 26-33.

wmmercer.com. 2001. "Work-Life Programs, Key to Retention." *workspan*, June, 14.

Young, Marjorie and Roach, John. 2003. "Accentuate the Positives." *workspan*, May, 50-52.

Zagata-Meraz, Suzanne. 2000. "More Employers Offer Work/Life Benefits." *workspan*, July, 9-10.

WorldatWork Surveys (http://www.worldatwork.org/research/surveys)

Flexible Work Schedules (2005)

State of the Work-Life Profession Progress Survey Brief (2005)

Elder Care Survey (2001)

Books — WorldatWork Bookstore (www.worldatwork.org/bookstore)

Artemis Management Consultants. 2000. *ReInventing Work: Innovative Strategies ReLinking Life & Livelihood to Benefit Business & Staff*. Mill Valley: Artemis Management Consultants.

Fitz-enz, Jack. 2001. *The E-Aligned Enterprise: How to Map and Measure Your Company's Course in the New Economy*. New York: AMACOM.

Friedman, Stewart D. and Greenhaus, Jeffrey H. 2000. *Work and Family — Allies or Enemies? What Happens When Business Professionals Confront Life Choices*. New York: Oxford University Press.

Glanz, Barbara A. 2003. *Balancing Acts: More Than 250 Guilt-free, Creative Ideas to Blend Your Work and Your Life*. Chicago: Dearborn Trade Publishing.

Harvard Business School Press. 2000. *Harvard Business Review on Work and Life Balance*. Boston: Harvard Business School Press.

Kossek, Ellen Ernst and Lambert, Susan J. (Editors). 2005. *Work and Life Integration*. Mahwah: Lawrence Erlbaum Associates.

Jackson, Maggie. 2002. *What's Happening to Home? Balancing Work, Life and Refuge in the Information Age*. Notre Dame: Sorin Books.

Laycock, Angelina B. 2003. *Strategies for Reshaping the Workplace*. Ann Arbor: Roma Communications.

Merrill, A. Roger and Merrill, Rebecca R. 2003. *Life Matters: Creating a Dynamic Balance of Work, Family, Time & Money*. New York: McGraw-Hill.

Michaels, Bonnie and Seef, Michael. 2003. *A Journey of Work-Life Renewal: The Power to Recharge & Rekindle Passion in Your Life*. Wilmette: Managing Work & Family, Inc.

Rapoport, Rhona and Bailyn, Lotte: Fletcher, Joyce K. and Pruitt, Bettye H. 2002. *Beyond Work-Family Balance — Advancing Gender Equity and Workplace Performance*. Hoboken: Jossey-Bass.

Rosen, Lori. 2004. *HR Networking: Work-Life Benefits*. Chicago: CCH, Inc.

Tatara, Irene. 2003. *HR How-to: Work-Life Benefits*. Petaluma: CCHKnowledgePoint.

Woods, Warren "Trapper" and Guillory, William A. 2003. *Tick Tock! Who Broke the Clock? Solving The Work-Life Balance Equation*. Salt Lake City: Innovations International.

WorldatWork. 2001.*101 Turbocharged Work/Life Ideas*. e-book only. Scottsdale: WorldatWork.

WorldatWork. 2001. *Life at Work — Beyond Compensation and Benefits*. Scottsdale: WorldatWork.

WorldatWork Courses (www.worldatwork.org/education/work-life)

W1: Introduction to Work-Life Effectiveness — Successful Work-Life Programs to Attract, Retain and Motivate Employees

W2: The Flexible Workplace — Strategies for Your Organization

W3: Health and Wellness Programs — Creating a Positive Business Impact

B5: Managing Flexible Benefits

T1: Total Rewards Management

T4: Strategic Communication in Total Rewards

Glossary

Term	*Definition*
Americans with Disabilities Act of 1990 (ADA)	A federal law that creates nondiscrimination protections for people with disabilities, similar to Title VII of the Civil Rights Act of 1964, which is extended to other minorities. Under the law, employers may not refuse to hire or promote a person because of a disability, and employers are required to make "reasonable accommodations" to allow people with disabilities to perform essential functions. Regulations are enforced by the Equal Employment Opportunity Commission (EEOC).
benefits	Programs that an employer uses to supplement the cash compensation an employee receives. Benefits include income protection programs such as publicly mandated and voluntary private "income protection" programs that often are provided through insurance, pay for time not worked and other employee perquisites.
bona fide wellness program	As provided by the Interim Final Rules for Nondiscrimination in Health Coverage in the Group Market (2000), a wellness program that provides a reward based on an individual's ability to meet a health-related standard related to health promotion or disease prevention. See also Notice of Proposed Rulemaking for Bona Fide Wellness Programs — 2001.
business strategy	The broad principles and approaches that guide the day-to-day operations of the business, ensuring that the business supports the organization's mission, goals and objectives. The business strategy includes the advantage that the organization believes it has over its competition.

claims utilization report	Report summarizing the findings of an evaluation of employees' use of medical services under a health and welfare plan.
community involvement	Corporate citizenship — not only external community outreach, such as company giving (foundations or direct), but also a renewed focus on building a strong internal sense of community. Formal ethics programs, shared (or catastrophic) leave banks, and disaster relief funds are some of the creative new ways of taking care of each other.
compensation	Cash provided by an employer to an employee for services rendered. Compensation comprises the elements of pay (e.g., base pay, variable pay, stock, etc.) that an employer offers an employee in return for his or her services.
compressed work week	Work schedule that condenses a 40-hour week into fewer than 5 days or an 80-hour two-week period into fewer than 10 days.
core hours	Specific range of hours when all employees must be at work (e.g., 9 a.m. to 1 p.m.)
corporate culture	The norms, beliefs and assumptions adopted by an organization to enable it to adapt to its external environment and integrate people and units internally. It is strongly influenced by the values and behavior of an organization's management. In turn, corporate culture influences both the behavior of the members of the organization and the quality of the work experience.
corporate mission	What an organization needs to do to achieve its vision. The mission specifies an organization's goals and how to attain them.
corporate philosophy	A means of translating the present state of an organization into concrete policy action to achieve the long-range goals of that organization.
corporate values	The beliefs of an organization.
corporate vision	What an organization wants to be.
cost shifting (health care)	A strategy in which the cost of providing employee health coverage is transferred from one party to another. It can refer to the case in which employers pass price increases along to employees, or when the government limits or reduces Medicare funding, leaving the private sector to bear a greater proportion of rising health costs.

culture	The holistic interrelationship of a group's identity, beliefs, values, activities, rules, customs, communication patterns and institutions.
daily flex	Work hours differ from the workplace standard. For example, working 10:00 a.m. to 6:00 p.m. instead of a "traditional" nine to five.
day-at-a-time vacation	Mini-vacations instead of using one full week or more.
dollars for doers	A company contributes money to a nonprofit where an employee volunteers. Most have application processes. The contribution is based on a specific number of hours the employee volunteers.
eligibility for a plan	The basis for determining the individuals or classes of employees eligible to participate in a particular plan such as an incentive or a supplemental benefits plan. This eligibility may be based on salary, job grade, organization unit or function or a number of other criteria.
emergency flexibility	Fixed number of days off with pay for emergencies (allow time to be taken in hourly increments).
employee assistance programs (EAPs)	
	Programs that provide counseling or referral services to employees. Services vary by employer, but may include assistance with chemical dependency, and psychological, financial, legal, family and career counseling. Services usually are provided by a third party to protect employee confidentiality, but may be provided internally by some employers. Typically, participation is voluntary unless a mandatory management referral is made.
exempt employees	Employees who are exempt from the Fair Labor Standards Act of 1938 (FLSA) minimum wage and overtime provisions due to the type of duties performed. Include executives, administrative employees, professional employees and those engaged in outside sales as defined by the FLSA.
Fair Labor Standards Act of 1938 (FLSA)	
	A federal law governing minimum wage, overtime pay, child labor and record-keeping requirements.

Family and Medical Leave Act of 1993 (FMLA)

A federal law entitling eligible employees to take up to 12 weeks of unpaid, job-protected leave in a 12-month period for specified family and medical reasons. Specified family and medical reasons include: the birth and care of a newborn child of the employee; placement with the employee of a son or daughter for adoption or foster care; care of an immediate family member (spouse, child, or parent) with a serious health condition; or medical leave when the employee is unable to work due to a serious health condition. The FMLA is administered by the U.S. Department of Labor's Employment Standards Administration, Wage and Hour Division.

financial planning

A popular perquisite whereby a third party provides budgeting, estate planning, investments and tax planning and preparation to employees for a fee. Typically offered as a company-paid benefit to executives.

flexible work arrangements

Any one of a variety of alternatives that provide employees with options to meet work requirements through non-traditional scheduling (e.g., telecommuting, compressed workweek, job sharing, part-time, etc.).

flexible work schedule

Work schedule in which the workday is divided into core time and flexible time, and that permits employees to choose their arrival and departure times during the flexible time period. Also known as flextime.

flextime

See flexible work schedules.

global company

An organization with worldwide operations, whose strategies, resources and technology are utilized globally, regardless of national or geographic boundaries.

Health Insurance Portability and Accountability Act of 1996 (HIPAA)

A federal law, enforced by the Department of Labor (DOL), designed to protect individuals who move from one job to another, who have pre-existing medical conditions or who are self-employed, by imposing a number of requirements on employer-sponsored health care plans. These requirements range from limiting pre-existing condition exclusions to mandating that employers provide certificates of prior plan coverage. Acts and provisions under HIPAA include: Newborns' and Mothers' Health Protection Act of 1996, Mental Health

Parity Act of 1996, Women's Health and Cancer Rights Act of 1998, Administrative Simplification Provisions (Privacy Rules) – 2001 and Nondiscrimination Provisions — 2001.

holidays
Specific days when most employees do not work but are paid as if they did. Employees who do work on such days typically receive premium pay or compensatory time off. The number of paid holidays granted by employers varies considerably by industry group and, to a lesser extent, by geographic region.

hours of work
Under the Fair Labor Standards Act (FLSA), all time that the employer requires, suffers or permits the employee to be on duty at a prescribed workplace, including the employer's premises.

human resources philosophy
Management's values and beliefs about its approach to the employee/employer relationship.

human resources strategy
The organization's overall plan for attraction, retention and motivation of employees.

informal flexibility
Includes ways to reorganize the workday to allow employees more time to focus on critical tasks or have some "quiet time."

Interim Final Rules for Nondiscrimination in Health Coverage in the Group Market — 2001
A set of rules that prohibit group health plans from establishing eligibility rules that would discriminate based on the following eight health factors: health status, medical condition (physical and mental), claims experience, receipt of health care, medical history, genetic information, evidence of insurability and disability. The rules also prohibit group health plans from charging an individual a different premium or contribution than a similarly situated individual based on those same eight health factors.

job sharing
An arrangement that allows two or more employees, each working part-time, to share responsibility for a single job and arrange their vacations and days off so one is always at work during the normal work week.

long-term care (LTC) insurance

An insurance policy designed to provide a stream of benefits payments to provide assistance with daily living when a qualifying insurable event occurs. A qualifying, insurable event occurs when an individual cannot perform a given number (e.g., two of five) of daily living activities such as bathing, dressing, eating and moving from bed to chair.

mealtime flex

Taking a longer meal break and making up time at the beginning or end of the day.

metrics

A quantifiable means of monitoring and measuring key performance goals.

Notice of Proposed Rulemaking for Bona Fide Wellness Programs — 2001

Proposed rules within the Interim Final Rules for Nondiscrimination in Health Coverage in the Group Market (2000) that clarify the term bona fide wellness program. See also bona fide wellness program.

overtime

Under the Fair Labor Standards Act of 1938 (FLSA), nonexempt employees must be paid one-and-a-half times their normal wage rates for all hours worked in excess of 40 in any work week. Some states require overtime be calculated by other than a 40-hour week or at greater than $1^1/_2$ times normal wage rate.

paid time off (PTO) bank

A design option for paid leave that combines sick, holiday, vacation and personal leave time into one category of available time off that the employee manages with certain employer guidelines.

part-time schedule

Working less than full-time hours with full or pro-rated benefits.

performance appraisal

Any system of determining how well an individual employee has performed during a period of time, frequently used as a basis for determining merit increases.

performance measures

The quantitative basis by which performance is evaluated against objectives.

performance standards

The defined performance levels, derived from organizational objectives, that an organization expects from individuals and/or groups with respect to specific objectives.

performance targets	Tasks or behavioral goals established for an employee that provide the comparative basis for performance appraisal.
personal days	Days off with or without pay (usually a fixed number), to be used by employees for personal reasons.
productivity	Any index measuring the efficiency of an operation, usually involving a ratio of outputs to inputs or costs. Rewards frequently are tied to productivity-related measures.
qualitative measures	Measures that allow for a greater degree of judgment. Typically used for behaviors and assessments that are based on observation and perception.
quantitative measures	Measures that lend themselves to precise definition and assessment, with very little room for variability of data. Typically "number' based.
sabbatical	A perquisite that provides a leave of absence for a specific period of time (e.g., six months) to allow for pursuit of some outside endeavor (e.g., a civic or charitable project, or completion of an advanced degree).
shared leave program	Donating personal/vacation time to others facing emergency situations.
shift flexibility	Options for employees to trade, pick-up or drop work shifts with other employees.
sick leave	Paid time off provided to employees suffering from nonoccupational illness or injury. Usually coordinated or integrated with short-term disability (STD) plans.
strategic planning	The process of establishing or developing organizational objectives, environmental constraints and opportunities, competitive strengths and weaknesses, and organizational structure and culture, and using this analysis to develop policies and programs that are most conducive to achievement of key organizational objectives.
strategy	The science or art of employing a careful plan to achieve a specified goal.
summer hours	An arrangement whereby employees have reduced working hours during the summer months (e.g., half day on Fridays).
summer time flex	Work hours differ during the summer months. For example, starting work at 7:00 a.m. instead of 8:30 a.m.

telecommuting	See telecommuting/telework
telecommuting/telework	The process of allowing employees to work from an independent location (most typically from home) anywhere from one day a week to working at home full-time. Technology connects an employee to office and/or business.
total rewards	The monetary and non-monetary returns provided to employees in exchange for their time, talents, efforts and results. Total rewards involve the deliberate integration of five key elements that effectively attract, motivate and retain the talent required to achieve desired business results.
vacation	The amount of time off from work with pay given to employees by an organization. The amount of time off given for vacation is usually based on an employee's length of service.
vacation borrowing	Employees may borrow up to one week (typical) of vacation from the following year.
vacation buying	Employees pay for a specified number of additional vacation days each year.
vacation sharing	Employees donate their vacation to another employee who needs additional paid time off due to an illness or other personal situation.
work redesign	A method of assessing how work is designed and structured, determining which tasks are essential, creating an efficient work flow and eliminating unnecessary work and inefficiencies.
work-life effectiveness	A specific set of organizational practices, policies, programs and a philosophy that recommends aggressive support for the efforts of everyone who works to achieve success both at work and at home.
workplace flexibility	A variety of flexible work options that enable greater customization over when, where and how work gets done. The three most common full-time options are flex time, telecommuting and compressed workweek. The three most common part-time options include job sharing, phased return from leave and regular part-time work.